THE WORLD LOST A MAN

'

BY DAN EBERHART

THE WORLD LOST A MAN

THE LIFE AND LEGACY OF A COMPLICATED SOUL

SGM

The World Lost a Man

BY DAN EBERHART

THE WORLD LOST A MAN

THE LIFE AND LEGACY OF A COMPLICATED SOUL

SGM

The World Lost a Man

Dedication

To my sister Eve and brother Pete without whose love and support
this project would not have happened.
And to our sister Medley whose spirit continues to inspire us all.

TABLE OF CONTENTS

Word from the Author 9

Chapter 1 11

Chapter 2 27

Chapter 3 37

Chapter 4 59

Chapter 5 75

Chapter 6 85

Chapter 7 93

Chapter 8 105

Chapter 9 121

Chapter 10 137

Chapter 11. 147

Chapter 12 161

Chapter 13 175

Chapter 14 189

Chapter 15 203

Chapter 16 209

Chapter 17 223

Chapter 18 239

Chapter 19 245

Chapter 20 259

Chapter 21 269

Epilogue 285

Acknowledgements 317

Addendum 319

WORD FROM THE AUTHOR

I cannot take full credit for writing this book, my father helped to tell his story. In my research for this book, I uncovered a treasure trove of his poetry as well as lists of unfettered creations and aphorisms that he chose to collect and file away. Though most of them are rough-cut and unpolished, they portray—much better than I could—the workings of his mind about a myriad of emotions, meditations, and life in general. Including them has, in a way, made me feel that he was co-authoring the book with me, our words together telling his story. His poetic writings and other contributions are framed and interspersed among my paragraphs where I thought they might provide existential emphasis. Unfortunately, I found few dates on any of the works to place them on a timeline. Some were labelled as assignments for his college classes between 1945 to 1949, but details such as when he wrote them, are known only to him at this point. The numbering of most pieces are of my doing, for my fragile sense of organization and sanity. There are two exceptions to the bordered works: my grandmother's poignant and breakout article, as well as a letter from *Dear Abby*, that I feel significantly impacted my father's life and beliefs.

Throughout the book are italicized quotes from actual letters to and from Dad, as well as from written works such as his mother's unpublished memoir and some of his school projects.

I have included an addendum where the longer pieces can be read and appreciated in their entirety.

The complexities of my father's life and tenets of his legacy are there for us to mine, evaluate, and reflect upon in effort to understand the soul of the man I called 'Dad.' My chore is to interpret this rumination of his and run with it.

Musings 7

Here's to the man with a smile in his heart
Here's to what put it there

CHAPTER 1

My father liked a practical joke now and then, so with a bit of self-reproach, I couldn't help thinking that he might have found sinister amusement in dying on Friday the 13th in 1989. My mother called from Denver to tell me the news. In a strangely calm voice, she explained that Dad's worn-out heart had stopped beating when he was in the shower. She curiously added that it was difficult for the emergency personnel to get him out of the tub.

My family and I lived in Topsham, Maine at the time. The day Mom called, the afternoon sky was yellow-gray as the sun tried weakly to brighten a drab winter's day. Devastated though I was, the day was a yin and yang sort of experience. Earlier in the day, good friends phoned to tell us about the birth of their healthy baby boy. The two events occurred 3,000 miles apart, yet through my sadness crept a soothing sense of balance, as one soul had left this Earth, another entered. When my three children got home from school, I sat with them on the desert rose-patterned couch in the living room. I somberly informed the kids about their grandfather. They didn't get to see him very often, but adored him and his quirky ways, like being able to talk in a Donald Duck voice. Absurdly thinking I could soften the blow, I felt compelled to tell them about our friends' happy announcement. I'm not sure they grasped the same cosmic balance I wanted to think was there.

I'm not a crier, never have been. When I'm really upset, I choke up to the point where words cannot be forced through constricted voice pipes. The inability to shed tears must be a parallel symptom. The three hardest deaths for me to endure were those of my parents and Medley, the older of my two sisters. After each passed, I cried exactly once, and the tears came unexpectedly, not to be staunched. It was November of 1978 when I got the news of Medley's tragic death while visiting in-laws in Vermont. Though I slumped to the floor with phone in hand, the tears did not come until I was alone later that night in the car driving to Boston to pick up my family, whom I'd left with my mother-in-law, for the flight back to Colorado. When Mom stopped breathing in 2003, I was at her bedside in a hospital room south of Denver. Stepping to the window to look at the lights of the Mile High skyline, my shoulders suddenly convulsed, my cheeks became drenched and my throat tightened, save for the sound of wrenching sobs. My brother and sister came to my side and wrapped their arms about me as if to hold me upright.

After Mom's call that fateful day in January of 1989, I hopped onto another plane home as soon as I could. While looking out the window at blue sky, puffy clouds, and some part of the country below me, a vision of my father sitting in his recliner surrounded by books and magazines, watching three TVs each with a different football game, materialized in my thoughts. The memory was pleasant yet unleashed a flood of hard, silent tears. I was neither certain nor caring if my seat mate might have been wondering, "What's with this guy?" Recently and way too long after I shed those tears for him, I sadly discovered one of his poems that hinted at his inimitable legacy. I think it tells of a man, I'm not sure of who that man might have been, who tried to do right by the world, but in the end was left with too many unanswered questions.

The World Lost a Man

The world lost a man who helped in its winning
The world lost a city but continued spinning

The world lost a way but went on without it
The world lost an age and did nothing about it

And the poor old world became tired and grey
But his children were single and their minds were fired

Then the world lost itself and fell through the stars
And I, among others, hopped off on Mars

I'll find my rest, although I'm near dead
By keeping abreast and one world ahead

It's better than two in the bush, they say
And that I understand
But what in the world was I going to do
With this bird I have in my hand

The world lost Wilfred Perry Eberhart 161 days after his 64th birthday. January 26, 2015, was 162 days past my 64th birthday, meaning that I had outlived Dad by one day. By then, I was living back in our beloved Colorado, and on another cold, raw day, I was left to conjure all the lost opportunities, questions unasked, advice not given, and great ideas unheard. In my brain, one word burned itself into my psyche, "Why?" Our love and connection were strong, but submerged not unlike those icebergs whose stability and strength lie deep beneath the frigid surface. Regret left me floundering in the white desolation of loss on the day I outlived my father.

Events occurred almost thirty years earlier, less than a year before Dad passed away, that had powerful implications to be uncovered soon after he died. In June of 1988, I embarked on a 3,400-mile bicycle adventure with 300 some other diehards that began in Seattle, Washington and ended on the boardwalk of Atlantic City, New Jersey. Ceremoniously, I baptized the back tire of my bicycle in the Pacific Ocean, and seven weeks later dipped the front tire in the Atlantic Ocean. In between were many hundred-mile days, high mountain passes, hundred-degree temperatures, and stiff headwinds. Glacier National Park was stunning with its awesome scenery, and people cheered us through small towns in North Dakota. My bike rattled and my body thrilled to ride through the tunnels of old railroad beds in Wisconsin. After the steep hills of western Pennsylvania, I impersonated Rocky running with my bicycle up the steps of the Art Museum in Philadelphia. I was 37 years old, strong, and able to ride 12 or more hours a day. Though I don't remember him saying it in so many words, Dad must have been pretty proud of me when I called him from Atlantic City.

Sometime, a few years later after my big adventure, I came across a photograph of Dad when he was in his late thirties. Though my young sisters are holding his hands, he nearly fills the picture. He stood six foot two inches and weighed almost 300 pounds. His shoulders were rounded, in fact, his whole body seemed rounded like a large, upside-down bowling pin. Realization seized me with a talon around my heart that at the same period of my life, I had pedaled the breadth of the United States. I found a picture of me back then, tan, lean with bulging thighs, and exuding fitness, and put it next to the one of Dad.

Eve, Dad, Medley,
and Grandpa

Me doing my Rocky impression
with a bicycle

The stark contrast between him and me in the two photos was startling and profound. Subconsciously at first, then purposely, l began comparing my well-being to his at various benchmarks in our lives. I had pictures of him in the Navy that showed a lean, mean fighting machine, six-pack abs, wiry and cocky. When I was around that age, I was a long-haired, dope-smoking hippie, tall and lean but not because I was as fit as he was. As our ages progressed, he smoked, drank, and became less physically active. Though I acquired the family vulnerability for the taste of liquor, I did start playing rugby, which developed into a lifelong addiction for exercise. Add to that long-distance bicycling, hiking, and working out in local fitness centers. I may not be a model of fitness, but I've stayed more active than most folks my age.

Comparing the two photographs planted seeds in my mind that I had to know more about my father and our relationship. Notably, I realized that Dad's early demise left me in a lurch; we had unfinished business that neither of us had been ready to admit, much less address. I desperately wished we might have sat down face to face, just the two of us, sorting through all the big issues: our partners, our siblings, kids, grandkids, retirement, politics, our love of Colorado, and how I wanted him to be a mentor for my fledgling writing career. Oh, the things we could have pondered! Too many years later, I was left to speculate and come to grips with the fact that what we had shared was merely the ragged opening to a lost gold mine, like one he might have written about. I wasn't ready to declare it back then, but I was taking the first baby steps on a journey to find a father I hardly knew. Before I ever read Ode 1, I was coming to the conclusion that I wanted to make the world care about my father.

⊶⊷⊷●⊶⊷⊷

Ode 1

It overtook me from behind that moment of bliss,
But I lumbered through Eden unmindful —

Stepping on roses — blinded to beauty,
Intoxicating myself with yesterdays,
My head on a swivel drinking the sky behind me,
Above me — not looking down or ahead.
Again I sensed the thunder, but thunder always passes;
And I giggled and lumbered along my merry way.
Until the storm grew and came down on me
And beat me down stumbling into the mud.
I slid and slushed but could not stand;
I could only look back through the rain and the muck
To see the dismal path I had cut.
Wishing I could unbend each blade of grass,
Refresh the pleading rose and uncrush it,
I sighed and slushed ahead — crawling —
For the world little cares how a man dies after he is dead.

In life, Wilfred Perry Eberhart was highly intelligent, well-read, educated, principled, caring, opinionated, and boisterous, but not a politician. I knew much of this from proximity and seeing him in action, whether it was accompanying him on research excursions around the state, seeing him appear with the elite of Colorado politicians, or hotly debating his beliefs around the family dinner table. There were the books he published and mementos of his past, photos from his days in the Navy, boxes and boxes of photographic slides, letters to the editor, and friends as erudite and outspoken as he. There was a plethora of works and collected memorabilia around me from which I could reconstruct Dad's life, but little did I know at the time that I was barely seeing beneath the hazy veneer of a multi-layered soul.

Even with my scant pre-conceptions, it seemed like I was left with a million-piece puzzle to help me understand the man he was and what he meant to me. There seemed to be no straight-edge pieces to sort out. I began pulling out my memories of him, then I badgered my brother and sister for their recollections. Sadly, my mother and other sister passed away long before I could probe their reminiscences though Mom left behind a few small, simple journals. Only one of Dad's siblings was still around to impart family history to me, and I grilled him pretty incessantly. A few of my father's contemporaries and old friends remain to have their brains picked.

I'd known that my father had many accomplishments in life, many successes and positive contributions to the world around him. Because of them, I felt he was worthy of some sort of tribute, but for one reason or another hadn't received recognition consummate with what I felt was his impact on the world. His imprint was both public and personal, he profoundly touched the lives of me, my family, and many, many people out there in the bigger world. The last lines of Ode 1 utter a deep despair and fear that one's life will have meant little or nothing. Maybe I couldn't unbend blades of grass or refresh the rose, but I wondered if in some way I could carry on the work Dad had started. Having wrestled with enough bureaucracy and pompous people in my own life, I was too removed and uninspired to get involved with community issues. Gradually, the answer percolated into my brain; having one published novel under my belt and another in the works, I acknowledged that the flames of creative writing that burned in me could be a possibility. In fact, when I had talked to a couple of his old cronies, more than one of them asked if I was going to follow his literary footsteps. Embers of purpose stoked my artistic urges and coalesced with the need to honor the old man, spurring me to take on the mantel of telling his story. After many fits and starts, motivation became obsession.

As commitment blossomed, I knew precisely the first place to look for inspiration. Soon after Dad died, Mom imagined that all of the research, correspondence, and documentation he had accumulated should be useful to someone. We contacted Denver Public Library (DPL) to see if they would be interested in taking it. Not only were they more than happy to accept what turned out to be 39 boxes of stuff, but their staff expertly organized, filed, catalogued, and stored it all in their archives. When I recalled, nearly 30 years later Mom's reference to unfinished manuscripts, a fuse was lit and fueled the pursuit of my father's legacy.

I eagerly jumped into a routine of bicycling or riding the light rail once a week down to the Central branch of the library to dig through those 39 boxes and immerse myself in Dad's lifetime of work. To access the collection of "Perry Eberhart Papers," I traipsed up to the fifth floor, the distinguished and highly regarded Western History and Genealogical Research section. First, I had to store my backpack and jacket in a side room, only being allowed to take my cell phone—no writing utensils or notepads—into the special room set aside to view materials from the Western History and Genealogical archives. I would then present my request for one or two boxes from the catalogued collection of Dad's papers to the reference librarian, who would disappear into the bowels of the building to procure them. While he or she was on their mission, I would set myself up in the assigned room set aside for reviewing these special materials. I took a couple pencils and sheets of special paper that were provided for those of us pursuing our special undertakings in the special room. The reference librarian would deliver my chosen boxes and have me sign for them; it all felt so formal and important. I was then free to withdraw contents as long as I put them back precisely from where I withdrew them. Photocopying was verboten, but a tripod and display board were available to photograph items with the cell phone I was allowed to bring in with me. This setup proved very helpful for capturing images of maps, illustrations, and pages that were too many to copy or hard to read, so that I could undertake in-depth examination at home at my leisure.

Like excitedly prospecting in a mine shaft, I excavated the ore of raw data. My focus was primarily to find the unfinished manuscripts and delve into his historical research. While fervently hoping this treasure trove would provide a foundation for me to build upon, I once again became overwhelmed and intimidated. Guilt and hopelessness returned; there was no way I was going to write a sequel to any of his highly respected works. After much long, anxious introspection, I realized that with fiction being my thing, perhaps I might concoct an imaginary story based on Dad's wealth of collected facts, legends, and journalistic accounts. I began mulling over plot possibilities and attempted to draft a couple story lines based upon notes I scratched out from several trips to the library. My enthusiasm flared, prompting me to enroll in an online Historical Fiction class; the instructor was fairly complimentary about my efforts and offered, for a price of course, to edit my manuscript when

I got to that point. A plot began to formulate in my mind that would begin in New Mexico during the Civil War and work its way into the Colorado gold fields. I eagerly jumped into our new camper van and made excursions down to Fort Union and Glorieta to burn the landscapes into my mind.

Yet once more, my journey to Dad slowed and got mired in the muck of discouragement. Despite his voluminous cache of information, tons of research still loomed ahead of me to update and elaborate upon his work. Quoting him, perhaps I was becoming muddle-aged and feeling as if I were wasting my time. Weakened ambition once again was shelved in the back of my consciousness as I went on to promote my newly published novel and fish around for a newer, more benign writing project.

Sometime later, an event occurred that blew apart my vision of my father, trumpeted my ignorance, and put my expedition back on the fast track. The year was 2017. Not long after Thanksgiving, I received an email from a woman named Lisa that included a photo of my father and another man on board their ship in World War II. The picture was very familiar, I had grown up looking at it but never known who the other fellow was. Lisa informed me that he was Bob Biddle, her father. I was amazed, amused, and mostly dumbfounded. Dad may or may not have mentioned Bob's name, but I sure didn't remember it. That information was mind-blowing, but the biggest, hardest surprise was the other piece of news included in her email.

Lisa had recently come across a batch of letters her father had written to her mother during the war. They were mostly lighthearted and informative, though they conveyed nothing of serious consequence as he hadn't seen combat. His correspondence had also been censored for sensitive information such as ship locations. Lisa became intrigued by the abrupt cessation of her father's correspondence around May of 1945, soon before the war's end. The letters did resume the following spring, but their tone was more reserved and somber than the earlier batch. Lisa set out to uncover what had changed. She began delving into her father's other memorabilia from his military service. He had been assigned to the LCI (Landing Craft Infantry) 944 later in the war and had kept a list of its crew members, which prompted her to hunt down whatever shipmates she could find, one of whom was my father. She did remark that there were a few mentions in her dad's correspondence about this "Perry Eberhart fellow," who was a lively addition to the crew. In the process of Googling, she came across Dad's name and the fact that 39 boxes of his papers were archived at the Denver Public Library. Lisa and her family live in Baltimore, but as providence would have it, she ended up in Denver to attend a wedding, where she found a few minutes to check out Dad's stuff. Among a few corroborating items, she discovered a poem he had written about disembarking in Hiroshima one month after the bombing and touring the ruins.

Wait! What? Dad had seen firsthand the still smoldering devastation wreaked by the atomic bomb? And, how come I hadn't found that poem? More on that later, but to say I was stunned would be the world's largest understatement.

Lisa reprised the poem in her email. I read it several times, my chest and brain near to exploding each time until I could begin to even fathom what my father had seen. Along with the shock came the awareness that, to my knowledge, Dad had never said anything about that experience. My brother and sister didn't remember him talking about anything so momentous as Hiroshima. I have to believe that my mother knew, but sadly, she wasn't around to ask. Dad's last surviving sibling, Uncle Bill, vaguely recalled that maybe he'd said something, and that most likely he'd have shared the experience with their mother. Discouragingly, I discovered later that Dad had even tried unsuccessfully to get the poem published. How could that have happened and none of his offspring knew what he'd been through? I was shaken, heartsick, and ashamed to know that Dad carried this burden and who knows how many others to his grave.

Lisa and I have developed a wonderful friendship; I am her Ship Brother and she my Ship Sister. We began corresponding regularly, updating each other on discoveries about our fathers' war years. She deserves immense credit for the amount of information she uncovered. Included was her father's journal, which gave credence to the Hiroshima experience, as well digging up the 944's daily log. She also found a surviving ship mate, Ralph Rayner, and family members of others who were deceased. Her explorations led to the LCI Association made up of surviving sailors and more family members. She encouraged me, my brother and sister, other 944 relatives, and Ralph Rayner to attend the annual convention held that year in Portland, Oregon. The event was sobering, illuminating, and a grand social gathering, but the highlight was in the Swan Island Lagoon off the Willamette River. An LCI, the 713, had been rebuilt and restored. It was sitting peacefully along a pier next to a WW II era PT boat. We had a grand time exploring the exact replica of the boat our fathers had sailed on so many years ago. In the chart room, my sister, Eve, and Lisa even reprised the now glorified photo that brought us together.

My resolve to immortalize Dad crystallized. The desire was like molten rock, steel, and grit in my veins. There was so much I didn't know about the man, and with what I did know, the motivation to put it all together became imperative. I became driven to tell the world about this complicated man who inspired, antagonized, but most importantly loved me (though he never seemed to learn how to tell me). With renewed purpose and invigoration, I jumped back on the train that would take me to a terminus of fulfillment as a son, and bearer of my father's memory. The following Uncluttering gave me a sense that the going might get rough, but the journey now had obligation and light.

Unclutterings 12 & 13

I speak in smiles for my words are weak.

&

The stream of life:
Man is drifting down the stream that ultimately
Runs into the gulf of perfection and love

Realizing I had missed so much, I guiltily returned to the fifth floor of the DPL's Central branch and expanded my search beyond Dad's historical writings and research. I unearthed letters, journals, short stories, poetry, photos, meeting notes from his many community activities, correspondence with peers and public figures, certificates of accolade and recognition, newspaper clippings, book reviews, letters to the editor, and so much more. I took even more notes on the special paper and clicked more cell phone documentation, bringing it all home to parse, notate, and evaluate. One day, I looked up from the pile of stuff on my desk. Peering over my computer screen, as if I'd never seen them before, were three tall file cabinets that contained more of Dad's and Mom's stuff. The drawers stared back at me, daring me to come on in. I dove in to discover new buried treasure: family correspondence, report cards, high school assignments, a trove of love letters and even more creative writings. Much to my delight and amazement, I unearthed a 24-carat gem—a chronicle that Dad had laboriously compiled spanning the years 1950 to 1987, not long before his death. It was typed onto continuous feed paper on the Compaq 64 computer my brother had gotten for him and taught him how to use. I swiveled my office chair around to take in the shelf behind me with rekindled appreciation. On it sat the four books he published, the first in 1959, about Colorado's rich history, which has been sold worldwide. Not only did I reread them with heightened purpose, but my wife, Karen, and I have put them to use when we jump in our camper van to explore our beloved home state.

That I hadn't discovered this motherlode of information until nearly three decades after Dad's death was a gut-punch of guilt packed with a lot of disappointment. While I struggled to avoid being devoured by unforgivable negligence, a small part of me blamed him for not trying harder to share his history and fascinations. To be honest with myself, he did take me around the state on his research trips and subjected me and all the family to endless slideshows. Obviously, I wasn't paying attention and had forsaken too many opportunities to share the excitement while he was alive. I felt steamrolled by what I didn't know, should have known, and could have known. For a time that seemed to be eons but was maybe a few months, I gazed upward like Sisyphus at a seemingly insurmountable mountain of regret, self-doubt, and incompetence, pushing an immense boulder that consisted of all that Dad had saved for, what, posterity? Slowly, my despair began to fade into a wellspring of inspiration and focus. After all, I was the son of a writer who, despite his flaws and foibles, carved a path with big footprints for me to follow, and he had provided me with the resources and tools to do it. I can't say that I was engulfed in the euphoria of epiphany, but determination and confidence began to flow through my veins. I decided to write a book about W. Perry Eberhart, a colossal work that championed his noble efforts and educated the world about positive changes of which a complicated man is capable. My train had arrived at the departure gate of a grand journey, so I hopped on with high hopes of finding the gems and nuggets that led me to the motherlode—all the elements that made my father a complex yet extraordinary man.

CHAPTER 2

In 1979, my father had a business trip to Madison, Wisconsin. My mother was worked for United Airlines at the time, but they were on strike. She had time on her hands so she went along for the adventure. They decided to drive up in their new-ish Mercury, probably the nicest car they ever owned; it was very comfortable, Dad said, as well as having air conditioning and a tape deck! On the way, they drove into Wyoming looking for ghost towns and through the Black Hills of South Dakota. When business was finished in Madison, they took a detour on the way home through Yankton, South Dakota, where Dad was born. He figured he hadn't been back there in almost 50 years. They viewed landmarks such as his grandfather Mark's home, which still stood on College Hill, and the hospital where he was born (alas, no statue, he opined). Dad, ever the journalist, went to the offices of the Dakotan Newspaper and dove into their files. He found the obituaries for his maternal grandparents, Mark and Harriett Bennet; hers, Dad reported, was longer than his. Mom and Dad visited the cemetery with their graves, which were not far from several other Bennet markers.

In 2020, my wife Karen and I made a similar trek through Yankton. On a sweltering hot day, we rode our tandem bike past a couple of the family homes and visited family gravesites. The original beautiful buildings and campus of Yankton College had been taken over by the State Department of Corrections and turned into a low-security penitentiary. What a sight to see as we pedaled down the street that divided the campus in two: prisoners in shorts and tee shirts as if they were going to play tennis. I can just imagine what my grandmother would have thought of that!

Back to my parents' long-ago excursion. While in Yankton, Dad discovered that his long-lost Uncle John was living in Janesville, Wisconsin. In January of the next year, he and Mom were able to fly this time to Milwaukee, rent a car, and drive down in time to surprise Uncle John and Aunt Marguerite on their 50th anniversary. Dad was the one who came away with the best gift, an anthology titled: <u>History of the Eberharts in Germany and the United States (from A.D. 1265 to A.D. 1890—625 Years)</u>, by Reverend Uriah Eberhart. Subtitled: *With An Autobiographical Sketch of the Author, Including Many Reminiscences of His Ministerial and Army Life*, the book was published in 1891. The good reverend was my father's grand uncle. Way before 23 and Me, Reverend Uriah researched and catalogued the family lineage all the way back to the birth of Eberhard "The Noble" in 1265 A.D., in what was then Bavaria. Uriah concluded his effort with the claim, "I expect to be doing good to the end of my earthly pilgrimage."

Dad had his copy of the precious manuscript photo-copied and bound in a formal green cover. Each of us kids got a copy as well as each of his siblings. The book is replete with members of every generation from the middle of the 13th century to the end of the 19th century, as comprehensive as any roots Henry Gates might find on his PBS show. Suffice it to say, Dad found an invaluable record which has helped us all better appreciate the stock from whence we came. I am not prone to recap the book's contents, as that is another major undertaking, but suffice it to say that the work has provided a durable foundation for the most recent generations of the family. It helped me to uncover and reinforce endowments and eccentricities that were bequeathed to us to carry forward, or not. The first paragraph from History of the Eberharts states,

"All the Eberharts in this country or their ancestors, so far as known to the writer, came from Germany. They are very numerous both in Germany and America. They still obey the command, 'be fruitful and multiply and replenish the earth' so that to-day they are numbered in the thousands. And although the name has been written and pronounced in a great many different ways such as: 'Eberhardt,' 'Eberhard,' 'Eberhart,' 'Everhard and Everhart,' yet I believe they may all be traced back to one common parentage. This is evident from a resemblance in physical structure, mental similarity and religious faith, as well as in the sameness of their names, and views of social, religious and civil freedom."

* * *

Dad's place in the family history started more or less where Reverend Uriah's book left off. Much of it was chronicled in his mother's powerful and profound memoir, which unfortunately was never published. The book was titled, <u>A</u>

Bridge Named Harriet and paid tribute to her mother, the first of several powerful women that inspired my father. Harriet (Hattie) Christy was born in 1873, and by the age of 22, had earned both bachelor's and master's degrees at Dakota Wesleyan College, where she also become an instructor. In one of her classes, she discovered a student whose "burning conviction" intrigued her. In turn, that student, Mark Bennet, was captivated by her intellect and poise. Though they were a bit of a study in contrasts, Mark's family lived a hardscrabble life on the edges of the prairie while Harriet was raised in the more civilized confines of a college town, they would marry in 1897. Mark entered college as a shy young farm boy but graduated an inspiring orator and debater who loved to argue any side of a question. Almost every night, he would invite a crony or several for dinner to be followed by spirited discussion and argument. He was appointed postmaster of Yankton and would run for several political offices, including state senator. As a reformer in a dry, Republican stronghold, he was soundly defeated each time, eventually though, he did win the election for mayor of Yankton. Later, he bought the Daily Dakota Herald, which was considered the only Democrat daily in the state of South Dakota.

Hattie hosted her own club activities and became the paper's first society page editor, one of the first women in the nation to hold that position. My grandmother declared that her mother never complained and was a charming host, as well as a loving and understanding wife. Though she was often sick, she spent the day preparing for the night's banquet, the head count of which was never known until all the guests were seated. In all, Hattie had eight children but lost two of them.

Despite all his public activity, Mark found time to write long, loving poetry to Hattie.

Dad didn't see his grandparents much after his family left Yankton when he was about three years old, so he learned what he knew of them from his mother. After retiring from the dog-eat-dog world of politics, Mark bought a coal company that prospered until the Depression, when he nearly went bankrupt. He had to sell the house on College Hill, so he and Hattie moved into a small apartment on Main Street. Sadly, she died a short time later. Her obituary in the Dakotan listed her many interests and activities as one of Yankton's preeminent citizens.

I believe Dad developed a healthy reverence for his grandfather, though it was ambivalent. In a letter that he wrote from Paris to his mother after Mark's death, Dad reflected on special times when he was able to be alone with him. Those included walks in the woods, around the neighborhood, and even to downtown. He recalls a man, "straight and proud, unbending and honest. I shall always see his smile and hear his chuckle that never hurt anyone..." Dad's letter was curious in that he apologized for his "callousness" at not feeling grief in the traditional sense, and also that he was glad he was 5,000 miles away when Mark died. He explained his sentiment, "It would, no doubt, make me very sad and I try not to be sad as much as I can and I'm sure Grandpa would not be thinking it my duty to be sad." More intriguingly, "Death is only a superficial occurrence anyway to be used selfishly by those who view it." Reading this long-ago letter turned on the proverbial lightbulb in my mind, as it helped to explain why our family was never prone to indulging in memorial services and, especially, funerals.

The first born of Mark and Hattie's six children was Lucile Christy Bennett, who was born in 1898. She was the strong, powerful woman I would come to know as Grandma.

While at Yankton College, Lucile became enamored of a young football player who would soon leave to join the fight as a tank driver in World War I. That football player was Fred George Eberhart who was born in 1894 to Reverend Harry Pearl Eberhart and Belle Agnes Baker.

Despite the Hague Convention on Land Warfare that prohibited the dispersion of poisonous chemicals, Fred was gassed. He came home, received disability payments, and was in and out of VA hospitals for the rest of his life due to his injuries. Soon after his return from the war, Fred and Lucile were married at the Eastside Methodist Church in Sioux Falls by his father.

In her memoir, A Bridge Named Harriet, Grandma stated that, "The role models of my father and grandfathers was 'my way or the highway.' My grandmothers cajoled, ranted, prayed, and made their voices heard, [but] those were the days of paternal despotism of which so many of today's men yearn." Lucile claimed that her separation from her Papa's ideal began when she discovered boys. This would become bane and impetus for much of her life, as well as the rebellious keystone of her first marriage. When her father discovered that she had snuck out of the house to spend one more evening with her soldier, Fred, he forbade her from ever seeing him again. Little did he realize, that as Lucile put it, "…forbidden fruit to his willful daughter always tasted the sweetest."

When Lucile's infatuation turned toward marriage, Mark forbade any member of the family from attending the ceremony. He railed ceaselessly against the union, stating, "He was a womanizer of questionable honor."

To which young Lucile replied, "Papa, he is the son of a minister. He fought for our Democracy and was poisoned by gasses."

Hattie argued, "You have such a talent for writing, you should have stayed in school and developed a career."

"Mama, a career?" a distraught Lucile responded, "No, I want to make a home with the man I love and have babies to hold in my arms."

Despite the headwinds, Mark and Lucile got married in June of 1919. I, unfortunately, was unable to find if any of Grandma's family did sneak away to defy her father and attend the wedding. Lucile, only later in her memoir, admitted lingering pain from that sense of not living up to the achievements of her family. Her father had been Mayor of Yankton and a newspaper publisher while her mother was a well-respected academic and socialite. In their footsteps, her sister Ruth, brother Burke, and sister Jean all attended college. Lucile would sadly recall how Hattie would get tears in her eyes when Jean, studying music, and Burke, in the Glee Club, would sing together in the music room on College Hill. Ruth was the honor student while her brother Paul was engaged and helping in the family business. To quote Grandma's lonely lament, "It was only Lucile who had made such a muck of her life!"

The luster of Lucile and Fred's union faded faster than frost on a spring morning. Fred took up his father's profession as preacher and they moved to Davis, South Dakota, where she taught Sunday school. Despite fiercely defending her wounded knight against the ridicule of her father, romance and mystery quickly succumbed to the drab existence of struggling to feed and clothe themselves. She confided her dismay that the stolen kisses and clandestine embraces of their courtship became the ordinary couplings of married life. In starkly sarcastic and candid words, she complained, "Where was the romance? Where were my poems of love? Where was the excitement? Wham, bam, thank you mam [sic]!"

Fred traipsed off proselytizing around the Midwest, with Lucile striving to be the dutiful wife. He was far from a paragon of piety, as he lorded over his congregations with a little philandering and embezzlement on the side. She would later recount, "I had to save my first husband from scandal. I begged them, 'He has children to support, please let him keep his job. Move him to another state.' " When the Methodists transferred him to other outposts, he wrote to those who disparaged him, "Just try and get any money out of me now!'"

Was the following poem Dad's caricature of his father?

He Got the Jump on the Lord

He got the jump on the lord and played
    it for all it was worth
Figuring on starting a cold,
    hell right here on god's good earth
and when the mortals started coming they fit
    right into the plan
What with all the shooting and (?)
The echo of the (?) and (?)

But, lo, there came into the
    mountains one day
a man over fifty, lean
    lanky and gray
But he was lean and hard and
    had a fire in his eye
He had a bible in his pocket
    And his head in the sky

He came from Minnesota to
    Preach and work for hire
He was a traveling salesman
    for god, his name was
    Dyer

[(?) unreadable words from handwritten pages]

"I know how much I could have garnered at my parents' feet." With this line from <u>A Bridge Named Harriet</u>, my grandmother from her grave aptly portrays my guilt for not learning more about my predecessors. Was I not paying attention, feeling their words not important enough to remember, or just arrogantly ignorant? Why am I only now learning so much from them, when there's no one left to answer my questions? To my great regret, I hardly remember my father or even his mother talking much about his grandparents, or sadly have forgotten what they did tell me. I would have discovered and more fully understood the family inclination toward scholarly debate, journalism, and literary composition. My liberal roots, I would find, were planted in the hard-packed South Dakota soil. The family had a strong spiritual foundation, but it wasn't the product of regular church attendance or organized prayer, or respectable preaching, for that matter. Echoing great Uncle Uriah's assertion, "[We Eberharts had] a resemblance in physical structure, mental similarity, and religious faith, as well as in the sameness of their names, and views of social, religious, and civil freedom."

Dad may have been thinking similar thoughts to mine as he contemplated those that came before him. Whether we pay attention or not, they keep on marching.

<hr />

Musing 4

I looked back
And saw a generation coming
Abashed — I shouted and pointed
But on they came
Their superficial anthem
More polished that even mine
Smothered my words and they marched
In a frenzy dancing the same
Miserable trails I cut for them
I felt guilty but could only hope
That perhaps one of their ranks
Would straggle and perhaps look back
And could shout louder than I

<hr />

Ask the questions before it's too late.

CHAPTER 3

I'm looking back, striving to catch the generations coming before me. Like Dad, I'm shouting and pointing, a fervent hope is that I can get them to stop long enough for me to hear and learn from them.

In April of 1920, Lucile gave birth to her first child, John Robert Eberhart, who came to be known as Jack for reasons I'll never know. He was born without the support of her family in the small town of Davis, South Dakota, where Fred was trying to launch his preaching career.

Lucile went home to Yankton to have her second son, Donald David, in April of 1923. For a while, she had some family around to support her. Soon after Don was born, however, she and Fred moved to Bingham Canyon, Utah, where he was a preacher in the Methodist Mission church. She wrote that for a short time, "Our little family was happy there," but they left once again in scandal. When John, Fred's younger brother, wired funds to cover the shortfall in the church's coffers, Lucile opined that, "I would have been visiting my husband in jail."

Again, seeking solace from family, Lucile returned to Yankton for the birth of her third son and my father, Wilfred Perry, on August 5, 1924. Though Lucile lamented that she probably should have left Fred then and stayed in Yankton, she and her growing brood rejoined him in Loveland, Colorado. where he was preaching to yet another Methodist congregation. I would chide my father that as much he loved Colorado and showed his reverence to her many times over, he could never qualify as a native, which is a sort of badge of honor in our fair state. His amusement at the claim always seemed subdued.

In January of 1927, they welcomed the birth of their first daughter, Jeanne Ruth. Then, a series of events occurred later that year that would have profound impacts on Lucile's life. Though still suffering ill effects from his war injuries, Fred joined the National Guard, perhaps to add a few dollars to the family coffers. In the autumn of that year, Colorado Governor Alva Adams called out the militia to the town of Serene, where union coal miners (the Industrial Workers of the World, or Wobblies) were on strike. Fred became a sergeant in Company C where he met and would develop a friendship with a cavalry sergeant in the Denver Troop, Carl Howard Haberl. At the time, neither of them, nor Lucile, could imagine the implications of that meeting.

As dark clouds of the Great Depression rolled across the country, Fred became very ill and was sent to the VA (Veterans Affairs) hospital in Indiana. Thus began the darkest time for Lucile and her family. She would write, "...at a time, when back in Yankton, the old trees were dying and covered with dust." The stock market crashed and she found herself and her children on 'relief.'

When Fred returned, they moved to Denver, into an old house on Race Street, near what is now the Botanic Gardens. Things began to improve, though the family was still quite poor, and Fred returned to life as an itinerant preacher. Life wasn't altogether gloomy, though. At an early age, Dad began to roam. Despite the mischievous smirk and wonderful shock of white hair, his overalls are encircled with a strand of rope to keep him from wandering.

Perry at about 4 years old

Dad found a cadre of neighbor kids who loved to play in the streets. They would scrounge ice chips and produce from wagon vendors that plied the neighborhoods. The alleys they roamed were filled with hollyhocks, wild rhubarb, and treasures that included love letters in the trash bins. One of Dad's fondest memories was of the old radio that sat on the mantel in the living room. Someone must have given it to them, Dad recalled, because they never could have afforded to buy it. One can imagine four little children sitting cross-legged on the old wood floor and their mother in a well-used, over-stuffed chair, all in a semi-circle around this magical device that brought the world into their living room. They laughed heartily at the comedy shows and their saintly mother would lead them as they sang along to gospel music. Dad remembers her being terribly frightened by Orson Welles' ominous baritone reporting that Martians had invaded, and the tears she shed listening to Franklin Delano Roosevelt's inaugural speech.

Their second daughter, Patricia Harriet, was born on the fifth of April in 1931. Not long after, however, the fissures that had grown wide between Lucile and Fred erupted when he came home to find her in bed with Carl, the dashing young cavalry man from Serene. That was the end of the marriage.

The divorce was toughest on Dad's older brother, Jack. Apparently, Fred left without expressing any love for his eldest son. Approaching adolescence, shy yet cynical, Jack craved that fatherly affection but blamed his mother more than his father for the split. Jack still wanted her love, but neither of them knew how to honestly express themselves when they were face to face. As Dad would write later, "They went through life at arm's length, never ever finding the words to say."

After Fred left, Lucile again went on relief, this time with five small children and pregnant with her sixth. They lived in a couple of seedy, downtown hotels before finding a shabby two-bedroom house at the corner of 11th Avenue and Clayton Street. In the midst of that ominous and distressing time, William Peter was born the day after Christmas in 1933.

The house was small for a family of seven. The two older boys bunked on the sleeping porch, young Pat and the baby had one small bedroom, and Dad shared an old wire army cot with his little sister, Jeanne, in a corner of the kitchen. I can just visualize the two of them trying to get comfortable.

"Mom, Perry took all the covers again!" Jeanne would wail.

Dad would roll over and hold her chubby little cheeks in his hands. "Shush, or I'm going to stuff you in the ice box!"

The family made do with canned goods and a few staples from the relief agency. Dad recalls the runny oatmeal that actually tasted pretty good. The roving produce vendors would often give Dad and his siblings their slightly overripe vegetables. They subsisted on potatoes, lots and lots of them because they were cheap and weren't bad as snacks after school. Now, I know from where our family's veneration of spuds sprouted. Dad and his siblings wore hand-me-down clothes, though he recalled that his mother was a wizard with needle and thread.

Across the street was a fire station, whose crew took the little family under its collective wing. Dad wrote that, "Instead of having no father to call my own...I had several, all kindly and fatherly." The firemen would play ball with the boys, fix things that broke, and even carry him around on their shoulders. One of Dad's most exciting moments was the time they let him ride on the back of the hook-and-ladder truck, on the way back from a fire. Often, they would bring piping hot meals across the street that had real meat and contained a lot of stuff the family seldom had at their house. Dad came to idolize Fireman Bob, who he described as, "the youngest, handsomest, strongest, smilingist, funniest, and friendliest." He was easy to talk with and even let Dad help polish the trucks. One time, he actually prevented Dad's big brother from bullying him.

Many happy times were spent just talking with Fireman Bob, who became a special role model for Dad.

After a time, Grandma moved the family a couple blocks over to a slightly bigger, 100-year-old red house at 2420 11th Avenue. Lucile's fervent belief in the power of education compelled her to find a cheap home in decent neighborhoods so the kids could be enrolled in good schools, but that also meant they were the poorest kids in class. As a sense of stability settled over them, the kids grew up and into their own spaces.

That old red house still stands. It's a couple blocks from the Denver Botanic Gardens. I ride my bicycle past the house periodically, musing on the lives of my father and his family living there, almost 90 years ago. The other places where they lived in the neighborhood succumbed to gentrification. Even Fireman Bob's old station has been converted into trendy townhouses.

Lucile felt that Jack was of superior intelligence but carried a lot of contempt for the family's lack of money. He was medium height for his age but skinny with a defiant scowl seemingly cemented on his face. She implored him to use his intellect as a shield against the troubles of the world, but unfortunately, he created an impenetrable barrier that cut him off from those who loved him. The second oldest, Don, with piercing dark eyes and always smirking, inherited his charm from his birth father, but also his irresponsibility. He was loveable, schoolmates opened their arms wide for him, but he did many things that hurt himself and others.

With the square jaw that all the children inherited from their mother, round cheeks, and a mischievous smile, my father revered his older brothers while observing and striving to learn from their imperfections. That didn't prevent him from being a bit precocious himself. He recounted with some measure of tongue-in-cheek braggadocio, "Nobody was more spoiled than I. I was perfect. This is a fact that my brothers and sisters are still having trouble getting over. I was Mom's 'little man' until I grew up and became her 'big man.' I helped support the family even as a little boy. The first time I remember my superiority...I was in about the fourth grade. We needed money for food. It had also snowed the night before. Mother sent Don, 2 years older, to go out and shovel some walks. Don came back a half hour later, one wonders where he went. 'Nobody wants their walks shoveled,' he said in disgust."

Dad puffed up his chest and snagged the dilapidated old snow shovel. "I don't remember if I was sent out or volunteered. Inside a half hour I had shoveled three walks. We lived it up that day on the money I had made. Mother didn't throw it up to Don, but Don didn't need it thrown up to him. From that time on I made a good living for my family shoveling walks and taking care of lawns."

Dad grew to adore and develop an allegiance with his sister, Jeanne. Lucile always wanted a daughter for all the frilly, feminine reasons, but with Jeanne, she got a tomboy. Endowed with the family's deep dimples and penetrating dark-eyed gaze, she was rarely clean, played softball with her older brothers, and thought most little girl things were silly. Jeanne claimed that she inherited all of the best traits of her illustrious ancestors, but not the ability to lie. While Grandpa Mark and her mother praised Jeanne for treating everyone with respect, Grandma Hattie, on the other hand, would shake her head and remark, "she didn't do well with her school lessons and I cannot believe her spelling."

Younger sister Pat was the sibling all the others rallied around, as she suffered much during those early years. In an active, seemingly big healthy family, she was surprisingly fragile. She suffered several major afflictions as a young girl. The first devastated my father because he was the cause of the incident that scarred his little sister. At the time, she was six years old. He was demonstrating a magic that involved molten lead (what was he demonstrating?!). Accidentally, he knocked over the pan that held the concoction and it spilled across Pat's leg. She was severely burned and spent several days on the sofa; every movement caused her to scream out in pain and guilt to rile in my father's stomach. After several days Pat became quiet, lethargic and developed a high temperature. The doctor sauntered in as if he was there to treat a simple malady, and next thing Dad knew, an ambulance was parked outside and taking his sister to the hospital. Lucile held vigil at her daughter's bedside but would come home to check on the other children. She gathered them around the dining room table and they prayed—even Jack, the oldest, who had railed against God since his father had left. Three days later, Lucile came home to say that their sister was going to be just fine. Dad exclaimed that, "The house had never seen or heard such shouting as it contained that night."

Only a year or two later, Pat developed rheumatic fever for which she was hospitalized again and bedridden for over a month. When she was able to return home, Lucile hovered over her 24 hours a day, seven days a week. Dad became very protective of his little sister, an obligation that would extend far into their adult lives.

In those early years, Carl became a regular presence at the red house on 11th Avenue, and as Grandma's marriage dissolved, he became her bedrock of support. She would later write, "I know there are those who condemn me for my affair...I told Carl in my letters that I only wanted to be friends, that I would not demand anything from him." As Uncle Bill would later recount, Carl came over every evening and stayed until 10:30, but never overnight.

Carl Howard Haberl was born in August 1908, the first of three sons to Phillip John and Nanette Fehr Haberl. From all accounts, Carl and his brother had an idyllic childhood until Nannette died in 1915 during the great influenza pandemic. Phillip and the two boys returned to Denver after living a short time in Seattle. Carl was taking classes at the Colorado University Extension School in Denver when he made that fateful decision to enlist in the National Guard. He began working with the Colorado State Employment Agency during the latter years of the Great Depression. He brought a genuine empathy to the job honed from his earlier experiences. Despite having been on the other side of the Wobblies strike in Serene and the mining camps in Cripple Creek, Carl had misgivings about being called to put down the protests of hard-working men who were only trying to provide for their families. In the wake of the Great Depression, many of Carl's cavalry mates disparaged the onerous ranks of unemployed men with comments such as, 'If they really wanted to work, they could get jobs. They're just lazy!' Disgusted with such sentiment, Carl quit the service, and became one of the jobless multitude. For a great long while, he found that, indeed, there were no jobs to be had. Finally, he landed a laborer's position with the Colorado and Southern Railway. With the bitter taste of the cavalry men's derision, the vagaries of unemployment, and the experience being an exploited worker, he became an ardent supporter of the working man and woman. When Carl secured an entry-level position with Division of Employment, his skill and finesse at finding jobs for down-on-their-luck, hardworking folk made him the go-to guy as he worked his way up in the agency. Carl's experiences and example made not only my father, but us in the following generations, hardcore Labor supporters. So much so, that when we hear the informal union anthem, *Joe Hill*, we might be apt to put a hand over our hearts as a tear comes to our eye.

When the youngest of her brood, Bill, a brash 19-year-old, was in the midst of an argument with Lucile when she let slip that his father was Carl Haberl, not Fred Eberhart. In the story of her life, Grandma very candidly wrote,

> "What selfishness or pride is it that prevents me from telling Billy and everyone else the truth about his birth? I fought so hard to keep on keeping on. I had him, alone, at home without comfort of hospital or without his father holding my hand. Maybe I was ashamed that Carl had not done the right thing by me. Probably it was the old adolescent warnings to control my passion. After all I had endured, I didn't want to be judged. Fred and I were pretty much living apart since before Pat's birth, and of course much of the time before that. Carl and I had a wonderful summer together."

Had Uncle Bill know from the beginning who his father was changed the trajectory of his life? Even knowing the truth, he doesn't think so because Carl had been a presence in his life from early on. He had had a difficult childhood. It was discovered that he had a problem with his eyes from the time he was very young, which they later learned was Amblyopia, or lazy eye, and made him very self-conscious. My father and Aunt Jeanne tried to protect their little brother, but they were soon charting their own paths through life, leaving Bill to become introverted and painfully shy. Looking back, Bill says now that he didn't want to attract attention to himself. As an adult, Bill discovered that his vision problems could have been corrected by surgery, and that his parents were negligent in not trying harder to correcting the defect.

Front row: Bill, Pat. Back row: Dad, Don, Grandma, Jack, Jeanne

* * *

When Lucile and the kids moved to the red house, they were still on the dole. In addition to small part-time jobs, she started in earnest writing stories to sell to local newspapers, national magazines, and other periodicals. Dad remembers coming home from school to find her at her typewriter, the dining room table strewn with sheets of paper. Late in the afternoon, Lucile would run to the mailbox only to find boundless rejections. Her face would fall and she'd sit forlornly quiet for several minutes, but then turn back to the typewriter and resume pounding the keys.

One day in 1936 changed her life forever.

I imagine a day in spring with new leaves sprouting on the Elm trees in front of the house, Dad sauntering in from the kitchen and throwing his books on the old wooden chair in the corner. Edging over to his mother, careful not to disturb the stacks of typing paper and carbons, he leans over to kiss the top of her head. "Hey, Mother! How's the great American novel going?"

Between the clacking of the keys, she glances upward with a quick smile. "Just okay, Perry, just okay."

A low clatter on the front porch draws their attention.

She says without looking away from the ubiquitous typewriter, "The mailman."

Though he knew she was trying to act nonchalant, he offered, "I'll bring in the mail, Mom."

Dad placed the small stack of correspondence on the table next to her. Resignedly, she tediously sifted through the letters, when suddenly, she looked up at him with her eyes brighter than he'd ever seen them. She jumped up, wrapped her arms around his neck, kissed him on the cheek, and ran to the bottom of the stairs to holler at whoever was home. Jeanne, Jack, and Don tumbled down the steps. Pat and Bill rushed in from the backyard.

Lucile waved a single sheet of paper in the air like a victory flag and jubilantly cried out, "They bought my story! They bought my story!"

All the little faces momentarily went blank as they tried to process the letter and their mother's excitement. Then, Dad and his older brothers whooped and jumped up and down. The younger kids, whether they understood the commotion or not, joined in.

"They," was the Christian Century Journal. They accepted an article Lucile had anonymously written and titled, 'What Shall I Teach My Children.' It started, "My six and I, we live on relief," and went on to recount the struggles of being impoverished while trying to provide a decent and loving home. The story was a perfect counterpoint to the characterization of women on the dole as scourges of society, living off the public's teat, or "welfare queens," which they came to be called many decades later. With incomparable candor, she wrote,

> "I have heard it said that anyone worthwhile wouldn't take charity. I used to think so, too. I am proud and sensitive. I have dreamed dreams. I fought for months, trying to stave off this relief business. I looked everywhere for work. I wanted to take care of my family myself. But there isn't any work that would provide a living for one mother and six children and pay for competent care for

the children while I am gone, so that they would run the streets and get killed, or worse. So, we are on relief." (The article in its entirety appears in Addendum 1)

The story received an overwhelmingly positive response and was reprinted in the Rocky Mountain News. The editors of the paper sought out the identity of the anonymous mother who so elegantly pleaded her case. Ultimately, they tracked down Lucile, who by then was using her pen name, Eve Bennett. They were so enthralled by her frank and hard-hitting style that they hired her to be a staff member for the newly created women's department. Before long, she became its first female editor.

Though Lucile's income early in her journalistic career was meager, the family reveled in the newfound sense of stability and regular income. For my father it meant he was able to soak up all the excitement available to a young boy growing up in the city. He developed a band of neighborhood friends who would ride bikes, play endless games of sandlot football, and hone their boxing skills; Dad declared proudly that we was co-champion in sixth grade. Dad tells of one friend Donny, whose family was devout Christian, born again before it was stylish. My father, in his inimical way, reported that he wasn't born anything, just "a pagan weed in the garden of life." Then, there was Chet, the neighborhood bully. Brother Jack told his little brother to stand up to him and not back down. Which Dad did, and would later pass along the same commandment to me years later. Dad became a newspaper delivery boy, continued to mow lawns, shoveling sidewalks and coal in the winter so he could have a dime or two to join his chums at the movie houses on Colfax. He and his friends would slip through holes in the fence to watch DU football games.

* * *

In September of 1937, Lucile and Carl went to the Cotton Bowl in Texas to see Whizzer White, a standout for the University of Colorado Buffaloes who would later become a United States Supreme Court justice. Dad reported, "When they came back, they were married!" Lucile and Carl, who became Grandma and Pappy Carl to us, were together until she died.

Grandma and Pappy's influence on Dad was as inimitable as it was profound. She was his confidante and rock of stability. Carl, or Pappy, was the sage and mentor from whom his step-son could expect direction or even rebuke. Beyond their guiding lights, however, being the third of six strong-willed children in the family certainly provided young Perry further explicit and subtle life lessons.

Older brothers John (Jack) and Don presented contradictory influences. Dad looked up to his older siblings, as younger brothers will, desiring to follow in their footsteps, whether they be in the worlds of athletics, bravado, or, especially, women. While Dad's efforts endeared him to his mother, Jack and Don were not as impressed. They would bully him for being "Mom's Pet," or "an apple polisher." When Dad grew to over six feet in high school and taller than his brothers, he apparently exacted his revenge, though I never found out how. He still looked up to his brothers and followed them into the military to fight for their country in World War II. Jack was a dynamic and endearing personality who would later make his mark as a beloved educator in literature and the arts. His and Lucile's erudite achievements obviously inspired Dad in his zeal to become a writer. In later years, both Jack and Don became philanderers of sorts, casting off wives and children, which did not inspire Dad. In these comments, perhaps he is expressing the yin and yang of growing up in the shadow of two such idiosyncratic brothers.

Collected Quips and Sayings 12 & 14

Intelligence is the capacity to understand and to connect facts and ideas (unknown)

&

Life is like an onion you peel off one layer at a time, and sometimes you weep (Carl Sandburg)

Dad was closest to his sister Jeanne. She claims that "[Perry] was stuck with me more than the others." Being only two years apart in age, they also shared many of the same friends through school and around the neighborhood. Jeanne liked to tell how she never had to worry about boys bothering her. If they did, she just called over her hulking older brother. However, she admitted, that may have made it a bit harder to meet guys as well. Despite Dad's looming presence, at the tender age of 16, Jeanne met George Zavadil, a 20-year-old Chicagoan who was training at Lowry Air Force base in Denver.

According to her, after meeting him, "no one else mattered." Dad remained indulgent and affectionate toward his younger sister as their tight bond deepened over their lifetimes. That devotion passed onto their spouses and offspring.

Lucile was overly protective of Pat, due to her maladies, but became the prideful mother when her younger daughter took up family's literary mantel. As early as junior high, she began following in her mother's footsteps, blossoming into a columnist in her own right and even had her own radio show, 'Teen Time Tempos,' at age 16. Dad was proud of Pat's growing reputation, and perhaps a bit envious. Not unlike her mother, though, she left college and her potential behind to join the man who would become her husband, Jack Blosser.

Bill was young enough that he didn't spend much time with his two eldest brothers, but Dad and Jeanne did watch over him to the best they could in their own busy lives. In recent years, I've become quite close with Uncle Bill. As the last descendant of his generation of the family, I appreciate more and more the invaluable trove of history he represents. Spending time with him allows me to soak up the intelligence and world vision of a family that may or may not have been out of the ordinary, but was immensely original. The intrigue, stories, and hallmarks are enthralling and, as he likes to say, he lived through it all.

* * *

Dad's high school years were filled with adventures and anxieties not unlike those of most kids before or since. As always, there were myriad seeds for behaviors and beliefs that would blossom later in life. In particular, Lucile's love of literature encouraged her children to read, read, and read some more. My father wholeheartedly bought into her conviction as if it were religion. Duly inspired by her newfound success, he began writing stories and poems, many he sold to neighbors for a dime, adding to his kit of money-making strategies.

There was a time when a visitor called on Lucile, perhaps to ask her about a column she had written. Noting how spiffed up the front room of the old house was, Dad took the cue to show off his worldliness, talking about books he'd read and his opinions on local events. "Putting on his sickly sweet," his sisters called it.

The visitor commented, "That boy is going to grow up to be governor one day."

Dad took those words to heart, remembering them well as he grew older. When he saw that some governors were, "lousy," he wasn't sure that was the best thing to be. Other times, he thought it was something to shoot for, "something that would make [his] mother proud!"

As time went on, part of his disinclination to politics prompted him to think of himself a "lousy" speaker who hated the spotlight. His first negative experience involved standing in front of his more well-heeled, seventh grade classmates to talk about gifts he had received for Christmas.

"Well, I got a modern pen that contained ink," he said shakily.

Immediately, the other students began giggling and neighbors nudged each other. Before long, in Dad's mind, the whole class was laughing uproariously. He wanted to melt away and disappear, the blush on his cheeks like fire. Only after he'd slunk down in his seat did he realize his fly was open.

Fortunately, an instructor took Dad aside in later years to tell him that he was talking about things he knew or cared little about. When he began talking about topics about which he was knowledgeable or cared passionately, he gained more confidence. Though he always disliked the spotlight, his chops as good public speaker greatly improved and served him well later in life.

Dad was small for his age until he reached high school, then he grew to be over six feet tall. Football, boxing, and other active pastimes kept him fit and trim. His sisters were even proud enough to show off their big brother to their friends. In his yearbook, one girl he liked wrote, "To my idea of Adonis." Dad had to look in the dictionary to see who this Adonis guy was. Despite the compliments and adoration, Dad claimed he had not one date in high school. He even proclaimed to his little brother that he was a "kissless wonder." Among the pages of his nascent memoir that he would pen many years later, he admitted to dreaming of "warm and sometimes sizzling relationships." Feeling second-class in his fairly affluent high school, he could never get up the nerve to ask a girl out. There were several girls with whom he was quite friendly, buddy-buddy or brother-sister things, he recalled, but when the friendship hinted at something more, he got cold feet.

"Perry, why don't you bring your friend home for dinner, just to get acquainted?" his mother would ask.

When his younger sister said she had a girlfriend who was crazy about him, and that he should ask her out, Dad brushed off the idea, saying, "Why would I want to go out with a silly young thing?"

Instead, Dad would dress up and pretend he had a date on a Friday or Saturday night. He'd take a streetcar downtown and go to a movie...by himself. After treating himself to a grilled cheese sandwich and chocolate malt, he'd come home and report to his mother what a good time he'd had.

This is a sad, desperate poem. My heart weeps to think that Dad felt he had to give everything to get love. That he would be so vulnerable and not being loved would leave him empty, a shell.

Unanswered Love

I want to be your temple, your confessional, your rosary.
I want to be your nothing
   - like a robin singing on the sill.
I want to be your all
   - like the torrid sun you cannot escape.

Please draw from me.
I want to be like you are to me.
I'm only happy serving you;
I'm only happy being like you want me to be.
How can I pierce the wall around you — of doubts and fears and hurts.
If I were but God and could say to you.
Like I must say to you -
Like I cry to say to you -
Eloquently, crudely, profoundly, silently —
   - I love you

Epitaph

Now I look back and see what I wanted to be.
I wanted to be God — but what is God?
A storybook love that little boys dream of;
Fed by books, and movies, and music.

But love is like a mountain
That only changes as the snows come and then
the summer.
Little boys can't change nature,
And when they try, they only change themselves.
I forced and strained the love from my body
And drained myself of love and of me –
I lost myself to you –
Until there was nothing left for you to love.

One day in his senior year, Dad and his friend Dick Bray were boxing as they did most every Sunday in the little garage behind the big red house. It was warm, despite being early December. They had worked up a pretty good sweat, when his mother came out and excitedly shouted at them to come in the house. Dick and Dad quizzically looked at each other and ran into the kitchen to find Pappy and the other kids crowded around the radio.

"The Japanese are bombing Pearl Harbor!"

CHAPTER 4

"Why don't we just bomb the hell out of Hanoi, and get it over with," I raged.

It was 1966 or so. American involvement in Vietnam was reaching a zenith. I was an all-knowing sixteen-year-old who had all the answers, as did every teenager since the dawn of time. Leaning against the kitchen counter, I defiantly crossed my arms around my torso.

Dad sat on a stool at the other end of the counter. With a look of sad amusement on his face, he responded, "You really think that's the way to end the war?"

Dad's reaction confused me. I just shrugged my shoulders and left Dad to his nonsense. My naïve self didn't understand my dad's answer because, after all, he had been in WWII, where the US helped defeat an evil despot and the aggressors of Japan. About all I knew of his service was that he learned to drink, smoke, and play cards in the Navy, and that he brought a Japanese rifle back from Okinawa. Sadly, he never spoke of the tragedies he saw, nor the fears he faced. It would be 50 years and long after his death that I would learn about him and his shipmates stepping ashore in Hiroshima. As well, there was a rich military history to our family: my grandfather drove a tank in WWI, was gassed and lived with the effects for the rest of his life; my father and four uncles were in WWII; Dad's stepfather was in one of the last active units of the US Cavalry. Of them, my father, step-grandfather, and two uncles developed strong anti-war beliefs after what they'd seen and experienced.

The United States did bomb the hell out of Hanoi in 1968, and again in 1972. The destruction during each of those events was horrendous, but they did not end the war.

* * *

Like those of us who remember exactly where we were and what we doing when JFK was assassinated or the twin towers fell to the ground on 9/11, Dad never forgot where he was and what he was doing on December 7, 1941. He was seventeen-years old at the time and had yet to comprehend the impact that day would have on his life.

In my excavations, I came across a term paper Dad wrote when he was a high school senior in 1942. It was titled, 'College or War.' In a way, he displayed the same naïveté and ignorance that I showed in our suburban kitchen some 20 years later, however his paper showed much more depth of thought. 19 pages is far too much to include here, but a few snippets demand citing:

> "Unlike many boys my age, I knew what war meant... because I had a father who had been a sergeant in the first world war...had been gassed, shellshocked, and wounded by an exploding shrapnel shell...his closest

friend had his head blown off in the tank just ahead of my father's tank. Many other stories of his...made me fear and hate war."

"Statistics show 1 in 20 Americans that go overseas never come back...if there are those who must die on foreign battlefields, they chose the best way of dying; to give up one's life for his country and in the cause of freedom is the greatest thing one can do."

"A higher education will be the most important factor after the war in building up the world which will be pretty well in shambles."

"I don't know which would be worse — going to college until the war is over and miss serving my country; or going into the army with the plan of going to college later, only to have the war last many years so that I would be too old for college and would not be trained for any peacetime occupation. In either case, I would be quite displeased and feel left out of things. I would feel that I have been denied something I wanted and needed to do."

Young Perry was definitely torn, and certainly heavily influenced by what was happening around him, including the fact that his two older brothers had already enlisted in the military. Like a good deliberator, he carefully lined out the pros and cons. Arguments in favor of the Army (he used that as his default, though he alluded to the Navy as well) included: fierce patriotism, immediate financial reward, technical training, and the benevolent care of a thankful government (pensions, healthcare, etc). The case against included death and dismemberment, of course, as well as losing ground to those who got their educations first. I find it quite interesting that Dad was able to rationalize mortality as justified if life is sacrificed to the honor of country. He scorned being, "run down by a car, or breaking your neck by slipping on a cake of soap...or falling down the basement stairs," because then one would not have the satisfaction of, "serving your country and the right cause."

While his brain leaned toward going off to war, Dad's heart might pulled toward the walls of ivy. His mother and stepfather were stalwart champions of education, as well as already having two other sons going off to war. Based on his recollections, I can only imagine a kitchen discussion not unlike the one Dad and I would have in the future.

Lucile might have said, "Perry, you must go to college now! That has been our dream for you."

Dad would have replied, "But mother, the country needs me now."

"You still may have to go into the military anyway," she asserted, "but if you go after college, your training and being older will only make you a better soldier."

Pappy Carl would have been sitting in the corner, smoking his pipe, not saying much, but Dad would have been unable to ignore his wizened gaze.

Even older brother Jack, who had enlisted in the Royal Canadian Air Corp because the Americans disqualified him due to his eyesight, wrote Dad advising him to continue his schooling. "Let the older men take care of the war," he said.

College, Dad figured, offered social relationships, contacts, and new friends, "All of which gives you a poise and understanding of life at its best...can also be accomplished in army, but in college you have more time to perfect this side of the picture and acquire some of the culture which you cannot very well get any place else." It also offered him the opportunity to pursue his dream of playing football. The drawbacks to campus life were significant in the face of patriotic fervor. He lamented, "[I] could stay home, be safe, have a good time, and yet prepare for my future. Yet we do not think much of men who do that. There were men in the other war who did that and it took many years to live down the shame of it."

19 pages of soul searching and analysis in the end boiled down to one ultimate conclusion:

> "At least I do not intend to go into either the army or to enter college unless I have decided what to do that will satisfy my conscience. I believe that my conscience is the most important thing to consider, as you can live without money or without a leg or an arm, but you can't live with a bad conscience."

* * *

So, how did Perry Eberhart get from high school senior contemplating war or college to a hard-bitten, sagacious father facing a belligerent son who was confronting the same life and death conundrums he'd stared down? He started by keeping his conscience clear and soon after his 19th birthday, enlisted in the Naval Air Corps, with dreams of being a pilot like his brother, Jack. On April ninth in 1943, Dad reported for basic training in Ely, Nevada. Six months later, he was assigned to flight school in San Luis Obispo, California, and later, Corpus Christi, Texas. He caught the fever of aviation and was terribly excited by the possibility of touching the heavens. At this point, however, his story took an abrupt turn. For some reason I have yet to uncover, he left the air corps. I have some memory of Dad saying that he "washed out" of flight school because of his eyesight, very similar to his brother Jack's story. Scouring all his papers for possible mention of his time in flight school, I came across only a couple flight training manuals for the SNJ-3 airplane and a couple short exams. His scores weren't particularly stellar: 80% on one, 60% on the other. Those results were perplexing because my father was rather intelligent and should have been capable of better. Had his study skills suffered being out in the adult world with all its distractions? I wouldn't be surprised that the Air Corp would have had minimum qualifying scores, and perhaps it was higher than 60%. My only other discovery from that period was his flight logs. Between March and July of 1944, he flew over 160 hours, almost 70 of them solo. In his journal, there's an obscure mention of "the Navy suddenly slashing its pilot training program..." Uncle Bill recalls that Dad never said much about why he left flight school, though he thinks he might have confided in their mother. Dad had seemed pretty depressed about whatever happened. I would have thought he'd have mentioned it to my mother, but she never fessed up. Not querying him about this episode in his life served as yet another lost opportunity for me to know him better. Many years later, whenever this was written, it's obvious that he never lost the desire to soar above the clouds.

Musing 8

If I could climb the blue again
Into the fresh blue heavens, and all by myself
Lose the bands of Earth and soar closer

To heaven than the dusty, dingy, discouraging Earth
The ground where man has to stop for fences
And stop lights
    Away from a lost love that has in its
Beauty my whole life, now.

***

The Navy wasn't the only thing on Dad's mind in the early 1940s. After calling himself a kissless wonder in high school, his love life seemed to take off once he began flight school. Despite Dad's anemic self-perception, there's plenty of evidence that romance wasn't desperately lacking or deficient in his life. Uncle Bill may have only been nine years old when his older brother went off to war, but he retains some memories of the girls that Dad talked about or brought home. Then, there's the bundles of letters from various women I discovered in his vast collection of papers. Frustratingly, I found only correspondence to him and not his side of the conversation, though there's many allusions to his written comments. The letters contain some endearments, lots of flirtation, hints of conflict and not a little bit of exasperation that my father seemed deviously averse to commitment. Of note, the letter writers often mention meaningful connection to his mother, Lucile. Apparently, his women friends would spend time with her when he was away or otherwise occupied. There's some basis for speculating that his mother furnished a buffer that allowed him to keep fawning women at a distance. In that regard, he probably wasn't that different from other members of our gender who had wonderful mothers. In the following uncluttering, Dad might have blamed those little faults for his inability to attain the lofty nirvana where he had placed his mother.

⊷⊶⊷◆⊶⊷⊶

Uncluttering 14

I see a reflection of me in your eyes
The words you speak are mine
Your little faults that stab my heart
Are made from my design

⊷⊶⊷◆⊶⊷⊶

Peggy's[1] letters don't start until Dad is in California for flight training. Apparently, their relationship started in high school but warmed considerably when he left home. Early on, she wrote, "I like you better than any boy I know. As for me, I'm not in love with anyone I know, unless I am with you and for that I'm sure only time will tell." Later, after he'd been to exotic places like San Francisco and islands in the Pacific, she wrote, "Have you, by the way, an identification bracelet [that I could have]?" Her reasoning was to let other girls know, "Hands off, he's mine...Or maybe a sign would be better, easier to read you know. I think it's a good idea to have you 'hog-tied.' " That last comment would have sent a few shivers up a young man's spine! Things seemed to hit a rocky stretch in early 1944, as Peggy wrote, "It took quite a bit of serious thinking

---

1   First names are being used in case the women or their families ever get hold of this book!

to answer your letter. Perhaps both of us were flying off the handle at little things." In an undated letter soon after that one, "I'm sending your wings [badges of flight school] back. I'm sorry, maybe if we had known each other better things might have been different. Oh yes, there's just one more thing. Would you please return the photo I sent you? Thank you, Peggy [she used her full name]." Dad did send orchids for her birthday in July of 1945 and there was some friendly correspondence after that. The depth of his feelings for her is hard to gauge, as well as how they spent their time when they were together. She would beg him for letters, then be delighted when she got them right away or regularly, which seems to have been a pattern with other women as well. Through the course of the correspondence, Peggy first signed off as, "your friend," then "love," and finally, in her last letter (1948), "as ever."

Is this Dad's recollection and meditation on a first love?

Ballad 1

The rise and fall of an epic love
    Chorus:
    I loved you thoroughly, I loved you long;
    I loved you truly, I loved you strong;
    My only sin, I loved you wrong
    For I wasn't used to loving.

Dad may have characterized himself as "kissless," but he certainly seemed to be stealing hearts, and from more than one woman at a time. In another batch of letters from the war years, Adele's correspondence went from kind of snarky, to blushingly lovestruck, "Darling really I'd give anything if you could be here now. But I'm awfully proud of you and happy that you were here as long as you were...never a day goes by that I don't think of you," to complimentary of his mother, "Really I think you have the nicest mother," to appreciative of his composition skills, "Who taught you to write such swell letters?" At one point, she chided him for "being mean," and confessed that she was going out with someone else, but then recanted by admitting that she was only kidding, and always wanted to go out with someone named Butch. I can only guess what Dad thought of Adele's meandering affection and superficial rebukes, but he sure had her wrapped around his finger; she even claimed to have been going steady with him. In February of 1944, her letter ended with this wistful admonition, "Perry, we used to be friends and tell each other everything didn't we? I'm beginning to feel like a stranger for all that I know about you. I haven't really known anything about you since about last year. Honest Perry, I would like to know what you've been doing and the things that have happened."

In a letter soon after that one, Adele included this commentary which is quite alluring and plaintive but almost a lecture, "I was just wondering, do you think I am a bad influence on you because just the other day Barbie told [your] Mom that I didn't bring out the good in you like she could have if she had been going with you. I didn't think the good in you needed to be brought out. I liked you the way you were. Do you think I ought to start reforming you? Shall I??? Now listen here young man you should take that twinkle out of your eye, it makes you look like a [unreadable]. Well anyway and the way you have a very disconcerting habit of winking at a person when they are looking at you and trying to be angry. It weakens your resistance. Oh I don't think I'll say anything more because you might start reforming me..."

Dad must have been caught in a vortex of desire and apprehension spawned by Adele's mixed messages. In one of her last letters, postmarked April of 1945, she wrote, "Darling, no one here means half as much to me as you do. I love you. I still do only I guess actions talk louder than words and mine haven't been very good lately. I don't know if you still feel the same. I wouldn't blame you if you didn't. Perry if you have met someone else or even if you haven't please tell me. I promise I'll always tell you, I was going to, only there wasn't. I just wanted to tell you that I still feel the same as when you left."

In this poem, possibly written after he'd spent time in France, Dad writes about the shadowy woman who haunted his darkness. Does this woman he calls the "the night" exemplify all the wiles of adoration and commitment that intimidated and kept him at an emotional distance from women he cared for and who cared for him?

⊶⊷⊷◈⊶⊷⊷

La Nuit

The night is a lovely woman with a crescent in her gown
Whose limpid eyes share my laugh and wink in the looking down.

Once I waltzed my way to heaven rapt in her embrace,
And felt a bit immortal with her breath against my face;
Then for only a pause in the music when came the
sober day,
I carried that night in my pocket to better light my way.

But the night is a jealous woman with black and
wavy hair,
Her trailing robe is a satin shroud woven of my despair.
Cradling to her fickle bosom the laughter born of lust –
The shallow music taunts me and turns my tears
to dust.
Somewhere in this musty corridor flows a never-ending
stream
Recalling the echo forever, the echo of an empty dream.

For the night is a wanton woman in a sinister disguise
Her feline fingers choke the fields and light the
savage eyes.
Behind her every pagan veil her cohorts look askance
For a hollow in her wicked womb to do their
devil dance.
The rustle of a silent scream with the mornings warning
tune
Goad the shadows on to frenzy beneath the
mummified moon.

Now the night is a lonely woman whose languid lyres
bewail
Her timid trek to wasted lands along a deserted trail.
In mute disgust, the nodding boughs whisper to see her
pass
That such a needless errand dare disturb the
weeping grass;

Then with a sigh as the tedious ritual had so recently begun
She must cower in the corner to await the passing sun.

In the collection of his amorous correspondence are some intriguing letters from Camille who, as close as I can figure, was friend of Adele, girlfriend to Bob, and Dad may have been sweet on her. She doesn't have any qualms coquettishly reprimanding him: "I have really enjoyed your letters. The ones I haven't ever gotten! Listen you worm, I know you have lots of gals to see...My reason for not answering your last letter is rather evident as I realized that you are not serious about anyone and I would just be a passing fancy..."

Apparently, Camille read Bob's correspondence with Dad and recounts this little gem from one of their letters: "I hear the blonds are really thick up there so go to it man!" How many women was Perry Eberhart entertaining?

Camille must have had a good inkling and offered this advice, "Don't worry too much about that other gal who signs her letter, 'As ever.' " Was she referring to Peggy, Adele, or someone else? My take is that Camille was a confidante of sorts to Dad, but that he was still pretty fond of her.

Is this mysterious lover real or imagined?

Jane

The land below is asleep in the lap of night.
In the distance, the giant jewel box of a city...
Sleeping,
Rubbing its tired feet,
Complaining of an unknown tomorrow,
Sweeping up the scraps of yesterday,
Whispering softly in a promiscuous corner.
    Here and there an unnamed strand of dime-store
    beads
Thrown casually on the dresser-top of night.
    There is a light...
Just one light –
A farmer with a daughter named Jane
And a cow with the colic.
The cow's name is Mildred.
    All else is nothing...
The color, the patchwork of life...
Nothing.
    I sit back up there...
On nothingness.
    I see me below,
Sleeping in a giant jewel box,
Complaining of my feet,
Fearing tomorrow,
Whispering things I haven't whispered in years.
    I see me reaching out from the dresser top...
Yearning to travel beyond...
But afraid of the dark precipice...
So I sleep.
    I want to meet Jane...

I love her...
God, how I love her.
But, then, only a few can have their love...
And they are afraid.
  I am full of feeling...
For Jane and myself...
Below.
  I hope all goes well with them.
  One can hope better in the dark...
Up there...
Not touching anything.
And not being touched.

Love is a muse that inspires many a poem!

CHAPTER 5

"Navy porn!"

My ship sister, Lisa, coined that term. She was referring to photos of our fathers and the other shirtless sailors aboard their ship, the LCI (Landing Craft Infantry) 944 to which Dad had been assigned in late 1944, after mysteriously washing out of pilot training. He and his crewmates were slender, sinewy, and fit. My father, 6'2" and around 180 pounds with chiseled, suntanned physique, jet black hair and piercing dark eyes, indeed looked hot and sexy.

Lisa is the woman who shoved open the door to my father's wartime experiences. She compiled an admirable record of the 944's exploits, from her dad's letters and journals, actual ship logs, and keepsake memoirs from families of the other crewmates. In particular, she gleaned stories and details from 90-some-year-old Ralph Rayner, who had been the 944's commanding officer. The ship's activities included mine sweeping, transporting troops and supplies, destroying enemy munitions and gear, and devastating weather. Despite never being involved in actual combat, the ship and its crew experienced plenty of tragedy and drama. One event occurred when the 944 was stationed at the harbor in Manus, New Guinea. An

American munitions ship, the USS Hood, was moored nearby when it suddenly exploded, raining debris and worse down upon the sailors; Dad and his mates had to clean up the mess. The 944 and crew were also caught in two devastating typhoons during the latter part of 1945.

Detonation of atomic bombs over Hiroshima and Nagasaki brought the war to a brutal and merciful end. While Dad, Bob Bittle, and the rest of the 944 crew were joyous, they would still be stuck on the ship for many more months. Most of the time, they were engaged in mundane and thankless tasks, though there were a few memorable events.

In an article for a military newspaper, Dad and Bob Bittle were interviewed and quoted as saying, "Naturally...we would like to get in on a beachhead landing one of these days like other landing craft do, but we realize our little job is an important one and we are satisfied." Hence, Dad and the crew of the 944 wrestled with the age-old conundrum of fighting men who don't get to fight, but witnessed the utter destruction that comes from war. Some call it survivor's guilt. Others might say, "You were damn lucky, celebrate that!" Those of us who have never been in their shoes will never comprehend the enormity of that burden.

Lisa unearthed an interesting side story to this photo, the one that connected us. It was taken for a story that would appear in Stars and Stripes, the military newspaper that served all in the armed forces. Apparently, Dad and Bob were instructed to avoid indicating on the map where the Japanese fleet was determined to be. The two rogues decided that anyone looking at the picture would think they were being deceptive and thus Bob's finger is actually pointing at their precise location.

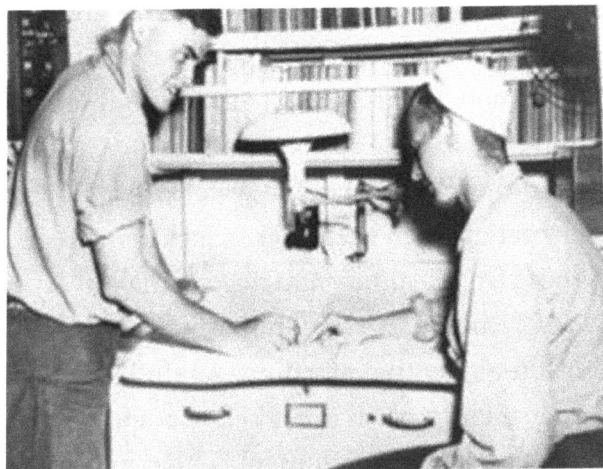

Dad and Lisa's father, Bob Bittle, in the chart room of LCI 944

My ship sister educated me in a way that my father never did about his experiences in the Navy. As I've mentioned before, what I most remember him saying is that he learned to smoke, drink, and play Bridge during the endless hours his ship spent at sea. I do recall Dad talking about sailing into Okinawa days after the war ended, and retrieving the Japanese rifle as a souvenir that hung on the wall in our home for as long as I can remember. There was also the white Navy fatigues and cap that seemed impossibly small that he wore back then. It all seemed pretty harmless.

If I knew, I forgot Dad telling me about one happy coincidence that occurred when the 944 docked in the Philippines. He and a friend were walking the docks when they passed a vessel whose name Dad recognized. It was the ship on which his brother was sailing. He went aboard immediately, located Jack and they had a joyous reunion. In a letter Jack later wrote to their mother, he said, "I thought you might like to know that I just saw Perry. I was very proud of him. He's grown so much more than since I saw him last, smokes to beat hell, swears a lot, but has a natural poise and taciturn manner about him that is admirable in the Eberhart clan."

Together, they went ashore to watch the VJ (Victory over Japan) celebration, then went back to Jack's ship. "We...talked of everything from Jeanne's marriage to the way it used to be when we were home. He then had my bed on the ship and stayed for breakfast this morning. Again I say, I was really proud...These Philippines are a hell of a spot, and now I've seen two men that I knew in them, which makes it more livable. I was ever so glad to see [Perry] again. The whole bunch on the ship did their damnedest to make him feel at home, they're a nice gang that way."

Jack had been discharged from the Royal Canadian Air Corps when the plane he was captaining crash-landed in England. There was some question as to whether Jack had ditched the plane, but we'll never know. In any event, he turned around and enlisted in the U.S. Merchant Marine on a ship that took him to that fortuitous rendezvous with his younger brother.

* * *

The most unfathomable, momentous event in Dad's time aboard the 944 was that day a month or so after the bomb obliterated Hiroshima, when he and a few others stepped ashore into the wasteland of that devastated city. Had Lisa not contacted me 70 years later, I may never have known. Captain Ralph Rayner would casually recall so many decades afterward, "[I] did not know much about radiation, but...thought it was probably not a good idea to walk around in the rubble. [I] went around the city in the bed of a dump truck to witness the power of the bomb. Others, like Bob and Eberhart, probably walked in the rubble."

Hiroshima in ruins (taken by one of Dad's shipmates)

Despite Rayner's detachment, I can hardly fathom the gruesomeness and tragedy those men saw. Needless to say, Dad was profoundly affected and would after the war compose the poem I would not discover for another 60 or more years. He painted a tableau of the visions, sensations, and emotions that swept over him as he picked his way through the ruins. I believe the poem was written for a college class and that he tried to get it published. When that didn't happen and it failed to arouse much abhorrence or outrage, he must have buried, deep in his mind and away from his family, the horrors he saw that day. Oh, how I wish I could have talked to him about what he saw that day and properly acknowledge the magnitude of his elegy.

———◆———

Hiroshima

The buildings along the dock were untouched and busy.
I was so happy that the world was untouched.
Then we walked a block and it hit us –
Across the street was another world,
A world extending to the hills miles away
The rubble of a city lay at our feet –
A different rubble, for we had seen much rubble.
The city had been inoculated a month before,
And it was still unconscious and unmoving.
It lay like molten dust hugging the ground
With only lonely charred and twisted trees,
Like the black naked props in a Frankenstein movie,
Standing above as eerie monuments.

As we walked and saw deeper into the wreckage,
We saw the ruin as it really was — a molten mass –
Not crumbling and dusty like the others, but smoothed over
Like brightly-colored mush, frozen and lumpy;
Between the lumps a substance had run.
It had hardened as it ran — like peppermint candy.
But the recipe called for different ingredients –
The heated fusion of the elements-
A man's house, a man's furniture, a man's child.
A shipmate joyfully found an unbroken vase –

With a big glob of peppermint hardened on it.
He would take it home and place it on the mantle,
And wind proud tales around it for all
interested listeners.
  This was Hiroshima to a few victorious sailors.

{see the entire poem in Addendum 2}

Having learned too late about the travails Dad navigated during that crucial period in his life, my new knowledge and the poem stimulated me to see deeper into the soul and torment of Perry Eberhart. One of the ramifications from his war experience that I uncovered was the tearing down of his belief in God. He went into the war thinking God was on his side, only to look in horror upon the wrath that He could inflict. With roots sown as the son of a pastor and a very spiritual mother, the foundation of Dad's spirituality was shaken to its core. He would ask how a benevolent god could wreak such havoc on the world and so many innocent people. He floundered for quite some time, until he began to put together the essence of a higher being that would provide him solace and maybe some answers he could not find in empty preachings and self-serving religions. This poem is so intense in its questioning and cynicism that one can only imagine the memories and recollections my father had. What does not need imagining are his conclusions and implications.

God Wore No Uniform

I left the green valleys of youth,
I left the hills of happiness and love,
I left God –
When I sailed to a world at war
- in the beautiful South Pacific;
To trudge through dust, and heat, and fear,
Dark fear — dark jungle fear,
Fear of a leaf, a godly ripple,
Fear of a star-filled night,
Fear of myself.
My only protection was the right to kill
My only possession was a weapon.
My luck was not with God
For the dead died with their faith –
The bloody stump on the beach
Had once been lifted in prayer.
The helpless and twisted dead
Lay in godless mounds.
Knowing only blood, and dust, and sweat

{see the entire poem in Addendum 3}

Now, when I reflect back on my indignation at Dad's per-
ceived brush off in that long-ago kitchen confrontation, I'm
almost surprised that he didn't excoriate me with fire and con-
descension. After what he had seen and endured, he instead
coolly disputed my assertion that "we should bomb the hell"

out of anything. I think he saw in me the capacity to lose my innocence and rationally come to understand his belief that war is no good for anyone. Of course, in my continued naiveté, the true nature of his lesson dawned on me too late, to the point where I might have, if not thanked him, at least accorded him the courtesy of polite discussion. It's not that we didn't come to take the same side in the extended family arguments, or that he wasn't supportive of my anti-war activities, but in retrospect, I now feel I never took the time to truly understand what he had experienced in war. I never opened the door for him to share the profundities he endured and carried with him to his death.

Dad was not alone in his travail from youth fueled by patriotism to hard-bitten veteran. Many families I know celebrate and venerate their military heritage. And they should; I have come full circle from disparaging the warrior to respecting his or her combat service. Yet, my family history does not justify the continued support and blind loyalty to war. Especially, since President Eisenhower's supremely prescient admonition has proven accurate many times over: "Beware the Military Industrial Complex."

Despite my family's robust record of military participation, my predecessors who saw or experienced the horrors of war came down on the side of, "Never again!" Those, like my fathers, uncles, and step-grandfather, who abhorred warfare, were not naïve and never thought that those wars to end all wars would live up to their billing. Uncle Bill remembers, at the tender age of twelve, going downtown on VJ (Victory over Japan) Day, watching the wild celebrations and being swept up in the patriotic fervor. Yet, he'd heard enough of the inhumanity and horror stories from his older brothers to know right then that he could no longer believe in war. He, his brothers, and others in the family did what they could by voting their consciences, backing the right causes, and one day supporting their slow learning, yet actively involved son and grandson. With their support and on the backs of my own experiences, I now disavow the need for any war, though the Hitlers and Putins of the world savagely test my convictions.

I wish I had read Dad's term paper and Hiroshima poem while he was alive. For one, I could have genuinely expressed my gratitude, empathy, and consensus. For another, I so dearly miss the strengthening of our bond that would have been inevitable as we explored the true depths of our beliefs. Somewhere in our explorations, perhaps I might have found a small opening for him to talk about his demons. Then, maybe, I could have offered some outlet and small measure of comfort. Yet sadly, all that's left is another profound lost opportunity. I can only imagine our discussion surrounding this rumination,

---

Musing 1

Today is Tommy's lucky (happy) day
They pinned a medal on his grave

CHAPTER 6

Dad was discharged from the Navy on the 11th of March, 1946. His homecoming to Denver was joyous and exhilarating. Don, Jack, and new brother-in-law George were back as well. Uncle Bill well remembers the first gathering that brought together the whole family once again under the same roof. While the celebration was raucous and filled with sentiment, Bill noticed changes in his big brothers. They were loud and boisterous, cussed unabashedly, smoked cigarettes like locomotives and especially, drinking alcohol, lots of it. Nobody even seemed to pay attention when their thirteen-year-old little brother cadged a can of Coors and snuck off to a quiet corner to drink it down. In retrospect, Bill recalls that day as a sort of watershed. Alcohol became an ingrained indulgence at family gatherings.

My father and his brother Jack enrolled in the University of Colorado at Boulder that fall. They were the pioneers of sorts, as Sister Pat and the following generation followed their footsteps into the hallowed halls of that beautiful campus at the foot of the Rocky Mountains. Even Pappy Carl took classes at CU. Though commuting from Denver for the first semester, Dad threw himself with gusto into campus life. He pledged the Sigma Chi fraternity, went out for football, and immersed himself in classes, particularly literature and composition, setting the foundation for a future career as a writer.

Fraternity life and the rigors of football soon fell to the wayside as Dad was becoming too enamored of the party life. In the spring of '47, he moved into the Baker dormitory. His roommate was a tall drink of water named Bob Rolander, who Dad affectionately—but probably to Bob's disdain—nicknamed Boob Rollover. Rolander at 6' 7", played basketball for the Buffaloes, and was teammates with future Colorado coach, Sox Walseth. Though Dad was no longer a participant in organized sports, he became a diehard sports fan, then and for the rest of his life. His penchant for Colorado football carried on to his indoctrination of his eldest son, me. I fondly recall him and me heading up the Denver Boulder Turnpike many Saturdays when the Buffs were playing at home on Folsom Field. To this day, where the highway drops down into the valley beneath the specter of the red sandstone Flatirons and the lofty peaks on the horizon, special memories flood back. Until, I swear, I was twelve years old, Dad would tell the ticket taker that I was only six, though tall for my age, so I could get in free. We would take up our seats on the wooden bleachers that, at that time, faced east toward the red brick stands for alumni and students. One game, in particular, was memorable. In 1957, the Buffs hosted the Falcons of the newly established Air Force Academy in Colorado Springs.

"Dad, they're pulling down the goalposts," I yelled as the final whistle sounded.

The uprights were made of wood back then, and easily succumbed to the efforts of celebrating fans.

"Sure. Why not?" Dad sorta mumbled. He was usually pretty well potted with Coors beer by the end of the game.

I ran onto the field, and attempted to do my part to pull down the goalposts. As they came down, one of the uprights splintered and I came away with about a two-foot-long, jagged piece of wood that I knew would be part of history. That piece of flaking white, slivered goalpost stayed on a bookshelf in my bedroom until I went off to CU as a Freshman. By then, the goalposts on Folsom field were constructed of lead pipe.

Perhaps because Dad was busy studying and socializing, he didn't capture or write down more grist of college life for me to discover in the future. The most significant find was the surfeit of writings he produced for his composition classes. There's a thick folder of poems, some of which are found in these pages, a good collection of short stories which could prompt a sequel to this memoir. In a few years, Dad did attempt to get some of his works published, including the Hiroshima magnum opus, without much luck. Among the findings are the starts (but no completed manuscripts that I found) for novels and other longer works. Then, there's several spiral notebooks not unlike the ones all college students everywhere used back in the day. Makes me think when some son in the future is researching for a book about his father, will laptops and digital files be as adventurous to excavate? In any event, Dad's notepads were filled with class notes, seeds of ideas, and doodles.

I like this poem as it neatly portrays the artistic mind. Dad was trying hard to marshal all the forces of inspiration and finding the return on that investment too often inconsequential.

Creative Genius

I opened the door to all the past,
Switched a light on Pompeii
And moved on;
Rousing Shakespeare and all the others
From a gentle sleep — and they collaborated with me;
All the doctors of progress held a consultation
To diagnose my case;
I thumbed through the dictionary of my days;
I sought among memories and reactions;
Rested my feet on the farthest hill,
Sat back on a cloud,
Used fancy as a periscope,
Dipped my pen in deduction and induction,
Pushed it with emotion,
And I wrote
   - but a line

There might not have been much more to discover about his academic life, but there were lots of letters from smitten young women. I'm not sure most of them would qualify as love letters, but they were awfully flirty. I imagine back in the days before texts, emails, and social media, when you weren't with that special someone, you wrote letters. Personally, I rue the demise of handwritten correspondence. A lot gets lost in the efficiency of today's communications. So perhaps letters to the man who called himself a kissless wonder were more newsy and intimate because that's what they did when distance separated them from their quixotic "friends." Sadly, but not unexpectedly, I found none written by Dad himself.

The letters, including those mentioned in the previous chapter, spanned the period from 1942 and spilled over into 1949. Additionally, the timing for many of them was not exclusive to one woman at a time; they often overlapped. Of course, the words of the letter writers were discreet, if there was anything more risqué than smooching, I wouldn't know. They did not, however, shrink from being cutesy, mushy, lecturing, rejected, or demanding. The letters opened with greetings such as Ducky, Ebby, Eversharp, Perry Darling, SS Man, Gruesome (?) and Pooky Took. One woman, Joyce, addressed hers to "My Hubby," and closed with, "Your loving wife." I'm pretty sure my father only had one wife in his lifetime! Many other letters were signed, "With love," "Your sweetie," "Forever," and "Always." It is hard for me to imagine how close Dad got to these women, how he stayed uncommitted to any of them, and if he was stringing them along. Makes me think that he had quite the journey from kissless wonder to Navy Porn to BMOC (Big Man on Campus, a slang phrase used to designate the popular guys).

Dad wrote this poem to "A Friend," but it sounds like he's describing a lot of the women I found in his letters.

A Friend

She lavished her way with glittering gold
And paid the fiddler with a kiss.

Thinking the things she couldn't hold
    Were the things she wouldn't miss
By standard rights she was a queen
    She had a material wealth of beauty
She insured security but she lost herself
    And her happy earthly duty
She molded her manners from a book
    And knelt to a tinkling bell
She existed here in a hollow heaven
    And gave her happiness to hell.

I found one series of letters that came from Barbara in 1948. She and her correspondence stand out, because I think I knew her as the woman my father and, later, my mother called Bubbles. Many of her letters are mailed from California where it seems Barbara spent a good amount of time. A good indication that theirs was a pretty serious relationship came when she reveled in a significant milestone of collegiate devotion, "Just think we have been pinned three weeks, isn't that just wonderful, just think this time next week we will be celebrating our fourth anniversary together."

Barbara, as did the others, thrived on letters from Dad. When they must have been amorous or interesting, the women nearly swoon; when there were long periods of time between his letters, they were discouraged and depressed, as exemplified in Barbara's thoughts: "You certainly have been sweet about writing. Thank you so much, the letters are making my vacation a little more enjoyable"; but then, "No letters from you for the past few days so I have been kinda down in the dumps." She claimed that she didn't usually dream, but at one point wrote, "Did you know that [you] are haunting me...since I have been out here I have dreamt of you every night, don't get me wrong, I love it, the only thing wrong with it is that I wake up in the morning and it ends there, we will have to do something about that."

Like all the others, Barbara was enamored of Dad's mother ("I just got through talking to that wonderful Mother of yours..."). He must have gotten in pretty tight with her parents as well. When they travelled to Australia, Dad had written them a letter to which Barbara's mother took the time to respond on January 20th of 1949: "...nice to receive your letter... Mr Young and I are happy that B has you as her best friend... [Mr] feels sure that you and B are old enough to always do the right thing and in that may gain more and more respect for each other...express my appreciation to your mother for her many kindnesses to B."

Intriguingly, the last letter I found from Barbara was postmarked just the day after her mother's note. In it, she mused: "I sure do miss you Perry, honest I know this vacation is going to do us both so much good. Just a week from today and we will be back together again and I know things will be fine again...I do miss you a lot and still love you." If Barbara was indeed Bubbles, Dad carried a torch for her late into his life and even my mother seemed to have enjoyed her friendship. Might Bubbles have been the inspiration for these Unclutterings?

Unclutterings 8 & 11

Nature, please be your best for Barbara
The symphony of nature that I shall conduct.

&

I could not love you properly if I did not love all life
  the same

CHAPTER 7

In the years after World War II, all undergraduate students who lived on the University of Colorado campus in Boulder had a curfew and were not allowed to have cars on campus. Amazingly, this was despite many of them were military veterans who had traveled the world serving their country. Consequently, Dad, Bob and their friends in Baker Hall had no wheels to cavort around town or drive up into the hills. They were dependent on those who lived off campus and had cars.

Dad, like many of the other vets, took summer classes to make up for lost time. One day in early June of 1949, Stan a friend of Dad's, invited him to go swimming with a group at Allen's Lake, outside of town. The best part was that he knew a woman who could give them a ride. She was a graduate student who lived in downtown Boulder and thus was able to have a car. When she showed up at Baker Hall to pick up the two strapping men, they ogled her as she stepped out of the car. She was tall and slender, had long wavy brown hair and lively dark eyes. The boys' chauffeur turned out to be a fiercely self-reliant woman with an effervescent smile who hailed from New York City. In Dad's words, he got to know the driver "real" well, but how could he know then that he would end up married to her for almost 40 years and raise four children together? That fortunate series of events almost didn't happen, as on the way home from the lake, Dad and Stan were fooling around with, of all things, talcum powder, which made a mess of the car's interior. Their chauffeur said she wouldn't be driving them anywhere again if they didn't clean it up. History shows that they must have completed the job to her satisfaction.

The driver was Helen Tecklin, who insisted on being called by her nickname, Sandy. She was born in Brooklyn, NY, on December third, 1925, to Carolyn and Max. They were Jewish and unfortunately in those days, Jews were often treated as second-rate citizens, even in New York City. Max, despite being a highly regarded tax accountant, was never able to become a partner in one of the firms on Wall Street. Many Jews sought to remain under the radar by shrouding their family background. Carolyn, aka Carrie, a very intractable and status-conscious woman, kept her daughter from attending services at the local synagogue but enrolled her in well-heeled private schools and ladies' finishing societies. In striving to maintain the standards of an affluent lifestyle, Max and Carrie purchased a vacation home on the lake's edge in Watermill, on Long Island, within spitting distance of the Hamptons. Sandy spent endless hours in the water, which led to a lifelong love of swimming.

Being the only child of a domineering mother, Sandy struck out to find her independence after high school by attending Duke University in North Carolina. Going to school in the South with all its formalities and appearances was quite the learning experience, but Sandy developed friendships that she maintained for many years thereafter. After graduation, she moved back to New York City and worked for Time Inc. for a while before her mother's badgering drove her away again. She headed out to Colorado to indulge her love of skiing. To add some sense of accountability, she enrolled at the university in Boulder to get a teaching certificate, therefore being a graduate student able to live off campus and have a car.

Sandy Tecklin, aka Mom, circa mid-40s

Perry and Sandy's first official date was on his birthday, August fifth, when they went to a "beer bust," at the foot of the Flatirons in Chatauqua Park. Dad reports they drank a lot and endlessly sang 'The Tennessee Waltz,' which was very popular at the time. To celebrate his birthday, he was "crowned with a pan of beer," which then prompted a swimming trip to Baseline Lake so he could wash off the suds. On the way back to campus, Dad fell asleep in the back seat of the car and Sandy left him there for the night. Perhaps the red flag had not yet started to wave, as he did the same on their second and third dates. The latter occasion was a party at the Kappa sorority house, where Sandy apparently danced the night away with a dorm proctor who would go on to become a Colorado Supreme Court judge. I'd like to think that Dad realized a good thing when he saw it and penned this poem as a plea to accept him as he was and that his heart was in the right place.

Unnamed 3

Please be the Queen in my kingdom
As minor as it might be
But of all the worlds of every time
It is the greatest one to me
Please take every little second
That made the life I live
Of all the life of a million years
It is all I have to give
You have given my life the mettle
To organize my soul
You have given my life a reason
You symbolize my goal
Please take all the life forever
And lacquer each living part
And guide me
With the gold within your heart
And please take the love I offer
I pray I can build the (?)

I could not love you more.

Not long after that first date, Sandy got to meet Dad's big, boisterous family on the day of his graduation from CU in 1949; his brother, John, received his master's degree at the same ceremony. Graduation ceremonies were held in August that year due to the high number of WWII vets who returned and enrolled in college like the Eberhart brothers. The day began inauspiciously as Dad and Sandy were invited to a friend's house for a pre-celebration that included martinis. Neither he nor she favored the cocktail, particularly in the morning, but the friend was proud of his martinis.

Hence, Dad had trouble staying awake during the graduation ceremony and apparently, according to Sandy, "lumbered across the stage to get his diploma...but, at least, he didn't look drunk!" Afterward, in front of Mackey Auditorium, she met his whole family. Before heading to the family home in Denver, they stopped by the friend's home for a couple more cocktails. In retrospect, Dad realized that his new girlfriend, an only child, was rather intimidated by the large clan. She clung to his arm for protection, glassy eyed, and said very little. All ended well, as the more the family got to know her, and her them, they would get on famously and laugh about the infamous introduction. The only detractor was Pappy Carl's father who would talk about "those damn chews (his ascerbic pronunciation of Jews)," then add, "Not you Sandy, you're nice."

Many hours of the nascent love affair were spent in Timber Tavern (TT) at the corner of Folsom and Arapahoe in Boulder. Again, despite many of the male students being war veterans, older and world-wise, they were still underclassmen not able to stay out beyond curfew. After my father and his buddies returned to Baker Hall, Sandy stayed to dance to the juke box with the Tavern's owner, Max Gold, while his wife, Tess, cleaned up. The crowd at TT loved to sing boisterous songs and ballads, many of which Mom and Dad collected in a small book, <u>Colorado Sings</u>, that was later printed by Dad's future publisher, Alan Swallow's Sage Books. 20 years later, as a freshman at CU, I went to work for Max and Tess who recounted good times with that crazy Perry and lovely Sandy.

* * *

In November 1949, Perry and Sandy went to Albuquerque for a football game between CU and the University of New Mexico. The next day, which was the 11th, on the way home, they took a quick detour into the small town of Raton and were married by a Justice of the Peace. That I know of, there was never a celebration or party, but I was born nine months and six days later when Sandy officially became, "Mom," and Perry, "Dad."

Before I came along, Mom stayed on campus to finish her teaching certificate, while Dad moved back to Denver to grow their nest egg at such jobs as lumber yard laborer, seed sorter, and fertilizer bagger, visiting Boulder on the weekends. When Mom finished school, the newlyweds moved into a basement apartment on South Pearl Street in Denver. The honeymoon's afterglow burned strongly as Dad penned this missive of infatuation and promise.

Pome* Number Two To Sandy (Valentine Division)

Feb 14, 1950

Strange things can mock the chopping block
All ages will reveal.
A most gentle breath, like a kiss of death,
Can crumble a shield of steel.
No tale can outdo a story true
Witnessed by western skies,
A tale of passion, making others old-fashioned
Like by them poet guys.
So I ordered more beer, and leaned close to hear,
Oblivious of the din and smoke,
And I felt a chill like the world stood still
As the aged observer spoke:

Part One and Conclusion

It was the tale of a bird — not one of the herd –
But a Most unusual guy.
Who's world wore wings, and unseen things
   - the 'Indestructible I'
He loved from here to the San Pedro Pier,
As scattered hearts will bemoan.
Always ready to smooch then down his hooch
And travel on alone.
Oft times he grinned, like he ruled the wind
As on its wings he'd fly,
Always happy and proud, he could lease a cloud
   - the 'Indestructible I'
THEN — OUT OF THE EAST, like a rampaging beast,
But as soft as the summer hue,
Came a girl so gay, there was heaven to pay

\- the lady that's known as You.
Armed but with the grace of a pretty face,
And pretty scrumptious hips
Her dancing eyes, like spring-colored skies,
Looked down on luscious lips.
But these were the tools that made other men fools
Of which I never knew,
But it was the extra-large heart, that was the potent part
Of the lady that's known as You.
And I lost my might under the soft moonlight
And the laughing stars above.
I lost to the charms of a woman's arms
And the weapon that's known as love.
Always great men can unveil some hidden trail,
But always they shy from this:
Why great men will cower from the unknown power
Concealed in a simple kiss.
But who cares for reasons, like the sun and the seasons,
Humble men can't apply;
But if you want the result, you can always consult
The 'Indestructible I'.
For I'm here to tell, that come heaven or hell
The whining winds know it's true –
I thoroughly enjoyed, being totally destroyed
By the lady that's known as YOU.

   * Actual spelling by Dad

Soon after Mom and Dad were married, the parents from whom she'd fled to Colorado to escape, moved to Denver anyway. Momma T, as Dad would call her, apparently spent much of her first several months in the hospital for many unspecified ailments. Max, aka Papa T, commuted back and forth to the Big Apple to finish up his work there. My grandparents, who would become known to me as Granny and Grandpa, bought their daughter, her pie-eyed husband and their darling young grandson a Chevrolet convertible that chauffeured me around, shuttled them to their jobs, took them skiing and on a few trips around the state.

Mom came to straddle different lives. Her mother didn't particularly like my father, or anybody much. Short, round, and always scowling, she was very demanding, especially with her husband who she bossed mercilessly. From her, I came to comprehend the phrase, "henpecked." Grandpa was meek in her presence but professional and approachable away from her. He was tall with rimless spectacles perched on a bulbous nose but always neatly dressed. I was a beneficiary of his thick head of hair. Being the first grandchild, I also benefitted from happy, meaningful times with him. He and Granny lived in Northeast Denver, near a YMCA with an Olympic-sized swimming pool. During the summer, I spent many a sunny afternoon at the pool where Grandpa taught me to swim and do the back dive. One of my fondest memories was when just he and I took the train to Glenwood Springs, stayed in the Hotel Colorado, and luxuriated in the huge, hot-spring-fed pool. I must have been 10 or 11 years old. When I had my own grandchildren, I vowed to take each of them on a similar adventure. I did so with my first on her 10th birthday, but alas, the others were out of state when their time came and the logistics prevented a continuation of the ritual I'd hoped to continue.

Granny and Grandpa lived in a part of Denver that soon became the "colored" part of town. They were the last white folks on the block but were unabashedly kind and friendly to their neighbors. The family of world champion boxer Sonny Liston moved in across the street and became close friends with my grandparents. My brother and I visited often and developed many friendships with the kids on the block who just happened to have different skin shades. Due to Grandpa's affability and, surprisingly Granny's generosity, we never felt different or out of place. Those experiences were major factors in the progressive values my family held regarding race.

Still and all, Granny was Granny. Mom and Dad tried periodically to get beyond her toxic orbit by heading off to the mountains. One particular weekend, they fled to Grand Lake to get away from Mama T's constant complaining about Papa T. When they got home, she was furious because they hadn't told her they were going. A few days later, she informed my father that she cut $1,000 out of her will that she'd set aside for him. According to Dad, she also strictly controlled finances so Papa T couldn't invest in lucrative adventures, make a fortune, and leave it to them.

* * *

After I was born, Dad got his first white collar job at the Bureau of Public Affairs, overseeing the cases of 75-100 "unemployable men," a position wherein he met many nice people but felt the work was depressing. He took night classes to keep up his G.I. Bill[2] in hopes that he could use it to study over-seas. On the weekends, he worked at the Colorado Historical Society (CHS) museum as a guide but spent much of his time reading old newspapers and the organization's magazine. He wrote in his journal that, "since I didn't know anything about it, I spent much of my time in the office reading old newspapers and the CHS mag which started my interest in Colorado history." Dad had another stint as an information specialist at the Bureau of Reclamation, which was across the street from a US Geological Survey map outlet. Because government work was "bad and dull," he found lots of time to copy slides and photos from the society's massive collection. Those small embers flickered, smoldered, and flared into an enduring obsession with everything Mile High and Rocky Mountains.

---

2   The **Servicemen's Readjustment Act of 1944**, commonly known as the **G.I. Bill**, was a law that provided a range of benefits for returning World War II veterans. Benefits included low-cost mortgages, low-interest loans to start a business or farm, one year of unemployment compensation, and dedicated payments of tuition and living expenses to attend high school, college, or vocational school.

CHAPTER 8

The year was 2019 when I pulled our camper van into the Long Beach, California, parking lot. As Karen, my wife, and I climbed out, the Queen Mary filled my vision and my soul. Her burnished black hull stretched over 1,000 feet from stem to stern. The tops of her three red stacks rose almost 200 feet from her dry dock berth. I was overwhelmed knowing that I had beheld the same tableau almost 70 years before. Certainly, I don't remember it, as I was a mere thirteen months old, but my spirit could feel the connection shared with the Grand Dame of the seas. Clutched in my hand were four small, fragile black and white photographs that confirmed I had been on this magnificent ocean liner. Karen and I the next few days staying in one of the actual cabins, exploring the depth and width of the Queen Mary. One of our aims was locating the places where those ancient photos were taken. Much had changed, but enough was the same so that we found three of them. The experience was like entering a time machine that took me back to a magical time, not only for me but for my parents.

1951   2019

Me on the Queen Mary

* * *

On September 21, 1951, with G.I. Bill in hand and wife at his side, Dad carried 13-month-old me up the gang plank from the docks of New York City to the deck of the majestic Queen Mary. We were on our way to Paris, the City of Lights.

> "If you are lucky enough to have lived in Paris as a young man, then wherever you go for the rest of your life, it stays with you, for Paris is a moveable feast."
> —from *The Moveable Feast*
> (Ernest Hemingway, Scribner's 1964)

Dad wouldn't have yet read those words, but he must have absorbed the romance and intoxication of the City of Lights that had infected artists, philosophers, and Bohemian wannabes for centuries. Even the city's nickname offers some clues.

It was among the first European cities to use gas streetlamps back in the 1860s, making it literally a City of Light. Also, in the 18th century, Paris was a hub during the Age of Enlightenment. So, literally light for enlightened minds.[3]

I love this characterization of Paris by Alexandra Styron in her memoir about her father, <u>Reading My Father</u> (Scribner, 2011):

> "Americans — novelists, poets, painters, ex-GIs as well as the rich boys who'd been sheltered from the draft came to hunt the ghosts of the Lost Generation, and were streaming into Paris in the early fifties…Since the end of WWII, the battered French government had staged a strategic operation to lure wealthy tourists back to the City of Lights. Rules on black market currency were eased and tourist card requirements summarily repealed. But instead of big spenders, Paris got a flood of cash-strapped expats. My father arrived to a scene part Athens, part Woodstock, part Vincente Minnelli musical."

One of Dad's favorite folk groups, the Kingston Trio, encapsulated the fervor in their song, 'Raspberries, Strawberries':

> "A young man goes to Paris
> As every young man should
> There's something in the Paris air
> That does a young man good"

I'm sure my father's head and spirit were filled with all that allure and excitement. Where else would a young wannabe

---

3   Thanks to the blog, *The Earful Tower,* by Oliver Gee

author want to go? To boot, he had a wife who was hungry to travel and ready to follow him anywhere. Though I was just a mite, the bug for travel and its sense of adventure must have bitten me back then, leaving me with a lifelong affliction that resides in me to this day.

Fueled with dreams, Dad, Mom, and I sailed the Atlantic on the Grand Dame of the Cunard Line. In eight days aboard ship, there were new friends, lots of singing, many Bridge games and flowing liquor. Some rough seas, but mostly, the sailing was smooth. We disembarked at the port in Cherbourg. From there, our small family boarded the train that took us through the beautiful French countryside and into Paris. After only one day, Dad declared, "It is a beautiful and impressive town…Love the place." Imaginings and ambitions that were imbedded a half world away on East 11th Street in Denver began to blossom in the rapturous shadow of the Eiffel Tower, on the cobblestones of the Champs-Élysées and especially at the street cafes of the West Bank. The young dreamer had found the home of his muse.

When did Dad write this? During his ocean crossing, or later in retrospect? I think it certainly embodies a newfound wanderlust, though I think he knew where he was going.

Come with Me

Come with me, I'm going a-traveling
Somewhere across the sea
I don't even know the name
It's all the same to me.

There's some land that's awaiting
Unpainted by my eyes
Some music and some laughter
And different colored skies.

There's a world still a-wanting
For me to come along
There's a voice that has the lyrics
To the music of my song.

My folks landed us at a small hotel at 135 Blvd du Montpar-nasse, where the elevator was only big enough for two people and the "light switches are seldom where you would expect them." It was, however, located a few short minutes' walk from Luxembourg Gardens; "the largest, most beautiful park I've ever seen," Dad wrote in his journal. Amidst light autumn breezes and falling leaves, and with starry eyes, they would push me along the streets in my stroller. Apparently, I charmed everyone whose paths we crossed; "Regarde le mignon petit garçon (look at the handsome little boy)," they would exclaim.

We wandered beneath the dome of beautiful trees and past ornamental shrubbery of the square named for the famous actress, Sarah Bernhardt. At the crown of Montmartre, the highest point in the city, we strolled past the picturesque basilica of Sacré-Coeur during the soft, vibrant evenings. We drank in the mystical ambiance of the Catacombs. Mom and Dad loved shopping and sipping wine in the cafes along the Champs-Élysées. Of course, no one can spend time in Paris without strolling the grounds and reverently stepping inside the Cathedral of Notre-Dame.

Within a few weeks, my folks found a second-floor flat at 89 Rue des Pyrénées. The landlady was Madame Bamberger, "a rather erratic, talkative old gal," Dad recalled. Apparently, she had learned tricks to surviving on her own after her husband, a Jewish newspaperman, had been killed by the Nazis. Mme. Bamberger took our little American family under her wing and fussed over us. She went so far as to call herself my French grandmother. Though the living quarters were small, and I slept in a crate the first few days, we finally had a place to call our own.

My parents began learning how to live French. Dad bought his first wool beret, "to keep his head warm," Mom said. When he went into a store to buy some matches wearing his new chapeau, the storekeeper excitedly and rapidly started conversing with him as if he were a local. In a late-night club, the piano player told Dad that he was reminded of young Ernest Hemingway. You could be forgiven for thinking that Paris was sinking her claws in deeper.

Dad was a little frustrated that Mom picked up the language quicker than he did, and she didn't even attend classes. My first language was French because that was essentially all I heard. Sadly though, I have next to no memories of the two years we spent in Paris. One of the few things I do recall is trudging gingerly up the shadowy stairwell to our flat with a fresh baguette over my shoulder. In addition to the baked goods, Mom and Dad were also introduced to all sorts of French cuisine. A favorite was escargot, although their first time preparing them almost put them off the delicacy forever. The inexorable aroma of strong garlic sauce filled the small apartment, nearly strangling them. "We couldn't look at another snail for almost six months," Dad admitted. Fortunately, they recovered their fondness for escargot. When I was twelve years old and able to stay up later than the other kids, they shared their special treat with me as if bestowing a special honor. To this day, I keep my own collection of snail shells from special occasions when I reverently extract the plump snail from its shell, pour the garlic butter in which it was simmering onto a round of baguette, and sip a nice white wine. The ritual puts me in mind of a young couple indulging themselves in their small home in the city of dreams.

Soaking in the wonder of Paris

The first of the multitude of friends Mom and Dad encoun-
tered in Paris was Zdena Berger, our upstairs neighbor. A
concentration camp survivor from Prague, she had lost her
parents and all other members of her family, and later wrote
a novel based on her experiences. Despite her tragic back-
ground, she enthralled my folks with her ebullient spirit. She
and her husband, Ollie, became regular visitors at our flat, and
us at theirs. Zdena would come down almost daily to chat over
cups of cocoa. The couples cooked elaborate dinners for each
other, played cards, drank, and talked late into the evening.
Mom formed a strong bond with Zdena, later finding her a job
after she and Ollie split up. Apparently, I was most captivated
by our new neighbor. I loved Zdena—would sit at her feet
and look rapturously up at her when she spoke in her thick
accent, following her all around the flat. When she was gone,
I incessantly hinted about going up to visit her. Apparently,
my infatuation turned "lustful," Dad wrote, as I would lift the
edge of Zdena's skirt and kiss her leg. To this day, I remain
enamored of Zdena, staying in touch and visiting whenever
I'm in the vicinity of her home in California. 70 years later, she
still calls me Little Danny!

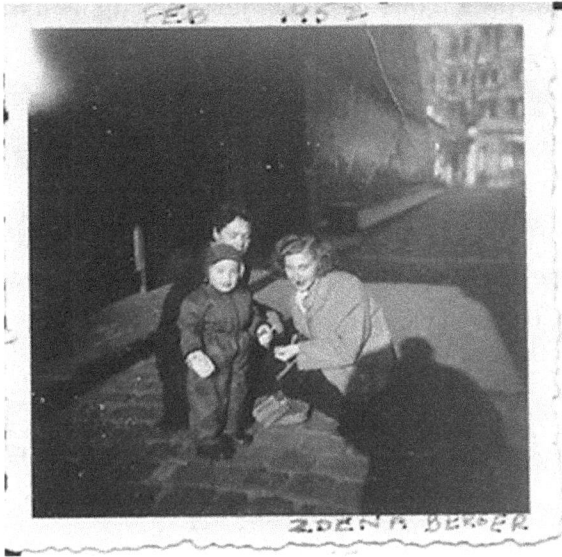

Me and Mom with Zdena on the streets of Paris

* * *

On October first, Dad started classes at the University of Sorbonne in their Cours Practique, one of two programs offered to foreign students. Alas, I haven't uncovered the reasons why he chose to participate in that program. Of the sixteen enrolled in the program, fourteen were from different countries; Dad was only one from the United States. Mom described his time there in a letter to Lucile:

"His classes are most interesting and sure keep him occupied. He is taking 17 hours and there is no definite homework therefore no test of any kind. His home study is completely of his own volition, as nothing is required.

However, if one wishes to just keep up with the classes, he must study a good five or six hours every night. He has classes in vocabulary, conversation, grammar, etc., and then lecture classes in geography, literature, history and the history of art. Everything is in French. It is really a good course for him. All the students are on the graduate level, and it is interesting to meet people of the same age from all over the world."

She later reported that he was so busy, he didn't have time to do the crossword puzzles his mother had sent from home.

In his spare moments, Dad wandered the city, finding and frequenting its many libraries and bookstores. He developed a proclivity for visiting the Quartier de Pigalle, known for its neon-lit red-light district and eclectic nightlife, with grand 19th-century neoclassical buildings and many notable art museums, and home to the 19th century cabaret, Moulin Rouge. He reported that, "I was only propositioned once." The muse led him through all the arenas Paris and time had to offer. One of his favorite hangouts was Le Dôme Café, the iconic meeting place for literati and Beatnik wannabes. Mom took art classes and would regularly paint while Dad would write. Her fascination rubbed off on him, as he liked to draw and paint, often self-portraits ("that were either gross or my appearance at [the] time was gross"), as well as renditions of the landlady and his beatific little son.

"Danny, sit still so I can paint a portrait of you!"

"Mais papa, je veux monter chez Zdena!" (But dad, I want to go up to Zdena!)

These were the halcyon days before television distracted everybody, allowing my parents to indulge in their various passions. They were voracious readers. Dad felt <u>The Diary of Anne Frank</u> was the, "most moving book I've ever read." After reading <u>A Portrait of the Artist as a Young Man</u>, he said that he was anxious to get hold of some more of James Joyce' work, and that, "[Joyce] is the most powerful writer I have read yet." Dad recalled and reviewed many more favorites in his journals and letters which also led to the wealth of literature that would overflow shelves, tables, and desks in any home he lived in for the rest of his life. He also devoured newspapers (Le Monde, Le Parisien, New York Times) as well as both English and French magazines.

Leaving me with various sitters, Mom and Dad delighted in the opera and theater, attending performances in French, English, and Italian. A favorite was 'Follies Bergère,' to which they would regularly take out-of-town guests. Music was another great passion; they loved jazz and live performances which included Edith Piaf, Charles Aznavour, and Sacha Distel. Dad bought a phonograph and immediately started buying and borrowing records, many of which made it back home to our collections in Colorado. Seeing Maurice Chavalier enhanced their love of dancing, which they did every chance they got. Mom and Dad also enjoyed going to the movies, both in English and French. Of 'An American in Paris,' Dad said that it was worth the long wait in line.

Singing was a regular part of every gathering it seemed— whether at home, at friends', or in the small clubs. Another of my earliest and fondest memories is when he would sing this lovely Irish ballad as held me on his lap in the old wooden rocking chair:

> 'O Danny boy, the pipes, the pipes are calling
> From glen to glen and down the mountainside
> The summer's gone and all the roses falling
> T'is you, 'tis you must go and I must bide

> But come ye back when summer's in the meadow
> Or all the valley's hushed and white with snow
> T'is I'll be here in sunshine or in shadow
> O Danny boy, O Danny boy, I love you so'

Though the lyrics and meter of Danny Boy are more often reprised at memorials and funerals, none of that mattered to me. Even now, I can recapture the emotion and security that stirred in me as Dad serenaded me with many of the other songs that became my favorites such as 'I Gave My Love a Cherry,' 'Alouette Gentile Alouette' and many others he crooned in French. I apparently got my start as a (bad) singer in Paris; Dad recalled I would throw my head back and howl with all my little might. That love of everything musical infused their future family life; I can't remember a time when there wasn't music or singing around all of the houses we lived in. In later years, I carried the torch forward and relished the opportunity to sing for my children and then my grandkids. They all seemed to treasure the intimacy we shared and didn't care that my singing was, at best, awful.

Being a gregarious toddler, I had trouble learning the strict customs of French children. They were not communal, and evidently never played with one another in the parks. They were given their own little area to play in quietly, but me being "limitless almost single-handedly severed international relations," Dad said. He recounted one example of me running after a rolling ball another child had missed. Le jeune français was surprised and furious that some other little kid would dare touch his ball and pushed me down. I, happily thinking this was the game, pushed him down in return. Obviously, the kid's parents, not at all pleased with the turn of events, roundly chastised me and my parents.

Social interaction was a critical component to Dad and Mom's edification. Zdena and Ollie were the first of their new friendships to be spawned in Paris, but they connected with old companions who'd migrated overseas as well. There was Hal and Bobby (short for Roberta) Tufty who lived at Rue du Pyrenees; Hal would, it seemed, regularly pour out his troubles to Dad over many glasses of beer and booze. Then there was Bubbles, the letter-writing friend from Boulder, who came to Paris on a whim and would often babysit me.

Bubbles used to stay with a family, the Tourats, in Tours, a beautiful city of ornate cathedrals along the Loire River. She introduced Marcel and Jacqueline to Mom and Dad, and me to their young son, Jean Louis. He was a year and a half older than me and became my best friend in France. Though his parents kept him spotless in the local fashion, wearing the usual white apron and pins to keep his hair just so, I was glad to have someone else to play with. Dad reported that the two of us had riotous times together and I would howl when the Tourats left on the train, because I didn't want Jean Louis to leave.

During those visits to Paris, the Tourats introduced us to close relatives, showed us the best of French traditions, and were proud of their American friends. Fortuitously, just before Mom passed away in 2003, she connected me with the Tourats when my wife, Karen, and I were headed off to Europe to follow the Tour de France. In response to my letter written to his parents, Jean Louis emailed me back saying that he and his wife, Edith, would not only pick us up at Orly Airport outside Paris, but take us the three hours south to visit with his parents. We had to email pictures of ourselves; who would recognize a playmate from fifty years ago? A highlight of the visit was a photograph taken of Karen and me with Marcel and Jacqueline on their porch that mirrored a picture taken of them with my folks during the early 1950s. Jean Louis and I remain fast friends to this day; he and Edith have visited us here in the USA a few times. Dad and Mom would be thrilled that we kept that French connection alive.

Another visitor to the flat on Rue du Pyrenees was a University of Colorado chum, Bill Baldwin. With a mad and adventurous bent, he stayed with my folks while he went in search of a motorcycle on which to circle the world. When he first dropped in, Dad was excited to see him, but apparently Bill soon wore out his welcome. Dad wrote of him, "disappointing having him here as I had always liked him before but now I have lost a lot of respect for him. He is a poor houseguest, self-centered, inconsiderate and short on gratitude. He is still quite immature, gets fed up easily and doesn't seem to appreciate anything he sees or does. In present frame of mind, he is bound to have a lousy trip — it is too bad, it is a wonderful opportunity for a lad." Ultimately, Bill ended up in

Africa and became a mercenary. He turned his experiences into a book called Mau Mau Man-Hunt (1957), the sub-title of which is 'The Adventures of the Only American Who Fought the Terrorists in Kenya.' Growing up, I heard tales of this guy and was enthralled by his adventures, even recalling seeing his book on our shelves. Only now, have I discovered that he was a bit of slug in Dad's eyes.

Dad developed a small circle of friends through the Cours Practique. One was a young man from Sweden who had studied for a year in the United States; for reasons I could not discern, Dad described him as a "gentle con man." He also became friendly with a fellow from Egypt, who he described as upper crust, strict in his actions and beliefs, especially about women. The pals would get together between and after classes to drink wine and discuss world affairs as well as course topics. Of the other people Dad met at the Sorbonne, he summed up his impressions of them when he attended a big party hosted by the school's faculty in the spring, "I was pleasantly surprised to see many people...let their hair down, as school is a serious business here and fellow students are meant to be starchy, but we made a lot of good friends."

Being inspired by top academics and minds from all over the world was exhilarating and galvanizing. Dad took it all in and though he got more laissez faire about going to class, and had this little ankle-biter demanding his attention, he kept up with his studies and began writing every day. Mostly stories and musings, but also articles that he would send back to his mother who tried, mostly unsuccessfully, to get them published. In June 1952, he took written exams and passed, though stating, "I think everyone did." That entitled him to take orals, which consisted of reading a short passage (in French) and answering a few simple grammar questions in front of two professors. He placed second out of the sixteen students. With that distinction, he earned his certificate of completion. He worked hard, yet appreciated the amount of discipline required to make oneself "learned," which may have inspired this appraisal.

Uncluttering 1

The ideal university has no examinations or grading system —
It is not compulsory to attend classes.

CHAPTER 9

"As fantastic as it may sound, I have definitely decided that I want to write which is a good reason to stay over a bit longer. I think I can but it will take a hell of a lot of work. As you can see, I have never worked so hard at it in my life. I have typed until my fingers are sore; and although, the typewriter and I are becoming much friendlier, we are still fighting each other. I have never had the opportunity to write like I have this year, and believe it or not Paris does have a certain stimulus. Anyhow, I have got to keep at it; it will take a lot of work and it would be very easy to be lazy again."

Dad wrote those words in a letter to Lucile in April 1952. Paris and the inspiration his mother had cultivated back in the red house on East 11th Street had taken root. He had witnessed the persistence and passion with which a single mother of six used to break into the world of journalism. Dad's pride in her success undoubtedly kindled in him a fever to put his own words on paper that people would want to read. The heady, wondrous environs of the City of Lights fanned the flames.

That summer, after having completed the Cours Practique at the Sorbonne and being bitten by the bug to be a writer, Dad persuaded Mom to stay in Paris a year longer than originally planned, which was an easy sell. She had been substitute teaching but found a more permanent position with the US Army Accounting Office. Dad also hoped to find a job but never did, so he earnestly threw himself into his writing. He approached the process resolutely by tracking the number of pages written per day, even sub-dividing the record by typed versus handwritten. At various times, he described his efforts as "being absorbed and not being able to quit"; "writing himself out and being high strung all night"; and "tying himself in sentences." With a workspace set up on the table in our small kitchen, and me off with a sitter, Dad challenged himself to produce at least one story or article a week, while forging ahead on a book manuscript with which he'd been dabbling. I uncovered an early and lengthy manuscript, but it was not dated, so unfortunately, I'm not sure if it was the one he was working on at that time. His journal entries portrayed himself as a workhorse seemingly able to write at all times of day and in few moments stolen between activities.

Dad would send articles and stories to his mother in hopes that she might find publishers for them. She never did, though he silently questioned her enthusiasm for the task. Despite her scholarly proclivity, which Dad sought to exploit, he would castigate her for her reviews of his work, "If I hear excellent, good or lovely (lovely especially) about my stuff again, I shall hit you (rhetorically, I hope!). Do give me some specific information and criticism. Did you like the idea for the poem (that was lovely)?" Must be that even an educated and professional mom can still have trouble being objective, or perhaps, she was trying not to tell him, "That sucked!" As are most writers, Dad was his own worst critic. After amassing 1,400 typewritten pages for the first draft of the "Great American Post-war Novel" he was writing, he edited it down to 600 pages and still called it, "awful." In The Moveable Feast, Hemingway said, "...how good a book is should be judged by the man who writes it, by the excellence of the material that he eliminates." Though most likely unaware of the master's wisdom at the time, Dad was snared in a labyrinth of that paradox. Though he deemed his initial effort unworthy, the exercise was invaluable.

Other disappointments tested his resolve. He lamented the time he submitted an article to the New Yorker, "Got bad rejection from them and had to pay 180 francs for it — can't figure it out!" When he tried to get work at the Paris edition of the New York Herald, doing anything, "the only responses were crank calls including a couple from women who wanted to know what 'anything' meant." His frustration and disappointment are clearly captured and poured into this very poignant poem.

<hr />

The Battle

O little sheet of paper,
O little plane of white,
Why are you staring so?
- Defying me to write.
You are little and lifeless.
I am big and strong.
Why — I could crumple you,
And wouldn't think it wrong.

It wouldn't take much effort,
And time a little more,
To disfigure you and darken you
With a stream of leaden lore.
The depth of my mind is endless
You should hear me talk.
My vocabulary is extensive and growing
- Knowledge from every walk.
I have a latent library of facts;
I gain a volume every day.
I can combine them and create
New facts and ideas to say.
Avidly I pursue discussion
To articulate my mind,
On various and sundry things
Leaving others behind.
Men and women and little people,
Sports and crime and sex,
Politics and history and art
And other things reflects.
On psychology, science and math,
The news, the reasons, the wit.
I'm profane, sensuous, eloquent or common;
Whatever I see fit.
And yet you sneer and stand your ground;
A might teasing the mighty
Your ego — my friend — is pitiful,
Terse, tickling and tritey.
Do you think you can humble
Or frustrate a man?
I should bow to your puniness,
How do you think I can?
You have no hand — cocky one –
In these beads upon my brow.

Tis not a look of fear
In my hollowed eyes just now.
I do not cringe or falter.
I do not shake my head.
I have not choked or cursed
Praying I were dead.
You are blind, vain and small;
You could never phase me.
It's in your audacious manner
That you amaze me.
I have not lost my power;
I have maintained my might.
My mind is throbbing with wisdom,
My fingers itch to write.
I yearn so to articulate –
To bubble with wit and lore,
But tis your petty defiance
I can't swallow more.
There is so much I could teach you –
So much you have to know,
But progress cannot penetrate
The shallow shield you show.
Tis a pity we couldn't be genial.
You have yourself to thank.
But I can't lower to your level –
I shall have to leave you blank

Dad continued wandering the city, finding inspiration in its many libraries, bookstores, and Left Bank cafes. Quite fortunately, the circles in which Dad and Mom revolved had their share of luminaries. While at Duke, Mom met the up-and-coming author, William (Bill) Styron, through her friend, Bobby Tufty. In 1968, Styron would win the Pulitzer Prize for The Confessions of Nat Turner (1967), the fictitious memoir of a slave who led a revolt in 1831. Another book he wrote, Sophie's Choice (1979), became a favorite of Dad's that he strongly encouraged me to read; I did, and it became one of my favorites as well. In the summer of 1952, Styron was passing through Paris on his way to collect the Prix de Rome for his first book, Lie Down in Darkness. The Prix de Rome is a monetary award and one-year fellowship program bestowed by the American Academy of Arts and Letters to top artists, musicians, and writers. His and mom's old friend, Bobby, was living in Paris with her husband, Hal. Mom and Dad were invited to join them for dinner with the newly famous author. Dad described the event, "...typical dull and boring...one consoling factor was Styron, the most genuine person there...spent most of the night talking to him. He is very well read and a very interesting person to talk to. We have invited him sometime soon and he seemed very eager to come." Bill did come to our apartment and Dad stated in his journal that he "hated to leave." He also joined us on a bus trip to Verdun, where Styron and I had a grand time swimming in the Marne River.

William Styron and Dad were both tall and slender with inquiring expressions. They might have had more in common, had Dad more carefully appraised his intellectual peer. He made this startling and specious entry in his journal after the time spent with the very promising young author: "Made me burn to write a novel because I figured if such an inauspicious guy [like Styron] could write one, I could."

Another up-and-comer who flew into Mom and Dad's orbit was George Plimpton. He moved into a flat upstairs from us on Rue de Pyrenees and would come down to visit us regularly. In later years, he became famous for "participatory journalism," wherein he trained and wrote about the New York Yankees, Detroit Lions and sparring with boxing greats Archie Moore and Sugar Ray Robinson. His stint with Detroit inspired his bestselling novel, Paper Lions, which was made into a movie starring Alan Alda. Plimpton also acted in a Western movie, performed a comedy act at Caesars Palace in Las Vegas, and played with the New York Philharmonic Orchestra.

Though Dad thought Plimpton "played the piano beautifully," he wasn't particularly complimentary of the young Harvard grad who had attended Oxford University. Not unlike his characterization of Bill Styron, Dad seemed to not discern the potential of Plimpton's talent, either. In his journal, Dad recounted, "George came down to play the piano and stayed to dinner. We had a long discussion. Maybe, I am out of step, but so few people over here seem to be real. He is a very nice fellow, but he is trying too hard to be an intellectual. He wants to write but I don't think he can bend enough. Maybe, he is smarter than I am. But he is like so many Americans...want to write but just don't sit down to do it or piddle around doing other things as a preliminary to writing."

Dad's portrayal went even farther afield when he wrote in another entry, "(Plimpton) is one of the editors who are getting together another literary mag [a list that included Bill Styron and other luminaries such as James Baldwin, Irwin Shaw, and Peter Matthiessen]; I thought he wanted me to subscribe but he just wanted me to submit some material." Dad declined because he thought the periodical would not last long, and maybe he wasn't yet convinced of his skills. That "literary mag," was the Paris Review which printed its first issue in the spring of 1953 with Plimpton as its inaugural editor-in-chief. What a miscalculation that turned out to be! The Paris Review became a highly regarded journal that remains alive and well today, having published works by such icons as Ezra Pound, Ernest Hemingway, T. S. Eliot, Jorge Luis Borges, Ralph Ellison, William Faulkner, Thornton Wilder, Robert Frost, Pablo Neruda, William Carlos Williams, and Vladimir Nabokov. I can only fathom the devastation and discouragement Dad must have felt, when in later years, realization took hold that he could have been in on the ground floor of the Paris Review. If only he'd acquiesced to George Plimpton's suggestion that he submit some work to the fledgling publication. His one big opportunity in a place he cherished quickly flew by the rearview mirror without having passed in front of the windshield. 'Escaped Thought' may be about fleeting ideas, but there too, is an inkling of the frustration he felt in missing out on great opportunities.

Escaped Thought

Under a flood of other things,
A thought escaped my mind.
When I cleared the way to pick it up,
The thought I could not find.
I looked around in frantic search —
The shadowed world I thrust.
I bared new thoughts that lay hidden

Shook others of their dust.
    The thought I could not find.
I can hear the music of the words
That set my soul to dance,
But can I bare the ebon cloak
The words I would enhance.
Perhaps you swim in the shadows.
Perhaps you shall return.
Perhaps you will find another mind,
And let the incense burn.

When I discussed this episode in my father's life with Uncle Bill, he quoted George Bernard Shaw saying that Dad "Never missed an opportunity to miss an opportunity."

* * *

Another reason for staying the extra year was because Mom and Dad decided they needed to see more of Europe. During the earlier years, we traveled around France, visiting Tours, where we stayed with Jean Louis' family, and Cherbourg and took a memorable ski trip to Briançon. During our extended stay, we journeyed to Amsterdam, Brussels, Switzerland, Germany, and Italy. Though the trips were often fraught with car troubles and lack of money, they were filled with adventure. Dad lamented after one excursion that he was "Sad to be home." Apparently, the drudgery of everyday life even in Paris necessitated escape now and then. There's no doubt that those excursions fueled Mom's wanderlust and further filtered into my DNA.

In the summer of 1953, having had enough of Mme. Bamberger's schizoid, moody antics, Mom and Dad moved us for a short while to 5 Rue Schoelcher. The landlady told of the house hosting lavish parties that included many celebrities such as Maurice Ravel, who composed *Bolero* and other works on "this very piano." Our flat had paper-thin walls and the woman next door could be heard cooing and sweet-talking during day, only to argue loudly at night. The next floor down, an attractive woman wearing a very sexy negligee would walk her husband down to the front door where she would passionately kiss him goodbye; five minutes later, another man came by, they would kiss passionately and go back upstairs. They apparently weren't the only clandestine lovers in the building; another tenant, who called himself a Shakespearean actor, had a mistress who would stay in his flat on weekends. An artist for the Paris Review, William Pene DeBois Jr., lived in the building as well; Dad described him as quiet, but his wife "was a bitch, who seemed not to like us because we were nobodies and had no talent." That must have stung and further tarnished Dad's impression of the 'mag.'

We then moved around the corner to a flat at 59 rue Froidevaux. Among the favored neighbors were Ed and Janice Pike, who had a baby girl whilst living in Paris. They named the cute little red-haired child Medley Ann. My parents fell in love with her and warned Ed that their first daughter would be named after her. The first of my two sisters was indeed bestowed with the lovely moniker. Mom and Dad would have been honored to know that they would have a great-granddaughter also given that name. My daughter, Mariah, was the only one of my parents' grandkids to know my sister before she died a far too premature death. Though she was less than a year old when they met, Mariah grew up hearing about the wonderful woman who she should have known as an aunt. She paid tribute by naming her second daughter Medley, thus carrying forward my parents' reverence for the name.

Reflecting on those times, Dad wrote that Mme. Foillet, our landlady at rue Froidevaux, was the only source of prejudice we experienced in Europe. She had thought Dad was kidding when he told her that my mom was Jewish. Dad didn't elaborate on the details of her arrogance, but a few days later, he told her that we had to leave sooner than we thought. The old biddy's abhorrent attitude wasn't the only reason for leaving rue Froidevaux; Mom was pregnant with my little brother, Pete, who would be born the following February.

In 2003, my wife, Karen, and I stayed in Paris while following the Tour de France bicycle race. Before she passed, Mom had given us the list of addresses we had lived for those two years in the City of Lights. Karen and I rented bicycles one day and hunted down the three different apartment buildings. Discovering that the latter two were across the street from Cimetière du Montparnasse, one of the city's expansive, ornate, and mystical cemeteries, I think I uncovered the source of Dad's lifelong fascination with graveyards.

* * *

In another excerpt from *A Moveable Feast*, Ernest Hemingway wrote:

> "There is never any ending to Paris and the memory of each person who has lived in it differs from that of any other. We always returned to it no matter who we were or how it was changed or with what difficulties, or ease, it could be reached. Paris was always worth it and you received in return for whatever you brought to it. But this is how Paris was in the early days when we were very poor and very happy."

Either through ignorance or forgetfulness, I don't recall Dad talking much about Hemingway or his books. Also being poor and happy, I do think he certainly came to love Paris in much the same way as Papa (the vaunted author's nickname). Dad seemed to have sought and found much of what he hoped for: an elite education, rich friendships, stimulating intellectualism with fine entertainment in an exotic, romantic setting. He discovered the beautiful muse, but also found that her hard-hearted sister, Reality, would be a formidable adversary. I'm not sure what prevented him from finding at least a modicum of success. He was, in practicality, young into his writing career, but what was the missing piece that vaulted many of his peers to literary heights? When he couldn't find stable employment and with Mom being pregnant, the decision to come home was sensible. Yet, it was also disappointing because he hadn't tasted the fruits of self-actualization or successfully completed the manuscript that he'd hoped to write when he first set foot in that "beautiful and impressive" city.

He took the fire of inspiration back across the Atlantic Ocean, with high hopes of creating a classic masterpiece. Less than ten years later, he would achieve a modicum of commercial success with his non-fiction works, but I think he had wanted to write something that could hold its own in the pantheon of Bohemian, archetypal masterworks penned by Hemingway, Joyce, Faulkner, Styron, and other celebrated authors of the era. With a young, growing family and real life coming out of the shadows, he fervently tried to keep the creative blazes ignited in Paris burning hot.

Of the keepsakes Dad brought back with him were the proper sense of determination and discipline he knew it would take to write something of worth. Much of that sentiment is captured in the letter to his mother, having never worked so hard pounding the keyboard until his fingers were sore and fighting with his typewriter. He learned the hard way that creativity meant writing shit sometimes and killing your darlings, but always persevering. That mantra was delivered to me many years hence, when he reiterated that writing had to be treated like a job. It had to become a routine that you stuck to regardless of lethargy, frustration, and disappointment. You had to persist until it became a necessity in your daily life, when a day without writing was one with a gaping hole in it. Though he's long since left me to discover the contours and structures of the writing life on my own, that piece of advice has helped me to accept writing almost as necessary to my life as companionship, community, and a beautiful sunset. The reward of that focus is the satisfaction of completing a work that can be shared with the world. To hold in your hand a book, an article, a poem that you have written, toiled, and sweated over, is nearly the pinnacle of contentment in life. For serious artists, the thrill of creativity ranks not far below the rewards of parenthood and having a loving companion. Yes, though the muse teased him mightily, I believe Perry Eberhart found her in Paris and passed her, or her daughter, along to me, even as a toddler; "Danny still persists on doing his own typing but he is enlarging upon his ability. Now he takes a piece of scratch paper, inserts it in the correct place, cranks the right crank to bring it around and commences to write out his thoughts. If my glasses are handy, he puts them on too."

As he knew he must, Dad would soon return to "real life," one where bills having to be paid, families raised and jobs created a mundane, work-a-day routine. I can only imagine quixotic, lofty memories spawned in the bookstores, cabarets, and cafes of an enchanted city forever haunting the deep recesses of his mind. Was he dispirited by the notion that this mordant lifestyle would trample dreams of distinguished, Bohemian literary success?

'The Search,' prefaces Dad's second book, <u>Treasure Tales of the Rockies</u>, published in 1961. Though it speaks to the quest for gold, such as the magic germinated in the streets of Paris, true success is found in the tedium of the quest.

***

The Search

What is the gold you seek?
Here in the muck and the mud,
Is it a crystal palace, clean and cared for?
What is the gold you seek?

Here in the naked cold of nowhere,
Is it warmth you seek?
This leather-hard skin,
This lean body, bent against the weather and the world,
Does it seek a softness, a velvet life?
In this narrow dirt gulch,
Do you seek refinement?
Beauty?
    From a handful of dust
Do you seek power?
Fame?
    What is the gold you seek?
In the stark, shrill aloneness of the night,
Do you pursue an ancient love?
A misty remembrance?
The warmth and tenderness of being wanted?
    This time-tortured body,
Bent with age and age-old hurt,
Does it seek the lost wealth of youth?
In this rocky corridor
Do you seek eternal rest?
    Do you see Heaven in the mud?
    If this be the gold you seek,
Keep seeking, keep searching.
The glitter is along the trail,
The search is the thing.
When the search is over....
    The glitter is gone.

CHAPTER 10

On October 21 of 1953, we left Paris for London. During the week we spent there, we watched the changing of the guard at Buckingham Palace, heard Big Ben toll the hour, strode across London Bridge and took in many other of the storied city's landmarks. There was more to the visit than sightseeing. Dad described a powerful lesson he learned, "... crossing the street, I looked the wrong way, [and] almost got run down!" Mom had her own memorable experience with socialized medicine firsthand, getting "free," much-needed dental work. Dad cryptically alluded to her problems, saying, "all of Sandy's teeth fell out." Growing up, I remember Mom having a bright, pearly smile. I knew she had some false teeth but never really knew why. She was very self-conscious about them, only taking them out in the dead of night when she felt no one was there to notice, except Dad, of course. When she was in her 70s, she became much less self-conscious about her false teeth. My sister and I would chuckle about how Mom and her roommate would take out their dentures and toothlessly chatter away.

From London, we sailed for New York and were back in the USA on November second. Bob Rolander, Dad's roommate from college, met us at the dock. He joined us as we spent a couple days touring the Big Apple including some of Mom's old haunts.

It was foggy and snowy when we arrived back home in Denver. Almost everybody from Dad's big, boisterous family was at the airport. Mom's folks, meaning Granny, were put out that they weren't able to meet us by themselves. It seemed her grumbling had merely been on hiatus while we were overseas. She had been upset when Dad took his new family to Paris because, as he would write in his journal, "Mama T figured I was wasting my time...all [my] friends and peers would become established in their fields and would be two years ahead of me by the time we returned." After the halcyon era in the city of dreams with visions of an illustrious literary career, Dad came home to her same haughty reproach. Despite her reservations about their naïve son-in-law though, Granny and Grandpa had a small gray and white house with a sharp pointy roof, built and waiting for us on Syracuse Street in Denver, a block and a half from the southwest corner of Stapleton Airport.

Though Dad appreciated the magnanimous gift of a house, he opined that, "We were home. And not much had changed." He captured a bit of his malaise in this ode.

Ode 4

What dams my stream of thought? Where can the outlet be?
Do I look too far and see a thing dimly?

Not focusing on a nearer gold.
Do I clutter my sight and all that's in me
By making my eyes too bold....

━━━◆━━━

Perhaps I shared a little of his melancholy, as he captured this musing from me in his journal: "It's terrible to be hungry and lonely when we live in Paris, France. Daddy took me everywhere and I got so spoiled." Old me can fathom the second part but has no idea where the first part came from, and alas, there's no one left to explain it for me.

* * *

"I don't see how you did it mother. I just have one little monster climbing on me saying 'Bye, Bye', and you had six," Dad wrote to his mother from France. He also included these gems from his friend, Hal Tufty: "...it seems like [Danny] is sitting right on the edge of a laugh all the time"; "...you should be thankful you have such a fine kid"; and "not everyone can have a kid like you do...hope we will as well."

In light of those glowing reviews, my status as the center of my parents' universe came crashing down soon after we settled into our new home. Little brother, Peter Mack, was born the following February. A chubby, happy little tyke, Pete did worm his way into my affection, but just like that, my parents took us from the world of Bohemian gadabouts and entered the milieu of young urban families striving to establish a future.

Dad's first job was, in his words, a menial job at a stationary store. Then, in quick order, he was hired as a cub reporter at the Denver Post, one of the two dailies in town, the other being the Rocky Mountain News that had launched his mother's journalistic career. Dad tried to handle both jobs but ended up leaving the stationary store and working "nightside" at the Post, where all new reporters started. He was paid $45/week, plus $4 for night shift differential. His boss was Mort Stern, who had some notoriety for busting the union at newspapers in Little Rock, Arkansas. Within a few short weeks, Dad felt he became a marked man when a dayside man, Thor Severson, leaned on him to get the night crew to join the guild (union). Consequently, Dad felt Stern and the "other bigwigs" always seemed to be keeping an eye on him. Another disadvantage was that, having taught himself to type, he wasn't as proficient as the others, especially when being watched. When his re-writes and re-typing kept the crew overtime, for which they weren't paid, Stern would get angry, one time even kicking a waste basket across the room. Dad became very insecure to the point that every word, especially names, looked wrong to him, which led him to think that he was getting ulcers.

Stan Thies was the head of the "cop shop" department, who Dad claimed was a poor writer, but an otherwise smooth cookie who sucked up to Mort Stern. Theis felt all nightside reporters should get their chops chasing down police activities. Dad was assigned to Theis and spent a couple of what he would call "the most depressing weeks of [my] life," either waiting for things to happen or observing lots of police brutality. When he tried to report specific incidents, he was told that the Post wasn't interested, obviously trying to stay on the good side of the Police Department. The highlight of his time in the cop shop was when he earned the handle, "animal reporter." He wrote a story about a German Shepard being run over and killed in the wee hours of the morning while his young owner was delivering newspapers. It got front page coverage, and the kid received a slew of offers for a new dog and a year's supply of dog food. For several days thereafter, Dad covered animal stories such as dogs sliding down slides and a cat that delivered green apples from a tree down the street at his master's feet. Despite this small measure of notoriety, Theis was hard on Dad; he even suspected that the man was feeding him wrong information. The final straw was when Dad spelled a name incorrectly in a story, a serious transgression for a reporter; Dad claimed he spelled the name the way Theis had fed it to him. In the end, Dad felt he was fired for his insecurities, union activities, and, what must have been terribly disheartening, because the editors didn't think he had the makings for a reporter.

My father's early experience in the rough-and-tumble world of journalism, I think, was a harbinger for the many disappointments to come. Not unlike his brushes with notoriety in Paris, he would fall short or miss the rousing, fleeting opportunity. This verse best portrays, I think, Dad's vexations and disappointments along the highway of career and livelihood.

Uncluttering 15

And although you all are so stupid,
I love you all the same.

The only thing that frustrates me
Is reading your name in fame.

—————⊰•⊱—————

A couple weeks after being let go by the Post and still only
1954, Dad began what would be an off-and-on, long-term rela-
tionship with the National Farmers Union (NFU). He was
offered a job in their information department. There were two
other men in the department, a writer and a cartoonist, both of
whom Dad called amateurs. They would soon be terminated,
leaving Dad and a "girl" to produce NFU communications.

To supplement the growing family's struggling budget, Dad
started working evenings at the Air Force Accounting Center
which had been set up in North Denver to centralize branch
records. He developed the adage, "When in doubt, discard,"
and apparently threw away a lot of good records. One of the
lasting benefits was that he got to work with Mabel Armstrong,
a gregarious woman with a permanent smile and married to
an equally outgoing guy, Bill, who was always nattily dressed
and had well-oiled hair. My parents got to be best friends with
Mabel and Bill, or William Henry, as my mother would fondly
call him. I have wonderful memories of hanging out with them
at our home or in the basement of their house, which was
decked out like a suave speakeasy, complete with wall-wide
mirror behind a polished, dark wood bar. Mom would be
twirled around by William Henry while Dad waltzed Mabel
into the wee hours of the morning.

In 1955, the job with the Air Force Records Center came
to an end, or "ran out," as Dad put it. His nascent inability for

being a typical, toe-the-line employee began to show its limits even in the denouement of this relatively mundane position. Dad was put on the committee to organize a farewell party, which at first was planned for the Aurora Veterans Club, but they wouldn't allow any dancing between the races; Mabel, his favorite dancing partner, was African American. So, the soiree was moved to the Democratic Club near downtown. The workers were supposed to be released at 8:00 p.m. on the night of the party, however, the officer in charge determined there was still some "piddling" work to do, so he wouldn't release any of the group. Dad led a walkout of a small number of fellow employees. I can just imagine him, haughtily getting up from his desk and announcing, "Let's go, gang! What're they going to do, fire us?"

Back at Farmers Union, they were planning on expanding their public relations department to produce a newsletter that would be sent to all its members. My father thought he would become managing editor. Alas, an old college friend, Bill Davoren, who Dad called a wheeler and dealer, and who also had connections with the governor, was given the lead role. Dad was assigned the title of Associate Editor, as well as a $25/week bump in salary. That wasn't enough because Dad felt he had as much experience as Davoren, so he gave them two weeks to pay him more or he would leave. They offered only another $25, so he left.

Serendipity for a change smiled on him during those last few days while Dad was cleaning out his desk. He got a call from Harry Kadish of the International News Service (INS), offering him a temporary job. At first, Dad thought it was a joke because Bill Davoren's brother, John, worked in that office; was Bill adding insult to injury? So, Dad played hard to get for Kadish, telling him that he had more experience than he really did, and "came pretty expensive." Harry took him seriously and hired Dad as a third-level newsman that he would later confess in his journal he didn't deserve.

President Dwight "Ike" Eisenhower had a heart attack while visiting his wife Mamie's family in Denver and was taken to Fitzsimmons Naval Hospital in nearby Aurora. What Kadish needed was someone on "death watch" to be stationed at the hospital for any breaking news, which became Dad's assignment. There were only minor items of newsworthiness, though Dad got a couple scoops. One was an inadvertent chance to meet and talk to Mamie Eisenhower. Dad reported she was personable and very gracious, though nothing of note was discussed. He was perturbed later when other newsmen asked him if she was sober; apparently, there were efforts to sluice out rumors and impugn her reputation.

Dad's other scoop was rather momentous in that it altered the scheduling of Ike's stay at the hospital. While hanging out, Dad got friendly with one of the president's physicians, Dr. Snyder, who Dad described as a "fine old gent with a head of white hair," reminiscent of his grandfather. They were both bored and reading the same book, which they would discuss at times. In the course of their conversations, the doc casually mentioned that Ike was putting golf balls for minor exercise, and that his primary physician was discouraging Ike from running for a second term. Dad also learned the exact day that the president was being discharged and that he would be slipped out the back door in efforts to avoid a big stir from the press. When Dad called in the details to the INS office, he was told they were too busy at the moment and to telegraph in his notes. A staffer called back to verify the information and it was submitted under the byline of a national correspondent. At the following day's news conference, the president's press director was peppered with details from Dad's account. He quickly shut down the news conference and later confronted my father in the halls of Fitzsimmons. The man walked away slapping his forehead, but ultimately, Ike was released on the date Dad reported. Dad later saw Dr. Snyder, who turned heel and walked away from him; Dad considered him a nice man, just naïve about the press and public relations. When Ike walked out the front door of the hospital, that was the end of Dad's temp assignment.

I have a framed photo of my father with President Eisenhower and treasure its vindication of Dad's capacity for flying close to prominence. He was proud of that moment and that episode in his life. Yet, like so many others, it too was ephemeral. Perhaps he was trying to encapsulate the convergence of impulse, revelation, and momentary fame in this poem, while sanguinely asserting that in the end you will always have your humanity.

<hr />

The Difference

It's easy to think it — it's folly not to;
It's something to do with your brain;
And thinking don't mean that you have got to,
For you don't even have to explain

It's as easy to say it — the air's full of words,
And some people might turn and stare.
The echo will soon fly away with the birds,
And the world's none the worse for wear.

It's different to do it — it takes the sorta
Act without talking, and dictate the day.
A man who becomes for a minute immortal
Whose steps the seas cannot wash away.

To live it — but, ah! — what's to compare?
For even the sun can't ignore you.
You may live on a whisker and dance on a dare,
But the world is better off for you.

—◦—◦—◁●▷—◦—◦—

CHAPTER 11

1956 was a year of significant change for both my parents. My mother started working with United Air Lines, feeding punch cards into their monolithic computer. I recall her being swallowed up inside this mysterious looking building on 32nd Avenue in Denver. Her desk was behind a huge wall of glass that made it look like she was sitting in a fishbowl. The sterile setting was to keep the monstrous data processor dust-free and temperature controlled; that beast would not be able to even compute the date on today's smart phone! Mom began squirreling away blank punch cards to use at home for 'to do' and grocery lists, which she did up to the day she died. A small stack of the precious rectangular cards, each with a corner cut and patterns of rectangular little holes, has been stashed in my desk drawer as well, only to be used sparingly and lovingly. Thus began Mom's 30-year sojourn with the airline, broken up by a few intervals to have babies and such things. She would do whatever to stay with them for the express purpose of flying free around the country and ultimately, the world.

When Mom went to work with United, Dad worked for a short while at the Sears department store downtown in the evenings and stayed home during the day with Pete, who was turning two, and me. One particular day during that time stands out. I had just finished kindergarten at Ashley Elementary, less than a block from our house. Across Syracuse Street from our house was Montclair Park, where we stars of the future played Little League baseball and football. Dad was sitting at the kitchen table with his ever-growing bulk hovering over his typewriter. I rushed out the door, heading across the street to start an illustrious baseball career that fizzled in my adolescence. Where I found it has remained an ancient mystery to me, but I was wearing a left-handed mitt. Dad called me back to say I had the wrong glove and made me exchange the one I had for a right-handed one. I'm pretty sure I was destined to be left-handed, but due to his inexplicable vigilance, I now am sort of ambidextrous.

My father was the consummate sports fan, especially when it came to football. His on-the-field experiences notwithstanding, the bug had bitten him hard and he let the fever infect me. On the same field across Syracuse Street, I pursued another illustrious athletic endeavor playing for the Montclair Orioles in an orange and black uniform, with a cardboard helmet.

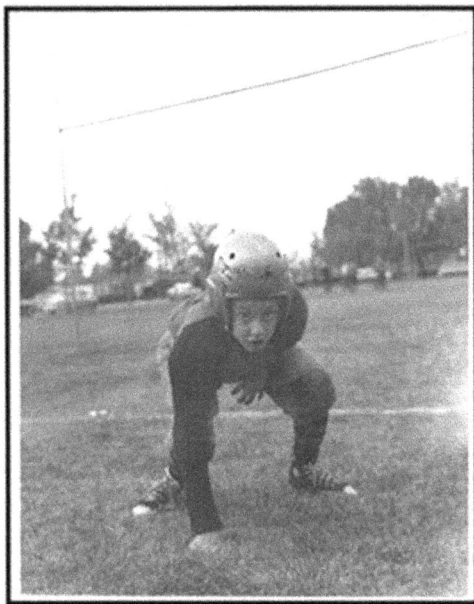

Future all-star?

* * *

Around Christmas, Dad got a call from Harvey Kadish, offering a permanent job back at INS that would start after the New Year. He, of course, jumped at it. When he returned to the small correspondence office, he found John Davoren still there, and three other staff writers. It was not long before Dad's maverick streak returned. Though no one ever came into the office, he and his cohorts were told that they had to wear ties, which my father was not inclined to do. After many suggestions and threat of a disciplinary write-up, Dad was instructed to wear a tie; the next day he came in wearing his best suit, replete with boutonniere and fancy handkerchief poking from the breast pocket. After that, a note was posted to the bulletin board that neckwear didn't have to be worn, but should be kept handy in case the odd important person came in.

Dad soon got bored producing what he called "petty stuff" and second-day leads, though he wrote a few stories that brought him distinction. One involved the 1956 Republican presidential nominating convention in San Francisco. A delegate from Nebraska, Terry Carpenter, did not appreciate being steamrolled into just going along with the party line. After Eisenhower was nominated to be the Republican candidate for president, Carpenter stood up and nominated Joe Smith for VP. There was no Joe Smith so Carpenter got ejected from the convention for causing a minor uproar. Dad dug a little deeper and found that Carpenter's wife was a Democrat, so he called her. In the next day's paper, he wrote that Mrs. Carpenter was quite proud of her husband and that the convention was just a "Pink tea party" anyway. I never figured out what that meant.

Another of Dad's big scoops involved the legendary movie star, Ingrid Bergman, and her daughter, Pia Lindstrom, who was attending the University of Colorado in Boulder. Dad was able to finagle an interview with Pia in her dorm, where she complained that she was tired of all the false rumors and innuendo about her not wanting to see her famous mother, and she wanted to set the record straight. Dad's story made the national papers.

Despite the few fleeting events, Dad was still not finding the satisfaction and exhilaration he'd hoped to find as a journalist. I can't know who Dad was writing about in this poem, but I see life's reality clashing with a glorified self-image of what had been. In reminiscences of a carousing sailor or a beret-wearing Bohemian on the banks of the Seine, was Dad seeking relief from the man he saw himself becoming?

Unnamed 1

I saw him in the shadows of the marquee
And for a moment he had dimmed the dancing light
He was but a musty bag of rags
Shambling nameless and aimless into the night
Unconsciously I wandered after him
A creature from an unknown land
A friendless land of night and cold
And hunger, a horrible hunger
Not for food, but for wine
Wine to soften the way, and warm the night
What world was he from
That made him so different from me?
Was he once a boy bathing in the sun?
Laughing and singing as all boys do.
Loving and hoping but mainly hurrying
Through the fields and the sunshine of his youth
I saw him a victim of an unchastened birth
Misled and misshapen by an individual world
Marking him from drudgery and wantonness
And an emptiness filled only by wine
Wine to smother the monster in the shadows
As he ran from hell into a lifeless limbo

Soon he became lost in the naked jungle of night
And I forgot him amid the gaiety and light

As 1957 rolled in, Dad's mother Lucile's star was burning brighter. She published I, Judy, the first of a series of teenage romance novels that would become quite popular. Her status as a renowned journalist and author was establishing her as a well-regarded member in Denver literary circles. Dad delighted in her success, but I also have to imagine, harbored a little jealousy.

That summer, Mom, Dad, Pete, and I went on a driving adventure to Disneyland in Los Angeles, which had opened just the year before. When we arrived, Pete started having trouble breathing, so Mom spent the day with him at the hotel while Dad took me to the theme park. The next day, we headed home as fast as possible, where Pete faced a battery of tests. Before the results came back, the doctor told my parents that their son had all the symptoms of cystic fibrosis. When the findings showed that Pete "only" had asthma, Dad was understandably relieved but wanted to "kill the bastard" who had unnecessarily alarmed them. Since I was also having trouble breathing through my nose, and was, in Dad's words, "apparently allergic to everything from chocolate to Thursday afternoons and especially small furry animals," he took my brother and me to see Dr. Tufts at National Jewish Hospital. According to Dad, he did more for the two of us in one week than others had done in months. Dr. Tufts was a specialist who had treated kids from all corners of the country, and one of his theories was that asthma was psychosomatic, as much psychological as physical. He told Mom and Dad not to overreact to Pete's wheezing, which proved extremely difficult during long nights where it sounded like each gasp would be his last. Thus began a very knotty component in Pete's relationship with our father. Thankfully, with medication Pete got better almost immediately, but Dad nonetheless concluded that most of his attacks were stress-related or attempts to get special attention. He came to cite as a clear example the distinct difference between our visits to Aunt Jeanne's and Grandma's houses. Both of them had dogs, but despite Jeanne's home being filled with cigarette smoke, Pete had fewer attacks and breathed easier. However, when he was at Grandma's, or even when she visited our house, he would start wheezing. In Dad's estimation, she became immediately concerned and fussed over Pete, despite Dad's protests.

"I hated the way dad treated me with my asthma. He would bully me as if I didn't want to work or something," Pete reported to me many years later. He felt that his active life really didn't begin until a neighbor gave him a whiff from a rescue inhaler. For the first time in his life, Pete said that he felt like running across the street. He recalled feeling as if that day might've been the first day in his life that his lungs were full of air. Dad would say that it was all in his mind, when what Pete really wanted to hear was, "I understand."

* * *

Pete's asthma certainly had many aggravating factors, but cigarette smoking could be considered a major suspect. It was endemic in the 50s and 60s—everyone smoked everywhere, in living rooms, their cars, doctors' offices, even on television. That I remember, Mom and Dad both smoked through my adolescent years. Perhaps the habit brought back memories of sitting in a café on the Left Bank in Paris, the elegant smoke of Gauloises swirling indolently into the air while discussing works of art in the Musée d'Orsay or latest production at

Cinéma du Panthéon. Mom never really quit, but it was almost like that was her only vice. She rarely actually bought a pack of cigarettes, but if someone offered her one, she'd gladly accept it.

Dad claimed he could quit anytime because he'd done it many times. Beginning with these journal entries from 1953, while living in Paris, he must have been seriously contemplating the consequences of his habit: "Stopped smoking this morning"; "Did not smoke cigarette all day"; and, "Smoked two cigarettes all day."

I came across this powerful admonition he wrote to himself. Although there are indications that it was written many years later, I'm sure he had been thinking these thoughts for a long time.

Notes to self:

Before You Light up that Cigarette

1. One will start it all over again.
2. I will just have to fight it again, and longer.
3. I will start coughing immediately, hacking, especially in morning.
4. I will get that soreness in throat, whatever it is, certainly isn't good.
5. Taste and poison in mouth, especially during night, when gag.
6. Stink up atmosphere, especially in close quarters, like Eve, Pete's and Dan's places.
7. Look and thoughts of Eve, Pete and Dan when I smoke.
8. If others don't smoke: Bill Bowser, Rick and others.

Reasons Why I'm Going to Stop Smoking for Permanent:

1. After huffing and puffing with a little exercise I remember how good my wind was when I had stopped smoking last summer.
2. The bad taste in my mouth all the time, the white coat on my tongue, and the brown on my teeth I didn't have when I stopped.
3. The cause of the sore throat and the spitting necessary, Sandy and nobody likes.
4. To end all the tension of whether I'm able to stop or not.
5. To show everybody what thinks I don't have the guts to stop, and to show them that I'm as good as they are.
6. To stop being a slave to all the ridiculous jingles and advertisements about smoking.
7. Even if there may not be a cause of cancer in smoking there is a chance of it which is reason enough to stop smoking.
8. To stop messing up the house, car and everything else with ashes and butts.
9. To save money, figure it will save up to $250 a year for me and as much for Sandy.
10. So I won't have to go out at all times of the day in all kinds of weather to buy cigarettes and feed my craze, and so I won't have to go out at halftime in sports events and sit in certain sections, etc.

There are more, but mainly to show people I have the guts.

Along with my parents' cigarette habit, I recall becoming aware of their indulgence with alcohol in the mid-fifties when I was six or seven years old. That vice as well was pervasive in those times; Steve Allen, one of the first talk show hosts on television, would have a cocktail sitting next to his cigarette smoldering in the ashtray on his desk. Advertisements for liquor and cigarettes were as prevalent as new car promotions on radio and TV. William Styron, in his memoir, <u>Darkness Visible: A Memoir of Madness</u>, claimed, "Cigarette smoking and alcohol consumption were de rigueur for the times." I remember neighborhood parties and other casual gatherings where beer, wine, and liquor of all kinds flowed like undammed rivers. There were times after raucous gatherings at Grandma's house or one of the other aunts' and uncles' places, when Dad and Mom would be so wasted that I to this day don't know how we ever made it back to our home. It was almost like DUIs (Driving Under the Influence) hadn't yet been invented because I never remember them being pulled over, at least when I was in the car.

As a young child, I could only peripherally conceive of my parents' cravings as serious problems. Mom, as I came to understand, was Dad's enabler and didn't seem to drink much, except when he wanted a partner in crime, so to speak. I would blunder through my teenage years thinking Dad was just getting smashed periodically, not unlike many of my friends' parents. Not until I had been a card-carrying adult many years later did I come to understand that he had a sickness, one that began to fester in those early years after he came home from the war and in those festive nights on the Left Bank and would eventually take over his life. The myriad details I uncovered squirreled away in notebooks, journals, and other writings that have become the foundation for this book provided me a better understanding as to why booze helped him medicate his troubles and memories, but also sadly made me realize that it had diminished the bond a son wants to have with his father.

* * *

In August of 1958, United Press International (UPI) bought INS. When the small Denver office was closed down, Dad still went into work on the last night so that they couldn't say he quit and take away his severance. He reported that sitting alone in that empty space, where all the teletype machines and furniture had been removed, was the longest night of his life.

It's not a big stretch to think that he could have written this poem with all that desolation surrounding him.

On Approaching the Age of Indifference

A revelation I wrought
From sudden thought
Is that my generation isn't lost, by damn –
I am.

I wander a wide circle amid wars and women and other
alliterated contemporaries,
But find them only temporaries.
I have fought, loved crudely, soused, thought deeply or
loosely in turn,
And still my heart would burn
To ride the steady rumble of an age,

To become absorbed in the rage
Of my generation
For which I felt a certain veneration.

I kept busy. My actions were not extraneous,
Still I felt more than a little miscellaneous.
I danced fleetingly with the future, lamented "les
neiges d'antan" *(the snows of yesteryear)* with the best
of them –
Always waiting for the rest of them.
I cursed my elders and flew with Sartre.
I haven't been a saint.
I wasn't a saint, but had the makings of a martyr.
I was pliable
And yearned to be reliable.

I felt like such an ass being "Zeitgeist" by myself.
In meeting my spokesmen, attempting to be persistent,
I did the talking — my spokesmen are not consistent.
This many-mindness I hate,
Although, I feel rather muddle-aged and as if I were
wasting my time of late.

---

* * *

Our family would be blessed on November 15, 1958 with the birth of my sister, Medley Ann. My folks followed through on their vow to name her after the cute little red-haired girl in Paris. I was thrilled to have a sister, but once again, the stature I'd maintained back then was diminished a bit further.

Consciously or not, my position in the family was subtly continuing to evolve from being the center of my parents' attention to the solemn role of protective, mentoring oldest sibling.

That next year, Dad began to think he should do something about his growing interest in Colorado history, particularly the gold rush and the ghost towns left behind. Deciding to explore these sites firsthand, he started planning trips around the state to places like Tungsten, Caribou, St Elmo, Romley, Hancock, and Cripple Creek. Brother Pete and I were beneficiaries of his impetus, as he would pack us into the family station wagon and head out to discover rustic locations, some easy to find and others more obscure. These were not highfalutin' camping trips, most of the time, we'd throw sleeping bags on the ground (no tent, mind you) or during inclement weather, wedge together on an air mattress in the back of the car. Dad would take our old green Mercury up dirt tracks and rocky roads into deep, piney woods or onto bald, wind-swept faces of high mountain peaks. I recall more than a few times people who had driven four-wheel drive Jeeps and Land Cruisers to what they might have thought was the outskirts of civilization gasping in disbelief and gesturing at our citified wheels. Dad loved chasing down librarians, old codgers, dilapidated wood structures, and ancient newspaper clippings that might divulge the secrets of towns or mines that once bustled with the excitement of gold and silver. Some of those places were barely evident on the landscape, a stone or two, maybe a pile of wood or a rotted foundation, but he'd find them. Dad used his journalistic chops to dig down, find the real stories, and retell them with reverence for their places in history.

CHAPTER 12

Before the UPI debacle, a coworker suggested to Dad that he put together a guidebook so others could find and appreciate all the historical and interesting landmarks he had discovered. Keen on the idea, Dad went to see Alan Swallow, who had been a cohort of his stepfather, Carl, during their rabble-rousing days. Alan hailed from Powell, Wyoming, and had spent time as a tour guide in Yellowstone National Park, where the spectacular environs engendered a love of poetry. He went on to receive masters and doctoral degrees in English and started to dabble in publishing as a way to offer his and others' works to the world. He called his fledgling effort the Alan Swallow Press. When he returned from service in World War II, Swallow began a new assistant professorship at the University of Denver and took the helm at the University of Denver Press. He purchased The Author & Journalist magazine. He continued publishing, changing the name of his business to Sage Books and expanding his catalog to include more Western writers. When Dad came along, Swallow was well situated in the genre and said he would check around to see if such a book was needed. Alan told Dad to put something together. "I did and he thought we ought to go ahead with it," Dad recalled.

* * *

With some sense of disappointment, I'm sure, Dad felt that the indignity of being jerked around by the news services as well as the mental and physical stresses were killing him. It was time for a change. He had been feeling that his knowledge and experience were worth sharing, and that teaching was a noble calling, so he decided to pursue a career in education. Needing a couple more credits to get a teaching certificate, he re-enrolled at the University of Colorado. At the same time, to bring in a few more bucks to the family bank account, he also got a job as night counselor at the Boys Reform school in Golden, an institution for convicted juvenile delinquents.

Right off the bat, Dad was advised that the only way to keep bad kids in line was by force, even brutal, because that was what they were used to and all they understood. Dad must've shuddered at that. One kid, Dad recalled, "to know him was to be disgusted by him." The worst part of the job was the last hour when he and the other counselors had to wake up the boys, march them over to the dining hall and make them behave during breakfast. The entire school population was in the cafeteria and the situation was ripe for altercations, as well as brutality from the guards. One of the few highlights for Dad was getting to know a doctoral student who was profiling young felons. He shared what he was learning with Dad about offenders' backgrounds: virtually all were from broken families, and most had single parents (mothers) and many other children in the household. The average IQ was about 75. He also noted that a disproportionate number of the kids were Catholics, which Dad concluded resulted "from large families with unwanted children." The only other upside to the job was that Dad had time to study in the wee hours of the mornings.

Dad clocked out of the reform school at 8:00 a.m., combed his hair, put on a tie, and drove across town for his student teaching stint at Golden High School. He taught in English, journalism, and speech classes. The latter was his favorite and the "mousey little first-year teacher" was more than willing to have Dad take over. On his first day, to calm the uproar he slapped a yardstick on the desk like a gunshot. When the pupils recovered from their shock and obediently stared at the big burly student teacher, Dad proceeded to tell the students that he was one of the worst speakers in the world, but that speech was one of most important courses he'd taken in his life. He added that their future success would well depend on how they presented themselves to others. I'm assuming with the mousey teacher's meek consent, Dad dispensed with "the book," and instead gave the students different topics on which to speak. Each of them would give a presentation on the topic, after which the rest of the class would critique their speech and make suggestions. Even the lazier kids, he recalled, participated at the risk of looking stupid in the eyes of their peers. One of the best students, Dad recalled, was a DJ at a local radio station. Another was a girl who was painfully shy; she mumbled a few words, turned beet red, and slunk back to her desk. Dad turned to the DJ and asked if he would laugh at her or do anything disruptive, to which he replied, "absolutely not." Dad made the girl get up and finish her speech, after which the rest of the class cheered her. He was very proud of how his system worked, and when he returned to visit the class after his student teaching assignment, the students gave him a standing ovation.

The Journalism teacher was "a fluttery middle-aged gal, heavily made up and spoke with society affectation," who Dad believed never got any closer to the subject than reading the daily newspaper. Again following his own instincts, he found success in letting the kids put together their own paper. The teacher embarrassed him in front of the other teachers in her fluttery way about innovations he was making, adding that, "Of course, he's had wide experience in that work, you know." Dad claimed that the English class was probably the best for him, and most difficult. The regular teacher was a longtime veteran with a wonderful personality who actually made the kids like English. Though feeling inadequate, when Dad took over the class, he taught them to write as they would speak; his newspaper experience did come in handy for that. The class was also taught Shakespeare. Dad admitted he was more scared than the students, but he made the teacher call on him to recite so he could confront his anxiety.

Back at the reformatory, Dad got fed up and decided to quit. When he gave the required two-week notice that he was leaving, the supervisor got mad and threatened that Dad wouldn't be able to get a job at any other institution in state, which Dad found amusing because he knew it was really hard to hire night counselors.

Soon after came the final exam for student teaching. Dad complained that it was probably the most "stupid and frustrating" part of the course. Instead of asking about the teaching experience and what he had learned, the test consisted of irrelevant and basic questions that were meaningless. The instructor gave him a C, but his mentoring teachers all gave him an A.

* * *

Dad landed a teaching job at Merritt Hutton Junior and Senior High School in Thornton, about 10 miles north of Denver, in September of 1959. The school's namesake was father to friend Tom Hutton. Mom and Dad sold the house on Syracuse Street and moved the family to a rental house not far from the school.

In October, Mom was expecting her fourth child any minute, but thought it okay for Dad to attend an faculty party. He waited for the call to come, but as the evening wore on and no call came, he decided he could drink more. Near midnight, Mom phoned to tell Dad that he'd better get home right away. There happened to be an autumn storm in progress, causing ice to build on the windshield and the roads. Dad made it home and even though Mom was in better shape than him, he said he would drive to St. Luke's in Denver because that was "[his] job." I was only nine years old at the time, and must have been asleep, because I don't remember that night, but now cannot fathom the implications of that situation. Mom must have been scared, perhaps angry, but in the midst of an onslaught of contractions too occupied for an argument. Judgement impaired, Dad took such incredible risks that, in retrospect, I wish I could have been there and aware enough to stop him. Whatever elements of fate there be, he was so fortunate that his nascent alcoholism didn't wreak unbelievable tragedy on our family that night.

Despite those inauspicious circumstances, Mom and Dad welcomed the second of their two daughters on October 17. They named her Eve Marie, honoring her maternal grandmother. Unfortunately for Eve, she was also given the nickname "Boo Boo," which we all used until she was old enough to defend herself. After she was born, Dad would claim that "Sandy found out where the leak was and closed it up so there would be no more boo-boos."

Once again, I took the further erosion of my share of parental attention in stride by setting the best example I could and gently shepherding my younger siblings through the vagaries of life. Dad provided me an early first lesson in that role when he explained to me, "Whatever you do to your little brother, I will do to you." The one time I violated that Golden Rule by lightly punching Pete in the back, Dad slugged me into tomorrow. I later found that I could lovingly admonish my little brother by lacing on the boxing gloves and pretending I was Floyd Patterson administering a little discipline to Archie Moore. There were also a few spankings administered to me and my siblings, but that was not uncommon for parents back then.

Despite not having had the role model of a solid father figure, Dad tried his best to provide structure, discipline and security to us kids. He enveloped us in his love of literature and music. We were scolded whenever we used the N-word, chastised when we used profanity in front of our mother and given curfews when we became teenagers. He instilled his love of sports in us, not only to accept the challenges of competition but to appreciate the mental and physical discipline it takes to succeed in athletics. Dad was not only our most loyal fan, but often the loudest one.

His heart and intentions were certainly in the right place when he wrote the following reflection. My heart hurts when I try and am not able remember him ever putting voice to its compassionate wisdom. In retrospect, I would've loved for him to throw his arm around my shoulder and share these sentiments with me when I had started my own family.

———◦—◦—⟨⊃●⊂⟩—◦—◦———

Musing 9

Man's 1st duty is toward his child, not in terms of financial security and material things but in cultivating his desire to develop his every capacity for good to the fullest. Give him love to develop his love and understanding, etc.
A human being is the most delicate and intricate mechanism there is, therefore his development is the most difficult.

———◦—◦—⟨⊃●⊂⟩—◦—◦———

Somehow, in addition to taking classes and working at the reformatory, Dad made time to write. After Dad received his teaching certificate in 1959, he submitted his manuscript to Alan Swallow. Guide to the Colorado Ghost Towns and Mining Camps would be published later that year and was the most popular book Sage had printed to date. When the book came out, Grandma gushed over it as expected, but his cantankerous mother-in-law had quite a different reaction. Dad recalled that, "She looked at it as if it were a dead rat, then said, 'When I think of all the time you spent writing this crap.' " However, the rest of the world loved it. At that time, there was basically one other comprehensive guidebook to Colorado history, <u>Stampede to Timberline</u> by Muriel Sibell Wolle, also copyrighted and published by Sage Books in 1949. Her book contained 198 illustrations, all exquisitely hand sketched by the author. Dad's book, on the other hand, contained photos he had taken and reprints of photographs from the myriad resources he'd uncovered. Additionally, making it a collaborative effort, he employed my mother and her artistic skills to draw the many maps that populated the book. Sales were so robust that Swallow remarked the whole edition might sell out in one year and they needed to start thinking about a second edition; there have been five printings since. For many years, it was the bible for the Jeep clubs in and out of Colorado. I've since run into people who were geologists, spelunkers, and plain old history buffs who've had Dad's book in their collections and swear to its excellence and usefulness. The <u>Guide</u>, as we all came to know it, has been sold worldwide and is still published as of the date of this writing, over 60 years later. Royalties from the book sales are disbursed among Dad's grandchildren.

I can just imagine my father having this esoteric discussion with the first jumble of ruins he found hidden deep in the hills.

Ask a Ghost Town

What do you ask a ghost town?
How have you been?
Did you have a nice visit?
Are you lonely?
Isn't it cold with those broken windows....

and the wind?
What do you ask a ghost town?
    Do old sounds disturb your sleep?
        What sounds do you recall?
        Which do you forget?
What do you ask a ghost town?
    Does rotting hurt?
    Does it make little sounds?
    ....about the smell of decaying?
What do you ask a ghost town?
    What happened to you?
    Where did the people go?
    What about their dreams?
What do you ask a ghost town?
    Any messages?
        Do you want us to remember?
    Do you want us to forget?
        And be alone again?

———◦∎◦———

While the <u>Guide</u> was taking off, Dad was teaching American and Colorado history to eighth graders and Journalism to high schoolers. He was apprehensive, as all new teachers are, but had high hopes of using his maverick instincts to, once again, connect with and inspire the students. In the history classes, he had the students undertake projects that covered various aspects of the country and state's evolutions. He and the kids found that many of the projects involved period dress, so the class decided to put on a fashion show. A "so-so" student was assigned to manage and coordinate the activities and flourished. The show was a big success, garnering accolades for Dad, the head of the History Department praising him for having gotten more out of his kids than about anyone he'd ever worked with.

The school had no good books on journalism, so once again, Dad improvised. He started by informing his students that journalism was one of the most important classes because a well-run democracy was based upon a well-informed electorate. That truth offended some of the kids. One "pretty school leader" got up and haughtily proclaimed, "My daddy is a good citizen, but he doesn't have time to read newspapers."

Despite that dubious admonition, Dad instigated the class to learn by doing as he had during his student teaching stint, resulting in a newspaper for the school, which they titled Thunderword. Potentially turbulent waters rippled almost immediately when the father of an aristocratic family who was on the school board wanted his daughter, who didn't even take Journalism, to be editor. Principle Tarver, "who knew which side his bread was buttered on," pressured Dad, who conceded to make her associate editor. The class also was populated by, as he called them, the usual oafs who figured Journalism was easier than English. One of them was Ronnie Palucchi, who was a champion wrestler. Other teachers called him "The Punk." When Dad made Ronnie a sportswriter, he caught the bug, went on to sell advertising, and become co-editor, then student supervisor. Dad lamented that it was too bad that Ronnie's abilities and talents weren't discovered earlier. I think he might have been thinking of Palucchi when he penned this reflection (I didn't discover who or what --- was).

Uncluttering 4

— had won his vengeance
He kicked a red, red rose

With the promise of a good job and royalties from the Guide, Mom and Dad bought a beautifully renovated custom home in April of 1960. It sat on three-quarters of an acre with an expansive view of the Rocky Mountains, the Denver skyline and high plains that stretched to the eastern horizon. The house was on Niver Avenue across the Valley Highway from Merritt Hutton High School in an unincorporated area that would become part of the city of Northglenn. It was surrounded by fields where we shot rabbits with BB guns and 22 rifles. In the winter, we sledded down long snow-covered hills and when the weather warmed, rode our bicycles on neighborhood streets and the sidewalks of yet-to-be-constructed housing developments. Ever the dreamer and innovator, Pete built a miniature golf course on the lower half of the backyard. We got paid a nickel for every dandelion we dug up in the massive lawn. A trampoline, aka The Tramp, became a fixture in the backyard and magnet to kids from all over Northglenn. Each of us kids acquired troupes of friends, most of whom enthralled Dad, most of the time. Mom now had a longer commute to Stapleton Airport, but she kept her job so she could keep us flying; we could actually see the airport from our house on the hill.

The best-kept secret at Merritt Hutton was the April Fool's edition of the Thunderword; Dad was amazed that the students could be so eager and excited, yet not spill the beans. The banner of the special newspaper was the Thornton Blunderwoid. Every story was a parody of something near and dear to the school system; the front page featured a large photo of a line of ballet dancers with faces of humorless teachers pasted on. Within minutes of the paper hitting the classroom, Counselor Jay Cayton and other administrators collected all copies in sight. The kids, expecting that would happen, squandered a few and sold them for up to $2 when they were usually 10 cents. The next day, Dad was called in to Superintendent Stukey's office. After listing good things he had done like working wonders with Ronnie Palucchi and the eighth grade fashion show, Stukey told Dad that he wasn't cut out to be a teacher and unceremoniously fired him. Despite being scorned by Principal Tarver, who had been head of military school and virtually had students marching down the halls, Dad was very popular with them and many of the "oddball, rebellious" teachers. The headline in the Thornton Sentinel, the local newspaper, read, 'School Paper Censored, Teach Fired,' with accompanying stories that even appeared in the Denver Post. A couple eighth graders, one the son of the acting head of the state Education Department and the other a smart kid who was one of the only black kids in the school, started petitions to have Dad reinstated. Counselor Cayton also collected all of those and ripped them up.

This is one of the few journal entries that is dated, and apparently was somehow attached to Dad's Advanced Comp class in college. The piece was dated, "Jan 13, 1949." As I was re-reading it for the umpteenth time, I was struck by the fact that he wrote it exactly 50 years before he died. What relevance that has, I'm not sure, but I've included the entry because there's an optimism and burgeoning sense of idealism born out of rejection. Dad carried that promise into the high school classroom and into his public activities in later years.

Revolution

I thought it. I blossomed as the sun blossomed, but no mortal
    breeze turned a leaf to nod in answer.

I said it. The leaves fluttered as my words drifted by to
    die beneath the minute ripple on the sea of life.

I wrote it. The words turned yellow and slowly turned to
    dust in a dark corner far from sight.

I did it. I smiled as the sun exploded, darkened, and reappeared
    warmly at midnight. I became immortal.

I lived it. And the leaves turned green, the corner brightened,
    As the world basked in the new sun I had created.

CHAPTER 13

Once again, my father was back on the job hunt. He was offered a position with the Littleton school district, a suburb south of Denver, with the caveat that, "We have a sense of humor here." I'm not sure what happened with that enticement other than he did not accept it. With a nascent desire to live on the West Coast, he and Mom drove to California looking for a teaching position, but it seemed that everybody wanted to teach there. He did find one job in the desert, which didn't appeal to either of them. Frustrated and disillusioned, Dad anguished over his situation, proclaiming that, "Teaching is the most satisfying thing I have done and the most work." He felt that teachers, despite being among the most important persons in our society and to the future, were the lowest paid of almost everyone else and got little respect. As well, much of a teacher's work, he bemoaned, is routine and bureaucracy that has little to do with the actual aim of educating young minds.

That mentality flowed to his next generations. I graduated college with a Bachelor of Science in Elementary Education. Feeling that the earlier you instill the love of learning in children, the more inspired they'll be as they grow, so I marched nobly into a first-grade classroom and thereafter, in the course of four years, also taught third, fourth and fifth grades. My brain and motivation were fueled with innovative ideas, but I quickly learned that good teachers are disciplined and organized, not two of my strongest suits. As Dad lamented, I also found that the drudgery of never-ending paperwork and following arcane doctrines took the shine off lofty aspirations. I had my successes but seemingly many more failures, and regretfully surrendered. My daughter, Mariah, has followed in our footsteps. She too graduated with a degree in education and a head full of great ideas. The ride has been bumpy for her as well, but she is sticking to her goal of helping children learn. I am supremely proud of the relationships she establishes with her students and the innovative ways she seeks to make learning fun for them. Alas, like her grandfather and father before her, she laments the stressful burdens of red tape, arcane rules and regulations. Despite the frustrations and impediments, Dad, Mariah and me herald the talents of a good teacher and bemoan society's lack of respect for them.

While my father was floundering in a whirlpool of professional enigma, George Bailey, a teacher friend from Merritt Hutton, called to say he had a contact Dad should call at National Farmers Union, where he'd worked before. He did and was offered a job back in the communications department. It was a good move for a couple years, during which time he became good friends with men whose names would become well known around our house: Wes McCune, the new PR Director; Stan Weston, a future VP; and CEO Fred Simonton, who Dad met at the national convention where President Lyndon Johnson was the guest speaker.

There was a very telling entry in Dad's journal from that time. At another later convention, Dad took Fred aside and asked, "What are we going to do about Stan? We've got a problem there." Apparently, Stan had confided to Dad that his doctor said he wasn't supposed to smoke and drink, but he didn't stop. Fred's retort was along the lines of, "the pot calling the skillet black." Stan died a short time later. Dad didn't follow up his journal entry with any indication that he had taken Fred's words to heart.

One of my father's big projects at Farmers Union was a collaboration with C. E. Huff, one of the original members and past president; they produced a book called, <u>The Friend of the Family Farmer</u>, a history of the organization. Despite that feather in his cap, Dad was once more the victim of misfortune as NFU experienced serious financial difficulties and had to shut down the PR office in Denver. He was out of another job.

Dad wrote this poem about the fate of boom towns, but in a way, I felt that he was also describing the houses of sticks he found in his own life. Hopes and dreams that were trammeled by the vagaries of whim and forces beyond his control.

The Old Town

Wasn't haphazard
There was reason there
There was life and hope
They planned each move with care
Lived from day to day
When there were people there
Valley resounded with living

Lost its promise with
    Cursing and a prayer
Walls of old cabin weary
For carrying load of years
Weeds over path
Dark mast of time
And in a hush left hope there
Gone but not forgotten
They left some of them behind
And took some of the old town
    With them

The Guide to Colorado Ghost Towns and Mining Camps was never meant to be a one-and-done effort. Dad had accumulated such an extensive cache of notes, clippings, and photos that it became his mission to continue writing about the state he loved. There was always more research to be done and legends to chase down. Not only did Pete and I accompany him on several more excursions, but abandoned boom towns and skeletal remains of old ore digging operations became destinations for family vacations and day trips. He and Mom would hop in the station wagon for a weekend jaunt, while later, my sisters took mine and Pete's places on many adventures. Much of the new was merged with old material and updated maps by Mom, into Dad's second book, Treasure Tales of the Rockies, which was published by Sage Books in 1961. It was on the local bestseller list for a while and to this day, is a favorite with many readers. It extolls stories, legends, and gossip about extravagant characters, folks who hit it rich and disappeared, as well as ghosts still rumored to be skulking over their old claims. Its fifth edition, <u>Treasure Tales</u>, is also still printed and new copies are available today.

I know my father was very proud of his second book. It allowed him more license to spin yarns in addition to providing statistics and driving directions. I'd like to think he dusted off some of those creative yearnings he uncovered in Paris. The book also burnished his stature as a writer and elevated his small measure of celebrity. The door opened slightly wider for invitations to speak to book clubs, recreational organizations, and even as a guest lecturer at local schools.

After <u>Treasure Tales</u>, Dad considered writing a book about the ghost towns of Montana but discovered that another highly regarded author was about to publish something along those lines. He then shifted his focus to the south and began researching the history of New Mexico. Pete and I were again the beneficiaries as we joined him on excursions all over the Land of Enchantment. Unfortunately, that book was added to the list of his unfinished projects.

There was an interesting, if somewhat harrowing sidelight to those research excursions. When we moved to the big house in Northglenn, Dad covered the hill on one side of our backyard with what became not only a hobby but a labor of love, a large rock garden with varieties of flowers, flagstone walkways, a small stream, and, of course, rocks. On our adventures around the state, he'd find and collect specimens of all colors, gem quality (or not) and sizes, some of them quite heavy for young boys to haul back from a hillside, creek bank or steep valley to the car. By the end of our journey, Dad could hardly see over the hood because the back end was so weighed down. I also remember a precarious and potentially tragic rock gathering event. After an excursion to the boomtown of Central City, the family picnicked on the way down Clear Creek Canyon. Under a cloudless Colorado sky, US 6 wove its way between the burbling creek on one side and a steep hillside on the other. We found a wide spot next to the river to set up provisions. Dad, after many beers and now rather overweight, huffed about twenty feet up the hill on the other side of the roadway, sat and started dislodging stones, rolling them down the slope for Pete and I to retrieve. Did I mention that the hill down which rocks were rolling butted up against the roadway, on which pretty thick weekend traffic was passing? Miraculously, none of the stones hit a passing car, while my brother and I managed to dodge our way across the road to the station wagon. I clearly recall Dad's inebriation and disregard for safety, though was still young enough to consider the incident just another stupid parent action rather that the red flag it was.

* * *

Meanwhile, the family was quickly settling into life at the big house on Niver Avenue. The newest member, Eve, didn't take long to establish her role in the family. Dad reported that she was growing up to be the "biggest devil of the bunch." Mom claimed that Evie was the happiest baby and would certainly be the "boss of this roost." Apparently, taking after her namesake, she talked and talked and talked, soon accruing some very quotable quotes.

Little sister chasing a crying big sister:
Medley: "Evie pulled my hair!"
Evie: "Here, take it back!"

After being put to bed and told to stay there until happy, Evie shook her finger at Mom and said,

"Don't you ever do that to me again—I'm happy now!"
And: "If I don't go potty, it comes out by itself."

Pete was the imaginative, go-getter child, or as my mother would say, "a number one nudnick!" He started taking piano lessons at an early age, embedding a fondness that he pursues to this day. Mom and Dad had somewhere procured an old, garish yellow upright piano and set it in the back of the living room. There came a point when Dad casually, but with aplomb I'm sure, remarked that Pete's banging on the ivories became rather oppressive, especially while the rest of us were watching TV. One day not long after, the rest of the family, upon returning to the house, noticed a big void in the living room where the piano had been. Pete had taken it apart, piece by piece and reconstructed it in the basement playroom, where it sounded as good as ever. Another time, Mom and Dad took the clan skiing at Loveland Basin, our favorite area. Mom observed Pete "maneuvering about on one ski." When asked if he had lost other one, he replied, "No, I'm just teaching one leg at a time."

Dad may have had my little brother in mind when he penned this line.

Musing 16

The sky is as wide as the top your mind

The Niver house was a rambling ranch-style dwelling with a full basement that Dad mostly single-handedly finished, complete with a full bar and rec room big enough for pool and ping pong tables. Mom did her part; not liking plain white anything, she painted colorful, stylish murals on the long hallway walls and down the stairway. As mentioned earlier, the view from the back porch was expansive and spectacular. We could watch Denver expand from the mountains to the plains. The house's flat roof proved to be boon for watching Fourth of July celebrations. It became an annual tradition for relatives and neighbors to set up lawn chairs on the roof to watch firework displays across the wide cityscape.

Perhaps, because the house was new and distinctive, the smell and stale air due to Mom and Dad's dirty smoking habit became a bone of contention with us kids. We regularly tried to get them to give up the filthy obsession, with little more than conciliatory efforts on their parts. Medley became the vigilante of vices and would regularly chastise our parents for their disgusting habits. In particular, she began harping on Dad for his drinking as well as his smoking. He feigned redemption, which only made her more vociferous but alas, unsuccessful. Interestingly enough, none of us offspring took up smoking other than a few odd encounters. I remember clearly being about 12 years old when some friends and I got ahold of some cigarettes and a cigar or two and headed to the fields to smoke them. Later that day, I was so sick I felt green on the inside and have never touched a cigarette since. As a result, I came to think that one day, when I had my own kids, a good tactic to keep them from smoking would be to have them smoke a whole pack all at once. Unfortunately, I didn't catch my older daughter, Mariah or her brother, Travis in time. I'm happy to report that she kicked the habit on her 40th birthday, and well, he's working on it. Pete smoked for a while in college, which was confounding due to the severity of his asthma.

* * *

Dad's reputation as a state historian and journalist started coalescing in the early 60s after publication of <u>Treasure Tales</u>. Through his widespread research, growing public persona and even his journalistic activities, he was developing a strong and lengthy list of contacts. When the local Farmers Union office closed in late 1962, he was put in touch with a fellow at the Regional Soil Conservation Services bureau (SCS) where he was hired immediately and put to work churning out press releases and pamphlets that had to be adapted for each of the ten states in the region. Interestingly at his six-month review, his supervisor told him that he was still acting like a newspaper man on deadline, reinforcing Dad's sardonic opinion that the aim of government work was not efficiency.

In the summer of 1963, Dad was sent to an SCS conference in Washington D.C. He used the opportunity to load Mom and us kids up in our new black and white Chevrolet station wagon for a memorable, cross-country driving vacation. We were all excited when Dad put a water-cooled air conditioner in the car. We reveled in the chill, until we hit eastern Kansas and the humidity that accompanied us all the way to the Atlantic coast. You see, water coolers aren't very effective when there's already a lot of water in the air. Our spirits weren't dampened for long, though. In Springfield, Missouri, we stopped for the night at a Holiday Inn, a first for us. The best part was the swimming pool, in which we all splashed until the manager probably had to come out and send us to our room. We stayed with Mom's college friend from Duke, Joyce, and her family in Bethesda, Maryland. While Dad spent his days at the conference in D.C., we made excursions into the nation's capital to see all the sights. The Capitol building, Washington Monument, Smithsonian and all the others were fascinating, but the highlight for us kids was the water park in Silver Springs.

Back in Denver, Dad was impressive enough in his duties that he was given more responsibility at the Rocky Mountain regional office. The position provided him many opportunities to meet influential people, as well as journey around Colorado and neighboring states. This allowed him to expand his vast trove of historical facts. In early 1965, the position with the Conservation Bureau became the next on the lengthening list of jobs taken out from under him. Budget cutting determined that SCS would have to cut one of the five regional offices, and much to Dad's amazement, Colorado was the one axed. He was offered placement at the national office in D.C., but not wanting to leave the West, he used mine and Pete's asthma as a hardship justification for turning down the promotion.

Dad's occupational cynicism continued to deepen as jobs came and went, leaving him high and dry. He wanted to support his family, beholden to high ideals of how people should be treated but at this point, the reality of "doing business" kept knocking the pegs out from under him. This satirical piece clearly underlies the disappointments and professional injustices he must have felt.

Business, My Boy

I'm glad, my boy, you came to me;
I've been in business since '23,
So I'm the man that you should see
About business, my boy,
About business.

It may be fine to have been a scholar,
But a ready smile and old wax collar
Is the way to trap that dancing dollar
In business my boy,
In business.

The big thing they don't teach in schools,
Is the money's there being spent by fools,
And needing a man with proper tools;
In business my boy,
In business.

So forget your lessons, forget your facts,
But keep a list of your best contacts –
It's easier climbing on others backs
In business my boy,
In business.

A 'frat' was good, you can sell your brothers,
And then go out and sell their mothers,
But get there first before the others –
That's business my boy,
That's business.

All friends are good, they all might sell,
And the 'glad-hand' is always sure to tell,
But many a 'softie' is poor as hell
In business my boy,
In business

Pick them up and give them a ride –
God and government are on your side –
And it takes persistence to turn the tide
In business my boy,
In business.

A family is needed for your show,
But love and nonsense have got to go –
There's only one thing you must know –
It's business my boy,
It's business.

Give to charity, but give 'out loud;'
Join clubs and churches — be in the crowd,
And it's 'easier pickens' on a cloud –
That's business my boy,
That's business.

And if ever you feel you've had your fill,
Don't despair, you'll get there still –
Just finger once a dollar bill
That's business, my boy,
That's business.

Never stop or set a goal –
If nothing else, sell your soul –
Money will easily fill the hole –
And business, my boy,
And business.

And when you gradually get your gold,
Befriend it well, but keep a hold –
You'll be pals when you both grow old
In business my boy,
In business.

In time, my boy, you may be as rich as I,
And there's not a thing that money won't buy;
But then, of course, when you die, you die,
But that's business, my boy,
That's business.

O, just one more thing before you go –
I always enjoy being a 'helpful Joe,'
But if you need my item, let me know –
It's good business, my boy,
Good business.

CHAPTER 14

Iwas in high school, probably 15 or 16, sitting on my bed and Dad in a chair facing me. He looked pretty nervous. Shadows seeped through the window of my basement bedroom and the concrete walls chilled the air.

Somewhat assuredly, he explained, "Now, you know birds and bees work together to pollinate flowers."

"Yeah Dad, I know, we read about it in Biology class," I responded, rather haughtily but eagerly because I was pretty sure of what was coming next.

"Well, humans sort of do it like that."

"Like what, Dad?

"Well, you know, the man pollinates the woman."

"Yeah, like how?"

With a bit of sputtering and looking out the window, he started slowly, "Well, the important thing is that women are beautiful creatures, and we must treat them with respect."

We both looked around the room, anywhere but at each other. While Dad never supplied the technical aspects, what sticks with me was his strong deference for women as complex, worthy human beings and not just tarts to be captured in centerfolds and exploited. I guess he knew by then that I had found some of his hidden Playboy magazines. The reverential spirit of his aborted birds-and-bees talk I took to heart and even expounded upon as I got involved a few years later in the nascent Feminist movement. Alas, his noble testimonial, when faced with the rigors of real life, untethered emotions and the free market doesn't always persevere. The intentions of us men often struggle between the zenith of respect and the degradations of misogyny. Dad revered women but particularly later in life succumbed to the vagaries of disrespect, especially with regard to my mother. Many tortured men, in their need to preserve some sense of authority and respect, venerate women only to belittle them when their own self-esteem is threatened.

Dad was a stud in high school and the Navy. He was intelligent, tall, and slender with dashing dark hair and piercing eyes. One could presume that his popularity with the opposite sex would have been validated, and perhaps admired. The voluminous letters he received intimated attraction and adoration. Yet, even in the earliest missives there are hints that he wasn't adept at reciprocating sentiment or that he suffered from the age-old complaint lodged against us males, the inability to commit. He didn't exactly string along his "darlings," yet neither did he securely wrap them in the comfort of his affection. Even when he met and courted the young, attractive woman from Brooklyn, he didn't seem exactly to shower her with effusive love; I'm sure sparks flew in the beginning and he admired Mom's pluck, but there seemed to be a fragility in his devotion. Mom was vulnerable in a strong, independent woman sort of way. She was the single product of the union between a smart, successful father and a domineering shrew of a mother. As a result, she adored her father yet had to confront his seemingly loveless and combative relationship with her mother. My father had many of the same qualities as my maternal grandfather, and not wanting to be like her mother, my mother made sure to honor him, for better and for worse.

As Dad had waxed eloquent about women being beautiful creatures to be cherished, an inconsequential incident during my senior year in high school conflated his reverence with real-world happenstance. At the time, my curfew was 1:00 a.m. and I was expected to come to his and Mom's bedroom to announce that I was in. One Saturday night, I walked down the long hall with lingering thoughts about a disagreement I'd had with my girlfriend, Micki.

Dad, sensing my agitation, asked, "What's troubling you, son?"

"Aah, nothing. Micki and I just had a bummer of an evening."

He sat up in bed, his eyes widened. He inquired pointedly, "She didn't let you get her pregnant, did she?"

After assuring him and Mom that they weren't going to be grandparents, I walked back down the hall, chuckling forlornly to myself. Micki and I had hardly began "petting!" Though she got along well enough with my parents, in retrospect, Dad's suspicion told me more about his conjecture about my sex life, and wariness about my girlfriend's motivations.

In his rough draft memoir of his early years, Dad wrote that his first love, Barbara Erton, stonewalled him in first grade because he didn't roller skate to her house that summer. That rocky start may have hit deeper and remained more entrenched, though he was only six years old. Did it underlie the conflicting feelings into which he would grow as an adult? His reverence for women was admirable, but there seemed a chasm between his virtue and his ability to demonstrate it. There were considerable overlaps in dates of letters exchanged with various women, leaving me to only speculate as to his fidelities. Later in life, the consummate pain of that failing was exacted on my mother, especially when he was in the throes of alcohol-fueled irrationality. What created such discordance in Dad that allowed him to put women on a pedestal, then treat them with such disrespect? The one woman that he truly elevated to a lofty altar of devotion was his mother, and that may have prevented any other woman from owning his heart or attaining such eminence. Booze most likely exacerbated and, for a while, protected his limitations but what underlying ailment of the heart was he trying to medicate that robbed him of knowing or accepting unconditional love? I think this poem expresses all those internal conflicts, the ones he never vocalized.

Unnamed 4

Our love it seemed was perfect
I loved her completely and unselfishly,
And I felt that she loved me the same
Each blissful moment together
Blinded me to all the world
Apart from her I felt like half a man
And thirsted for the moment, so far away
That we would be one world together again
More than all the gold in the world
I wanted her to be happy.
I lived for her smile and her laugh

I would mortgage all my vain pride
And petty ambition to establish this aim
I wanted her to forget all the ugly things
And to see only the beauty of love
To find her strength in me
I struggled to be perfect in her eyes
Not by my wanderlust (*or*) by my deeds
I was happy in my love and strength
I felt her happiness the same
    Then one day an unknown mood
Caught a foolish word from another world
A mood is feeling sorry for oneself

{see the entire poem in Addendum 4}

———⸺●⸺———

While Dad and I were working our way through the battle of the sexes, my siblings were continuing to compete for attention. My brother's asthma continued to confound our father, but as Pete managed to keep his ailment under control, in almost the same innovative ways he found to build and create stuff, he amazed Dad and the rest of us with the eclectic ways he found to injure himself. There was the time a metal clip inexplicably snagged his hand while on Uncle George's boat. With his life vest still on, we took him to the doctor for several stitches. Pete was also the entrepreneur in the clan. At age 14, he started delivering the Rocky Mountain News on an old Vespa motor scooter before the sun rose.

Medley also found eclectic ways to capture attention. There was the time when her long strawberry blonde hair got tangled in the electric mixer while mashing potatoes. Amidst her screams and flying spuds, her quick-thinking oldest brother thought to turn off the mixer. Though Med was the child who seemed to have the most ailments and disappointments, she had the biggest spirit and will to confront her challenges. A first major infirmity came about when her first-grade teacher noticed her sitting in the back of room and moved her forward. She did better but one of her eyes seemed slow to adjust. An ophthalmologist determined that she had intermittent exo-tropia, which we lay folk call "wandering eye." Med had an operation to tighten the eye muscle, which back then meant a couple days' stay in the hospital. The night after the surgery, with both eyes padded, six-year-old Medley talked her parents into going home, and that she would be just fine. For the next several months, she had to wear a patch over her good eye and do exercises to strengthen the wandering eye until she recovered normal vision. Medley being Medley, she wore the patch as a badge of honor.

A few years later, as she was maturing into an active young woman, Medley began to suffer serious nosebleeds and, more troubling, "attacks" as Dad would call them, which became seizures. Doctors were not able to diagnose a cause for them, but that, too, never seemed to stop her from doing what she had to do.

Eve, Medley, Pete and me circa 1966

* * *

Dad was doing some freelance writing but job prospects were again looking dim. Then Mother Nature stepped in. On June 16, 1965, the skies opened and inundated the South Platte River. The resulting deluge ripped through the heart of the city, resulting in the worst flood in Denver history.

Mayor Tom Currigan and the Denver City Council put together a small group, the Platte River Study Commission, to analyze the devastation and recommend redevelopment strategies. Dad was hired as the committee's publicist for $1,000/month, which was his best paying job to date. In 1967, the study group, renamed the South Platte Area Redevelopment Commission (SPARC) was expanded to implement strategies and coordinate with the state. Dad was named its Executive Director.

Among his many tasks were bringing in experts and speakers, writing a monthly newsletter for the Chamber of Commerce, and writing press releases to get coverage of SPARC's activities in the newspapers. He organized many PR events to highlight the river's importance to the city. One of his first activities was a hike along the river from downtown through railroad yards to the northern city limits; my brother Pete joined him as he pointed out all the issues and potential for the floodplain. Dad organized clean-up activities, tree plantings, and the introduction of fish into waters that had once been terribly polluted by industrial waste. To show how the water quality had improved, Dad organized a Boat-In where city elites and office holders would canoe a stretch of the Platte through downtown. The event had been planned to take place after the spring runoff but several days of rain turned placid waters high and fast, challenging the amateur canoeists who happened to include my young sisters. The boat in which they and a Denver Post photographer were paddling flipped, spilling them into the river. Dad, not being a great swimmer and loaded down with cameras, jumped into save them; good thing the water was only hip deep. Another admirable endeavor was Project Concern, where local companies were enlisted to pay half the wages for inner city kids to work along river; Dad deemed that a "great success."

SPARC became an ally in the construction of Chatfield Dam south of the city, which would be used to modulate the flow of the South Platte through the metropolitan area. When a large celebration was held to commemorate the closing of the dam's huge gates, Dad sat in the VIP seats and listened to then U.S. Vice President Spiro Agnew. Dad reported that he got a short Thank You" letter from Agnew, "probably one of his last written before he resigned in disgrace." For another notable project, SPARC partnered with the city and various business interests to create the Auraria campus which was anchored by the old Tivoli Brewing building across the South Platte from downtown. Auraria became home to three colleges that served commuter students.

My father's elevated profile at SPARC produced several other opportunities for him. In 1966, Roy Romer, who had served in the Colorado House of Representatives and the state senate, was nominated as the Democratic candidate to challenge incumbent U.S. Senator Gordon Allott for governor. One of Dad's old INS cronies highly recommended him to be press manager for Romer's campaign. The experience proved to be interesting if a bit bizarre. He met a host of fascinating people, worked many hours and traveled the state at the candidate's side. Unfortunately, Romer lost to Allard though he would go on to become Colorado governor a few years later. At the election watch party, Dad overheard someone state an axiom that stuck with him: "Democracy was too good and delicate an instrument to be left in the hands of the voters." On Romer's formal thank-you letter to staff, he handwrote to my father, "Especially you Perry, I am disappointed that I won't be taking you to Washington with me."

Fortunately, Dad had the sagacity to not send this whimsical flyer out to the public:

Romer's Groups

There is a group for you; please join — before it is too late
Join up and help pass out literature

Unemployed poets for Romer
Lefthanded catchers for Romer
Likeable umpires for Romer
Benchwarmers for Romer
Ineligibles for Romer
Dropouts for Romer
Non dropouts for Romer
Lint pickers for Romer
Sky writers for Romer
Rover boys for Romer
Romer boys for Romer
GS 7s for Romer
Lushwells for Romer
Ex-BMOCs for Romer
Tablehoppers for Romer
Aspiring socialites for Romer
Old-fashioned girls for Romer
V-5 cadets for Romer
Pool hall hustlers for Romer
Skid row rejects for Romer
Former bull fighters for Romer
Edsel salesmen for Romer
People over 90 for Romer
People under Five for Romer
People "in between" for Romer
Hula hoopers for Romer
Consistent losers for Romer
Unmarried teenagers for Romer

Misfits for Romer
Happy old maids for Romer
Unhappy old maids for Romer
Hermit couples for Romer
Adult fans of the Beatles for Romer
Teenage fans of Beethoven for Romer
Four Fs for Romer
Longhairs for Romer
Old-fashioned crew cuts for Romer
Baldies for Romer
Sonny Liston lovers for Romer
Wishy-washy car washers for Romer
Metrocal for lunch bunch for Romer
Snit-gnitz and Romerritz for Romer
Displace(d) Dodger fans for Romer

Roy Romer believes <u>all</u> the people of Colorado should be represented in the U.S. Senate

* * *

In addition to his community activities, Dad's reputation grew as an authority on all things historical around the Rocky Mountain state. Noted historian, professor, and author Tom Noel (aka, Doctor Colorado) told me that for many years my father was the "go-to guy" for questions about the state's history. Dad was in demand as a presenter and lecturer at schools, libraries, and community organizations such as the State Historical Society and Colorado Ghost Town Club. All of which fed his love of giving slideshows, the old-fashioned kind where you fed little squares into a projector and splashed them up on a screen. After his death, I pulled together eight huge boxes of his slides and have hauled them around the country, even through all my lifestyle changes. My goal is one of these days to go through them, weed out the family shots and, hopefully donate the rest. My Uncle Bill regularly remarked upon Dad's penchant for boring friends and family with his slideshows, but much of the rest of the world that was fascinated by Colorado and the West loved them.

'A Handful' *of Dust*, serves as an introduction to the <u>Guide to Colorado Ghost Towns and Mining Camps</u> and beautifully portrays Dad's love of the land.

⬤

A Handful of Dust

The mountains were there when man came west.
Shoulder to shoulder, they marched tall out of
the plains,
Their silent profile born of unheard fury and sound,
Their wrinkled brow washed by the snow of ages,
And whipped by the unheard winds of the millenniums.
Here volcanoes roared,
Storms were born,
First life crawled onto shore,
Mighty beasts lumbered over the land,
First man felt the sun's warmth briefly, and died.
Here in the mountains
All things lived and died.
The mountains were still,
The trees were green and full,
There was the same blue sky
When the red men came.
Their bronzed bodies walked through the centuries

And through the trees.
Here was their happy hunting ground,

{read the entire poem in Addendum 5}

———————⟨◦⟩●⟨◦⟩———————

CHAPTER 15

My grandmother Lucile was diagnosed with Parkinson's disease and later dementia which confined her to a nursing home in her later years. My cousins and I remember visiting Grandma in the big, drab, creepy house on Gaylord Street near City Park. Her sister, Aunt Jean, had also lived out her years there, afflicted with Multiple Sclerosis. My beloved grandmother died in September of 1968. Just before her passing, Dad carried her in his arms out of that old nursing home to the car and drove her home to die. A memorial service was hastily put together by the Denver Women's Press Club (DWPC) to recognize her journalistic work and publication of five teenage romance novels. Dad lamented that it was not a sincere tribute but Lucile who was not a joiner, treasured her membership in DWPC and Colorado Author's League. It was there she found the recognition and reputation she so richly deserved. I'm sure whatever the sincerity of the service, Grandma would have appreciated the homage.

Grandma at work

"Once I had fixed everything that was wrong in my world, it would be a simple matter to maintain it and keep it perfect.

And mother's life would be brighter from now on.

And she would truly know that I loved her."

Dad wrote about this vision he had as a small boy. He would lay "abed" in the early morning, planning out his day's activities, what to fix, what to clean, all with the aspiration of making the old house where they lived as good as it could be and fit for his mother to live in. In his eyes, she was hard-working, lonely and unhappy. With some sheepish frustration, he admitted that he wasn't much able to accomplish all he wanted to. Still and all, much of his life was spent striving to make her proud of him.

> "Maybe, all my plans, even in later life, after she had died, were for her to make her happy wherever she was, and to make her life more worthwhile."

Lucile rose from the ashes of a ruined marriage and single motherhood with grit and purpose that earned her third son's undying devotion. Dad's poetic epistle to his mother clearly exemplifies the love he had for her and fervent wish to gain her eternal approval; I don't know that she ever saw the letter.

To You Mother

Out of the torment before my eyes,
    In leadership so sublime,
Looms the figure I idolize
    That wonderful mother of mine.

Between me and bitterness
    Between success and despair
Is her model of righteousness
    Pointers in life's thoroughfare.

Oh! Lord, let me wander down the lane
    Through Heaven and through Hell
To the land of happiness and fame,
    To the land where great men dwell.

Send me deep into the pits of temptation.
    Emerge me proud and pure,

Strengthen my love for life and creation
    God, make me more like her.

Don't let me forget in each moulding place
    Where boundless faith melts into fear
The warmth that adorns her smiling face
    And the love that made her tear

And when decision leans its hated grace,
    Let me not falter before my goal
For her love and hope follows anyplace.
    A helping hand to a needing soul
So in the end when my pages are clean,
    From the skies in echoes loud,
She'll sing for all the world to hear,
    "My boy's done well, and I'm proud."

Love,

Perry

My sad presumption is that Dad felt he never measured up to her lofty exemplar, that perhaps he'd fallen well short of the mark. From early on, he strived to live up to her pet name of, "my little man." In the midst of the family's poverty and at an early age, Dad was the child who went out to find odd jobs to buy a few extra groceries or pay a bill. I can easily imagine him looking up at her, seeking and receiving that perfect smile that said, "Everything will be alright, Perry."

While Dad's adoration of his mother verged on worship, that devotion was not shared by all her offspring. While each may have respected Lucile for her mettle and determination, her brazenness could be counterproductive. Jack challenged and discarded her authority as many firstborn are wont to do. Second son, Don, took advantage of her kindness and deference, leaving her to defend him at immense detriment to herself. She fawned over her youngest daughter, Pat who rebelled not unlike Lucile herself had done so many years before. Bill, the half-brother and youngest of the clan, saw her as overpowering and stubborn.

In my eyes, Grandma was one of the most kind, gentle, compassionate and benevolent people ever. I loved her for her grace, wisdom, and a beatific smile that brightened my world every time I entered her orbit. This is a silly, little story but one that recalls Grandma's patience and acceptance. I was at the house on Quebec Street, maybe eight or nine years old and had a tummy ache. Grandma administered some Alka Seltzer and let me lay across her lap, with my butt in the air. While waiting for me to pass gas, she stroked my back and murmured soothingly. My embarrassment faded as I felt so loved in that moment. What other grandmother would do that, and seem so serene? And yes, I did fart and felt much better.

I was 18 years old when she died, woefully and mostly oblivious to the intricacies of her often difficult and yet inspirational story. All I knew was that her presence was the keystone for our extended family's tight bond during mine and my cousins' early years. Dad and his sister, Jeanne strived valiantly to preserve the magic by carrying forth the banner of their mother's benevolence and fortitude.

I also have to think the passing of his mother added one more, huge hurt that Dad tried to medicate.

CHAPTER 16

I got decent grades in high school and was in the National Honor Society, on the yearbook staff and pretty well respected by my teachers. In May of 1968, I graduated from Northglenn High School. Somehow, and I really don't know how this happened, my dream of becoming an architect turned into the miscalculated aim of studying Architectural Engineering, two vastly different fields. It may have been tied into the equally baffling notion that I could play football at the Colorado School of Mines in Golden. To Dad's immense delight, I ended up joining the third generation of my family to enroll at the University of Colorado in Boulder. Playing football fell by the wayside but I did start out in Architectural Engineering. That lasted a mere semester and a half. My creative brain couldn't handle all those equations and problems for which only one answer would do.

The Vietnam war had exploded full force on the American psyche, a daily feature in newspapers and on TV. Remember that cocky kid of 15 or 16, leaning against the kitchen counter righteously proclaiming that we, "Should just bomb the hell out of Hanoi?" Sitting across from him was a sadly amused father, who would opine, "What about all the innocent people who will die?"

On December 1, 1969, that kid came face to face with his own destiny. My name and those of every other American boy, aged 19 to 26, were thrown into the first modern Selective Service Lottery. Based on a totally random and arbitrary process, each of us was given a date with infamy, a reprieve or thrown into a provisional purgatory. Our birthdays were written on a blue slip of paper and deposited into a drum not unlike one from which Bingo numbers were drawn. The sequence in which the dates were pulled out determined our draft status for the following year. My number was 154, which meant that if I hadn't a 2S (student deferment) I would have been drafted in 1970 because they took numbers into the 200s. On that cold winter night, though I had a temporary stay from conscription, I made the decision to resist the draft when and if they came after me in four years. In addition to protesting the war in Vietnam, the early 70s were a period of enlightenment and Boulder was a hotbed for many other causes. Dad and Mom, being the impassioned progressives they were, encouraged my increasing involvement in the movements for civil and workers' rights; I also became a fervent women's libber, a Feminist.

Reveling in the Age of Aquarius and "power to the people," I became a peripheral hippie, which I define as growing my hair long, dropping acid and smoking a lot of pot, but I didn't drop out of society. In retrospect, I think those changes quickened the fraying of the father-son bond. Drinking alcohol was one thing but using chemicals to alter one's mind was beyond his sensibilities, as well as what he saw as our disdain for decorum. Imagine his horror when he invited me to accompany him to a Denver Broncos football game and I strode through the crowd with stringy hair down the middle of my back and a bowler hat and tattered jacket, ala Arlo Guthrie from the movie and song popular at the time, "Alice's Restaurant." Was he thinking of me when he wrote this verse?

Uncluttering 14

I see a reflection of me in your eyes.
The words you speak are mine.
Your little faults that stab my heart
Are made from my design

On a day during early summer of 1970, Dad was sitting as always in his recliner in front of the big plate glass windows that overlooked the skyline of Denver. The TV was probably tuned to a baseball game, and there would have been a stack of papers and magazines piled on the floor next to him that rose to arm level.

Me, almost 20 years old, "Dad, I'm not moving home for the summer."

"Oh?"

"Yeah, I've decided to stay in Boulder. A couple friends and I have rented a house on the Hill."

The pallor of agitation began to shade his expression. "Why are you doing that? Don't you want to come home and spend time with your family? Your brother and sisters always look forward to having you around."

"Well, that's just the thing, Dad. I love them and you and Mom, too, but I need to get out on my own. Y'know, make my own life, and well, little brothers and sisters kinda get in the way of that."

"So, you want to get away from them?"

Stammering, "Well, not exactly get away from them. It's like I just need my own space."

"You don't think I'd like my own space?" His face was blushing with the anguish of restraint.

Yet a few more threads pulled from the fabric of our relationship.

In the course of my research for this book, I came across a letter that Dad wrote to me. Across the top, he had written, "Didn't send when Dan [was a] Freshman or Sophomore." Apparently, it was in response to a letter I had written to him. I forget where in the files of his notes, musings, and unfinished correspondence I found the letter, but my triggering correspondence wasn't among those papers so I don't know if it still exists. In the far reaches of my memory, I can't recall what I wrote and that deprives me of much needed perspective. The only signpost that indicates when the letters flew is when he mentions Jaynie, a girl with whom I was involved during that summer of 1970. Perhaps I had written sometime after the scene in the living room, I'll never know. Dad's letter was four handwritten, legal-sized pages varying between apologetic, desperate, sad, lonely, then angry and insulting. The gist of his message was that the man he and my mother had sent off to college was now a "grass-smoking" coward who used profanity, slept with other people's daughters and had turned his back on his family. To say I was floored, appalled and hurt by his words these many years later would be an understatement. There is so much to unpack in the words he wrote and the ones unwritten between the lines.

"I was desperate that I was losing you and frustrated that I couldn't get through to you. Sure, it was all my fault. Talk about communicating, I've never been able to communicate — with anyone," he wrote. Can that statement be any more profoundly confessional? I have to believe that, in part, is why he didn't send the letter, it was too intimate, too emotional. A few paragraphs later, he lamented, "Somewhere along the way we lost touch — I'm sure it was my fault — that's the story of my life."

He accepted more blame and asserted his pain: "...how could I placate you to get back into your good graces. You see I need you — probably a hell of a lot more than you need me." He neither outright voiced that yearning nor intimated it, and I was too self-absorbed to have read the signs that might have been there.

He then went on to chronicle my fall from grace: "...I realized I wanted you the way you were...We worked hard at raising a man — not a goddam sissy. That's exactly what you have become." I have no idea where that came from, even when I try hard to clarify my recollections from back then, whenever that was. Now, taking that soulful look backward, my heart is so deeply pained that he never shared his concerns.

Dad concludes near the end of his letter that "Grass is the whole problem...it's a weakness...it's cowardly," and that I was dragging my little brother "into the mire." I suppose I must have tried to turn my brother onto the evil weed, but I sure don't remember doing that. This accusation of being a dope-smoking freeloader is particularly galling as well as perplexing. He apparently made no connection to his over-indulgence with alcohol or that its abuse in any way indicated weakness. Dad also penciled at the end, as if a note to himself, "Justify Easy Rider, Woodstock." I guess in a way, I was taking on the shortcomings of my generation.

I have to wonder why he kept his unsent letter and not the one from me that prompted such a response. How I would have reacted had he ever actually given or mailed the letter to me, I cannot fathom. I was sowing my young oats in the rarefied air of Boulder, so I likely would have been pretty confrontational. Dad may have been avoiding that scene, angry yet fearful and dreading the consequences. Our connection seemed already to be sliding toward ice during that period of time, the late 60s to early 70s. When I would come home for the requisite home-cooked meal and laundry to be washed, I vaguely remember dispassionate conversations and probably avoidance of being in the same room together unless it was to watch the Broncos on TV. At the time, I attributed his disgruntlement to being out-of-touch with the dynamism of the times and my experiences. Also, I was so goddamned self-consumed and focused on the bigger world, as were most of my contemporaries. It's not as if I didn't recognize and attempt to warm up our relationship. It was the era of the encounter group movement where a small group of like-minded Bohemians would sequester ourselves away to dig for and share our deepest anxieties. In one particular session that I recall, at the urging of the group, I was encouraged to take out my rage against my old man on a pillow, ending up in tears and hugging that stupid pillow father. In the end, Dad and I never dealt with the issues between us but I know our relationship weathered whatever storm it was and became stronger over the years. I can only imagine the doors that would have opened had he verbalized the tender sentiments in this poem.

Tell Me Son

Tell me son, where have you been
Your eyes are dancing so;
Here, come near, and take my hand
Perhaps that I may go.

Lead me to the music
That makes your laugh so clear
The land of precious sunshine
That makes each moment dear.

If I could understand the world
A field you far surpass.
With the answer in that pebble
And that blade of grass

Tell me son, that I can learn –
Together, you and I;
But you must take me with you
So I can laugh and cry

As 1971 approached, I was becoming actively involved in the peace movement. I was a foot soldier, not a leader or organizer but quite enmeshed in street protests, sit-ins, and in particular, the Day of Peace, during which we tried to get workers to not show up at work for one day as protest to the war. I also began working George McGovern's candidacy for president, as he was the anti-war candidate; alas, he lost in a landslide to Richard Nixon. Though I never rioted or was arrested, I definitely did not consider myself a REMF, ironically military slang for Rear-Echelon Mother Fucker.

At the start of what should have been my senior year in college I, for various reasons, would be short many credits of graduation. My 2S student deferment would expire the following June of 1972. The need to confront my impending fate became urgent. I had to decide what to do if I was drafted. Vowing not to be fodder in Vietnam or any other war, I had to determine my options. Being an Atheist, I knew I couldn't claim Conscientious Objector status, so I began accumulating my frailties: flat feet, asthma, etc., despite the fact that none of them hindered me from playing rugby. My last resort was a run to Canada. Mom declared that she would help me pack my bags; Dad, that I remember, silently supported my plans. By spring of that fateful year, the Selective Service Committee determined that they would only draft those boys who had numbers up to 140, so I missed being drafted by 14 arbitrary lottery dates. We didn't know at the time, but the authority to call up draftees would end after 1973, and the last drawing of the lottery would be in 1975. The closest I came to the military was wearing an army helmet while working at the Sink to protect me from bumping my head on all the low hanging pipes.

'Unnamed 2' is Dad's perfect portrayal of 'been there, done that," and why he'd never do it again. Had I read it, I'm sure it would have provided me great inspiration, affirmation and yet another opportunity to talk with and learn from him.

Unnamed 2

I'll have no more of hate and war -
I've served my time.
Now you are drumming things up again!
Play without me — let me be.
Let me retire into the love and peace,
And when you idiots seek out a hammer
Then you shriek my war cry
You pompous businessmen can feel my enthusiasm
    - and don my uniform
You pompous generals can win and wear my medals
You merchants and diplomats can suffer my wounds
    - and lose my blood.
And politicians can fill my grave
Let me be my own diplomat
This is my own body and life
There are my own emotions
This is my own blood,
What right has anyone to take them for his own?
It is mine, this life, let me spend it.
You fumbling and scheming children
Can go play tin soldiers with your own lives
Cowardice is reasonable amidst your loved ones
Or in the glories of nature
Bravery is childish on a blood-wet field
    - you hypocrites fight for words

Spend your money, devote your time, raise your voices,
And lose your blood — for words and for medals.
Let me be a coward amidst love and peace
  - and get tired after thousands of years.

⬥

While I was meandering through my travails, Dad's star was growing brighter. As the 1970s dawned, he was accumulating impressive engagements such as featured speaker at the annual conference of the Colorado Open Space Council, attending the grand opening of Larimer Square with Lady Bird Johnson, the president's wife, and being interviewed on local media outlets. A significant outgrowth from the Platte River valley redevelopment was the Regional Transportation District (RTD) which brought Denver together with several surrounding municipalities for the distinct purpose of assessing and improving mass transit throughout the area. Dad was asked by League of Women Voters to be Adams County's representative on the inaugural RTD board which he gladly agreed to do. One of the original tasks was selecting a president of the board; Dad was offered the position, but he declined. He enjoyed being on RTD as a board member in part because he was able to visit and observe many of the premiere mass transit systems around the country, including the Bay Area Regional Transit (BART) in San Francisco as well as the modernized subways in Washington D.C., Montreal and Toronto.

In spite of those highwater marks, by 1971 SPARC began falling apart to a large extent, because of a decline in fundraising. Though Dad was a great organizer and publicist, he was not a wheeler-dealer or political hack who could glad-hand and schmooze big donors. SPARC was quietly disbanded with its executive director once again swinging in the wind. All was not lost, as soon after Dad was named to the Colorado Environmental Commission which was put together to produce a comprehensive report on the state's efforts to reduce pollution, recycle resources and preserve open space. The initial account was presented to the state legislature, Dad said "they never looked at...it was a waste of time." Despite his misgivings, he was asked to be its executive director. As with RTD, he turned down another good-paying position. He never shared with me the whys, but I'm surmising he had been wounded and made gun shy by his experience with SPARC. I do know he was coming to despise bureaucracy and the personalities that wallowed in that swamp.

Uncluttering 20

You have robbed my mind of other thoughts –
My eyes of other sights.
You have laid waste some other days –
Discredited other nights.

While working with SPARC, Dad met and struck up a friendship with Phil Schmuck, who was Director of Planning for the state of Colorado. Phil had summited and taken photos of all the 14'ers (peaks over 14,000 feet in Colorado) and told my father that he was considering making a calendar. Dad's interest was aroused because he had an extensive cache of historic information on the legendary mountains. He suggested to Phil that they combine efforts and make a book. Phil liked the concept so Dad bounced it off Alan Swallow who was keen on the idea as well. Misfortune struck, almost scuttling the project. Swallow had asked Dad to drop off the manuscript and photos, but when he arrived at the house of his dear friend and publisher, Mae, Alan's wife sadly informed my father that Alan had died of a heart attack. He was only 51 years old. After Dad helped Mae sort out matters, she asked if he might want to take over the publishing business. Wes McCune, Dad and another friend, Bill O'Rourke came up with a plan to buy Sage Books but missed out by two days to a buyer from Chicago. In the transition, much of material for The Fourteeners was lost. Dad would have had to re-write the text, but his heart wasn't in it and he had lost his notes. One small lesson learned, he made sure after that to make copies of everything which he did in duplicate, triplicate and often more. The new buyer saw the project as a glossy book not a pamphlet and thus produced it in that format with Dad's unedited manuscript. Schmuck too was upset because the black and white photos he had submitted were rough copies and not meant to be in the final version. The book was published in 1970 and did fairly well but was never properly promoted and only saw a couple printings. To add insult to injury, in the sale of Sage Books, rights for the paperback edition of Treasure Tales were sold to Ballantine, and Dad never saw his share of the advance.

Riding the roller coaster of commendation and disappointments wore heavily on Dad. How much he shared his discouragement with anyone, even my mother, I wasn't aware. The effects weren't hard to notice. He put on more weight, got slovenly around the house and was becoming the unfit man to whom I would compare myself thirty years later after my cross-country bicycle adventure. Aside from few-and-far-between attempts to diet, nutritious eating habits went to hell. Regarding exercise, to the best of my recall, Dad didn't. He played his sports vicariously through his children's athletic endeavors; I recall him perched in the middle of the bleachers or on the sidelines, with arms crossed over big belly, a large Buddha cheering us on.

Worse than all of that, his drinking was getting worse. One day when I was home from Boulder, in an alcohol-induced haze, he stumbled and put his hand through one of the large plate glass windows in our living room. In a sad unusual twist, my father, who up to then would practically throw up at the sight of blood, sat there and giggled as we clamored to stanch the bleeding. Another time, I was in the basement and heard a loud thump. I ran upstairs to see my inebriated father sprawled beside the coffee table, against which he had fallen and broken his nose. Mom also told me years later that Dad was known to fall asleep in meetings which obviously didn't help his already tortured status in his various public activities.

It was also about that time that my sisters would call me and Pete who was also in Boulder, late at night to exclaim that Dad was yelling at and chasing Mom around the house. She was having to blockade herself in the bedroom until he passed out or semi-sobered up. My sister Eve confided to me many years later that our father would apologize to her and Medley but that she knew of, never to Mom. Those were years when my siblings and I felt helpless to intervene or didn't know how to. In retrospect, one only seems to find answers when it's usually far too late.

CHAPTER 17

Having dodged the bullet of military conscription, I suppose I let my fervor for studying go rather lax. By the end of spring semester 1972 yet still 20 credits short of graduation, I decided I needed a break from Boulder. A workmate at the Sink told me he could get me a job driving a cement truck in Boston. That's all it took, I was headed to Beantown. As it happened, a rugby teammate of mine lived in Foxboro on the outskirts of the city and offered to let me stay at his place. When we arrived there, his father informed me he had found a couple rugby teams that I might be interested in playing with. It took me only a few days to find a fifth-floor room in the Back Bay section of Boston and start playing with the Beacon Hill Rugby Football Club. I call the captain who welcomed me to play with them for their last weekend of games. Being virtually penniless at that point thus not having the fare for the subway, I walked across town to Southie (South Boston) where I ended up playing with the A, B and C sides, think top tier to novice. Afterward, at the requisite drink-up when the home team puts on beer for the visiting side and they all sing the dirtiest songs they know, I met the friend of the girlfriend of one of my new teammates. Her name was Diane. She was tall and slender, with long sandy brown hair and piercing dark brown eyes. She was a phlebotomist (technician in the blood lab) at Massachusetts General Hospital, very professional and stylish. She took pity on the poor kid from out West, buying me a grinder (sub sandwich) at North Station before dropping me off in Back Bay. I'm pretty sure she thought that would be the last she would see of me but a couple weeks later, who should show up knocking on her apartment door in Allston? Moi!

An interesting event occurred soon after that enjoyable evening. For Fathers' Day, I hitchhiked down to Washington D.C. to surprise Dad. He and Mom were staying with an old friend, Wes McCune, who was a journalist in the capitol city. He had a habit of going down to the office every morning to see what news stories were coming through on the teletype machine. Essentially, he was seeing what would be put into print that day. On that Father's Day, he came back kind of perplexed. He reported that for some strange reason, someone had broken into Democratic Party headquarters in the Watergate Hotel. Hence, my family and I were among the first to know about the biggest story of the decade.

Back in Boston, I successfully wooed the attractive young lab tech, and we became a couple. Our social life revolved around a great group of people associated with the Beacon Hill rugby club. The next summer, we did try to go our different ways, Diane to Europe and I to California. Within a couple months, we decided that we couldn't live apart. Despite my Atheism and with the aid of a Jesuit preacher who administered multiple dispensations, Diane and I were married in the Catholic Church in October of 1973. My family loved celebrating at the reception with our rowdy rugby friends. I'm sure that in Dad's eyes, marriage helped affirmed my march toward maturity and adulthood; Diane's mother, not so much, but that's another story. Diane, with her gregarious approach to life, also helped to dispel Dad's stereotype as an uppity Bostonian.

* * *

At one point soon after, Dad was appointed research assistant for the Colorado Historical Society where he was tasked with cataloguing over 1,000 of the state's historic sites. It was there he met an amiable doctoral student named Tom Noel who went on to gain notoriety as Dr. Colorado. Dad and Tom received a good measure of recognition and self-satisfaction from that project.

1976 would herald America's 200th birthday, and Colorado's 100th. Four years before that, the state legislature authorized creation of the Colorado Centennial Bi-Centennial Commission (CCBC), which was tasked with putting together events that would involve people and places from all over the state, as well as coordinate with national efforts for a huge celebration. Dad was hired as Deputy Director under Joe Albi, with whom he'd worked on Romer's campaign. His extensive knowledge was put to use commemorating the state's history and its historic sites. He was also put on the staff of the Heritage Commission with Dana Crawford with whom he'd worked while at SPARC. She would become one of Denver's premier developers after successfully fashioning Larimer Square from the wasteland of skid row into one of the city's shining lights. The work was exhilarating and highly rewarding, as Dad's expertise was highly regarded and utilized in the early stages of the group's development. However, and regrettably once more, Dad's professional demons came back to roost and life not only got worse, it got nasty. He and the powers that were at CCBC got crosswise and they parted ways, not amicably. Their divorce and its backstory garnered sordid press coverage as detailed in the abridged article in the Rocky Mountain News:

"Perry Eberhart, deputy director of CCBC, has resigned...rather than be fired...claiming the commission is riddled with nitpicking and people playing politics...[Eberhart claims] that he was eased out of [the] job because of philosophical differences with several commission members and [a] long-standing feud with the Governor Vanderhoof's chief aid and now, CCBC director, George Barrante [who had succeeded Albi]. He claimed the organization, '...needed someone more suitable to administer the deputy job'...Eberhart had been under fire for several months...for being unreliable and inefficient...when asked to detail his differences of opinion, Eberhart would say only that they didn't see 'eye to eye' on the way the commission was operating...several of them seemed only interested in 'picky' things like restructuring or small budget items... spending too much time arguing over details...the commission has a lot of work to do in the next two years and it's time it got started."

It's not hard to figure out why Dad wrote this admonition from Vince Lombardi in his journal: "If you aren't hired with enthusiasm, you will be fired with enthusiasm."

Yet, another thorn was lodged in Dad's side when in 1974, The Greenway Foundation was formed to carry out the monumental task of redeveloping the Platte River basin, essentially taking over where SPARC had left off. Greenway's Executive Director, Joe Shoemaker, had the connections and money-raising chops that Dad lacked. Revitalization projects redoubled after that transforming the South Platte River valley into a dynamic, scenic and treasured anchor for the city. Dad was appointed to the Foundation's board in the 1980s and named "Friend of the River" in 1988. He appreciated the recognition but, I'm sure, felt it a small reward for the inroads he and SPARC had made.

This is a rough draft of a poem Dad wrote for his Advanced Comp class in 1949; he called it an unfinished masterpiece. I can just imagine him being drawn to this old guy and sitting down on the curb with him. They could share their vexations and gloat about their small successes. Dad may not have thought it then but might he have anticipated that one day he might meet a soulmate and confidante in the down-and-out Bashby?

Bashby

Bashby sat on a curb where people walk,
And sulked to see them pass.
He prided himself that he didn't beg,

But cursed them that they didn't ask
He said people were selfish and narrow,
And he waited and laughed when one of them fell
Because he could laugh in a crowd and not be seen
Otherwise people would look at him and laugh.
He was able to fie the lout from a chorus and feel big
about it.
Bashby couldn't be big by himself with people around.
But once in a while he was thoroughly himself,
And showed his power and revenge on people
By pulling the wings from flies –
If he could catch the flies.
And he showed his control over nature and beauty
By crushing a red, red rose.

⸻ ⊶ ⊷ ⸻

In 1974, Diane and I left Boston driving our blue VW bug across the breadth of Canada, down the coast of California and back to Boulder. The times were good as Diane ingratiated herself into my big old family and I finally earned a Bachelor of Science degree in Elementary Education. Diane had gotten her teaching certificate so we parlayed our academic backgrounds into a program that hired American educators to teach in Australia. We were assigned to schools in Melbourne on two-year contracts. We made the most of our time there, exploring Sydney, the Great Ocean Road, vineyards of the Barossa Valley, the Great Barrier Reef and many more exotic places. Mom was tickled pink because she had a faraway destination for which to use her United Airline flying privileges. Her and Dad's joined us for our first Christmas Down Under.

As the seasons are opposite from the Northern Hemisphere, it was summer and we have photos of the four of us, sunburned and sitting around a traditional turkey dinner.

Our daughter Mariah, had the honor of being born at Melbourne's Women's Hospital on December 19th of 1977. Mom and Dad made their second excursion to Australia a couple months later. One of my fondest memories of all time occurred during that visit. We had an errand to run one afternoon. Mom decided to join us but Dad said he would stay behind to watch the baby. The three of us were a little leery so we rushed out and back. When I came through the front door, the house was dead quiet. I tiptoed down the hallway to our bedroom where Mariah's crib was. Dad stood there, one hand in his pocket, the other holding an upright bottle, feeding the baby. Her satisfied slurping sounds were accompanied by Dad softly humming an indistinct lullaby. He looked at me and said, "What?" I had a lump the size of a softball in my throat as my heart melted.

* * *

Soon after returning from their first visit to Melbourne, and with the fiasco at CCBC still fresh in his mind, Dad decided he'd had enough of other peoples' bullshit and vowed never to work for anyone again. His books were selling pretty well, royalties provided a nice annual boost to the family budget and he was still in demand as a speaker. Local colleges would invite him to teach a short course or two and he contracted to write articles for his old friend, the National Farmers Union. To show he could still be a thorn in someone else's side, Dad and a couple journalist buddies formed the anti-land developer cabal, The Friends of Alferd E. Packer. The infamous mountain guide remains the only person ever convicted of cannibalism in the United States. Dad and friends devised for the group such catchy phrases as, "Serving our fellow man since 1874," "I never met a meal I didn't like," and, "Take a land developer to lunch." As the impromptu spokesman, Dad would write letters to the editors about the inordinate sway developers had over city and legislative activities, signing the letters as Menu Chairman for the Friends of Alferd E. Packer Society. Legend has it that Packer ate only the Democrats in the party, inspiring this whimsical ditty by Dad:

Alferd Packer

One just doesn't eat people, Alferd Packer
Democrats least of all
That's somethin' your ma shoulda told ya
Afore you growed so tall.

We know them others is gristly
An' ain't got no taste a'tall
They's no agreeing with your taste buds

Granted a man gets hungry
And don't think before he acts
But Demmycrats are hard to come by
One's gotta face the facts
You coulda started a _____
There'd be a run on Demmycrats
Then where would we be?

At least you shoulda asked them
Or converted three of the five
And then alternated your eating
To keep the two-party system alive
You just didn't use your head
Now we gotta hang ya
Until you're dead, dead, dead

Activity swirled around Medley and Eve at the house on Niver Avenue, whether in raucous games of "tackle the man with the football" or during the countless hours of jumping, camping or just hanging out on the infamous Tramp. Years later, I would hear how that trampoline was a happy memory for several classes of Northglenn High School students. Both my sisters were tall, but very different in appearance. Eve had dark curly hair, cherubic cheeks and a bright smile. Medley smiled too, but there could be a mischievous shade to it. She complained that she had Grandpa's schnoz, but it was framed by glowing green eyes and long, straight strawberry blonde hair. The girls, as we called them, competed on the swim team but were highly regarded for their work as lifeguards and swimming instructors, particularly with the handicapped. Both Medley and Eve served as president of the Girls Letter Club in successive years and Mistress of Ceremonies for the annual athletic dinner. The dynamic duo gained notoriety for their toilet papering (TP) exploits. Their proudest moment came when one night, the Eberhart trees were adorned with streams of TP as payback. Another highlight of the nocturnal adventures was the night Eve, Med and a group of friends all claimed to be spending the night at each other's houses, only to come up the street at two a.m. to find an assembly of parents waiting for them on our front lawn. Very happily for Diane and I, both girls also came to visit us in Australia after they graduated high school.

The girls' relationship with their father was fickle, as was their brothers'. He was the biggest supporter of their athletic participation, often times the only parent cheering the team at swim meets. On the other hand, he would wonder why they were never at home, rarely having friends over and always spending so much time at their friends' houses. Eve recalls that when he made the decision to never work for anybody again, he worked from home so he was *always* home. Adolescents didn't hanker to be hanging around where overly curious parents were ever present.

During high school, my sisters went skiing almost every weekend with the school district club. Eve told of big sister Medley, racing down the slopes almost always out of control and insisting on getting a final run in just before the lifts closed. She would be the last one on the bus but then led the songfest on the way home. That was Medley, she took the world by the horns and shook for all she was worth. That included managing her father. Of the four of us kids, she held the most influence over Dad, challenging him in particular on his drinking.

Only eleven months apart in age, Eve and her older sister became the best of friends and partners in crime. Though forever inseparable, the dynamic began to change during Eve's last year in high school when Medley headed up to Boulder for college. Eve moved out from under big sister's shadow and the 'little sister' pigeonhole. Through her cousin Billy, she met his neighbor Rick Black who had a bit of Tom Cruise swagger both in looks and attitude. Beginning with regular dances at the King's Palace, a dance hall for Christian teenagers, a beautiful relationship blossomed that endures to this day. Dad was wary of the young parvenu who smoked, drank and was making off with the heart of his little girl. Dad would smolder as Rick hung out on the couch, watching TV while in his opinion, Eve waited on him hand and foot. After Rick enlisted in the Air Force and was stationed in Cheyenne, Wyoming, Eve's regular jaunts up there didn't sit well with the old man, evincing remnants of his puritan notions. As the young couple settled down, Rick proved himself to be very responsible and financially disciplined, gradually garnering Dad's respect. My sister became Mrs. Rick Black in September of 1979, and soon became parents of Lindsey, Nick, and Jesse.

For a while in his early 20s, Pete embarked on a journey of self-discovery that began when he dropped out of CU in 1975. Mom got fed up with his hanging around, scolding him to get the hell out of the house and go do something with his life. So he hitchhiked to California eventually landing a great gig in Santa Barbara as the head of facilities at a large retirement hotel. His duties included remodeling, plumbing, electrical repairs and what have you. He was in seventh heaven because he was provided a huge shop with all the tools most craftsmen dream about. In true Eberhart form, he got in trouble because he would do too much for people.

His meanderings helped him accept and understand as I did, Mom's passion for travel and the gypsy lifestyle. He appreciated her for fearlessly pushing him out there, "not all moms would do that." While in Santa Barbara, Pete found the opportunity to, as he said, "peel back the layers of life and existence," basically exploring spirituality in all its forms. He delved into Hinduism, Taoism and the works of visionaries who were en vogue at the time including Carlos Castenada and Herman Hesse. After much thought and meditation, he concluded that, "the path to spirituality is virtually the same for all, just different recipes." Pete found comfort in the correlation between Eastern and Western theologies which helped him to "stop expecting things to happen." His musings also prompted him to reflect on Dad's belligerent cynicism and crass rejection of organized religion. Having achieved a sense of harmony and clarity, Pete wrote a letter to our father explaining his enlightenment and taking issue with Dad's negativity. Dad noted in his journal that his son must have had a bad trip of the psychedelic kind. The letter placed a strain on their relationship. Fortunately, over the years and through the many trials they endured, Pete came to better appreciate his father's perspectives and convictions, the ones that heralded each person's individuality and principles. He claims that Dad helped make him more circumspect and not bow to false authority. Perhaps that attitude caused the three of us Eberhart males as much satisfaction as heartache. Our willingness to stand up for principles often collided with stodgy authority but in the end, made us proud of our decisions.

When Pete returned to Boulder, he met a free-spirited woman named Isabelle. They found much in common and a gratifying devotion. They were married in October of 1978 with a small gathering of families in my folks' backyard. After a marvelous six-month adventure via Asia and the

Mediterranean, Diane, Mariah and I returned from Australia in time to participate in the lovely celebration. Pete and Isabelle moved to Colorado Springs where she was a teacher and he went to technical school but was much more enthralled with taxi driving. They would soon have daughters Antonia and Emily, to add to Mom and Dad's flock.

* * *

My father's health issues escalated onto a roller coaster of ailments and malaise during the 70s. His chronicling of his medical history into mid-life was mostly perfunctory. With token allusion to alcohol and tobacco use, he mentioned his weight, some high blood pressure and concerns about stomach ulcers during his time as a newspaperman. After one particular check-up, he wrote in his journal that the doctor said he was "too healthy for his own good, but too heavy." Around the age of 50, he developed rashes and sores all over his body; to the revulsion of us all, he took to picking the scabs and, for who knows why, saving them in a pill bottle. For the first time since he'd had his tonsils out as a kid, he spent a lot of time in hospitals for all kinds of tests that apparently didn't reveal much. The top skin doctor took him off all meds with the caveat that if he took care of himself, he wouldn't need blood pressure medicine and would only have to take low doses of blood disorder medication. The skin problems did level off but that turned out to be just the beginning.

Soon after the rashes, an ulcer developed on the bottom of his foot. He misunderstood the doctor who, he thought, advised him to "loosely tie his shoes." Not long after, he and

Mom took a trip to Mexico City where they walked all over. Upon return, the little ulcer had gotten larger and inflamed. Doctors realized that the foot was not a localized problem but indicative of a larger medical issue that he would deal with for the rest of his life, diabetes. Dad noted that during one visit to the hospital the doctor prescribed Balsam of Peru, whatever that was. As his diabetes worsened, he began insulin injections. He "shot" himself four times a week and Mom would shoot him the other days. He quipped, "I could usually tell when Sandy was mad at me by the shots she gave—just kidding, we all know she wouldn't mix business with emotion."

On the trip with Mom to Madison, South Dakota in 1979, Dad started feeling lousy and losing sleep. Also, a "gawd awful thing" appeared on top of his other foot, opposite the ulcer. Back home, Mom took him to the hospital where they removed the growth. That fix lasted only a few years. Following another trip to San Francisco in 1981, he ended up back in the sickbay due to the spread of infection. He recalled, "...the doc cut the hell out of the bottom of my foot, almost to bone and tendon to clear out infection." Then in 1985, the rest of his toe was amputated only to be followed up a year or so later with the amputation of his foot. There was a curious, if not grisly aspect to all these surgeries. The man who once sickened at the sight of blood almost to the point of fainting had my mother take photographs of all the various, gruesome stages of his surgeries and amputations. Imagine my revulsion when I came across the envelope that contained all those pictures; thankfully, they were in black and white. The worst part, despite diabetes and amputations, Dad continued to drink through all of it.

As life tumbled him around like clothes in a dryer, I can see Dad signaling, 'Time out,' stretching out on a cushion of soft green grass, lacing his fingers behind his head and watching the sky. There, he adopted the cloud as a sage of sorts and put man in perspective.

The Cloud

Whenever I seek my sweet reward
Far from the vulgar crowd,
I sit a while enraptured
With his majesty — the cloud.
I see him in a grand parade
File by in endless might,
Shadowing the summer green,
Sliding silently by at night.
I see him ghost the dying moon,
And mingle with the stars.
I hear him chortle uproariously,
And hurtle lightning bars.
I see him sail the azure crest
Sailing on where nature stops.
I've seen one in my own backyard,
Another wrestling with the mountain tops.
Peacefully riding by unmindful
Of the dust on nature's floor.
Petty men bickering their doom
That die and live no more.
But the cloud sails on forever
One man can never see.
The same breeze that blows his dust
Blows through eternity.

What little things we are
As you noiselessly slip by.
How we emulate our littleness
With your bigness in the sky.
If we but had your vision,
If we but had your scope,
Our lives would sail on forever;
Our death would hold some hope.

CHAPTER 18

My sister, Medley Ann was extroverted, fun-loving and always ready to help or soothe the hurting soul. She was a grand partier who loved to sing; at the top of her lungs, she loved to sing! Her magnanimous personality lit up every room she entered and she considered everybody a friend. Unfortunately, that didn't always bode well for romantic attachments. Med had many 'guy' friends but got close to only one or two. Perhaps her inner loneliness propelled her to make sure others would not feel shunned or left out. Whether teaching disabled children to swim or volunteering at nursing homes, Medley rigorously ensured that no one would feel ignored. She graduated high school in 1977 with honors and headed off to University of Colorado with plans to major in physical therapy, which she felt was her best opportunity to help the most people. While she was ecstatic to follow the family tradition to Boulder and developed strong friendships, her sister Eve felt that Med seemed to have problems adjusting to her new life but would never complain.

The year was 1978. I was in Vermont staying with my new sister-in-law and her husband when I got the call. It was late on the night of November 15th, which was Medley's 20th birthday.

Mom talked low and slowly as she informed me that my beautiful sister died in a car accident that afternoon. I slumped to the floor, stunned. My brother-in-law followed me down the highway until at two in the morning, he and I felt confident that I could make it back to Boston where baby Mariah and Diane were staying with her mother. We caught the first flight we could back to Colorado to mourn with my family.

Medley had borrowed her roommate's red VW bug to drive down from Boulder to collect her birthday presents and go to an eye doctor appointment. On her way home, she slammed into the back of another car. Tellingly, there were no tire skid marks. The steering wheel had slammed into her chest, killing her instantly. Though it was never confirmed, we were pretty sure Medley had one of her seizures and blacked out. Only later did my parents find out because Medley didn't tell them that she had been told she shouldn't drive. Today, the medical world might precisely diagnose her as having some egregious form of epilepsy, meningitis or complications from a childhood brain injury. MRIs, CAT scans and other wonders of modern medicine not available in the 60s and 70s perhaps could have diagnosed the causes to Med's blackouts with treatments to manage them.

I'm not sure if there's a handbook on how to grieve for a lost family member. When we gathered at the family home on Niver Avenue, each of us shared memories of our vivacious sister and dreams for what she might have become. Individually, I think we each shed tears, but not so much sitting there on the living room floor. Afterward, the two in-laws who were there, Diane and Isabelle, stated with some amazement how calmly the rest of us reacted to the tragedy. Our family doesn't really do funerals and services, but we did invite all who knew and loved Medley Ann by the house. Everyone who came through the front door was sad, most tearful, all disheartened by the immense tragedy. Once amongst family and friends, stories about Medley, funny, uplifting, and affectionate provoked teary smiles, laughter and abiding love. People hated to leave the camaraderie and warmth; the sorrow they'd brought with them had turned to joyful remembrance. That was what Medley would have wanted.

One tribute deeply touched our family's collective heart but Dad's in particular, with his affinity for newspaper men. It's a column written by Steve Roberts, who was the sports editor for the local paper, The Sentinel Dispatch.

> "The sports department of any newspaper is often considered the 'toy department' and in most cases that is a valid observation.
>
> There are times, though, that working with kids in the prime of their youth can become less than the easy effort portrayed by the toy department image.
>
> This is such a time.
>
> About two years ago, maybe a little more than that, I received a letter from a Northglenn girl about the coverage of girls' athletics, not only at her own school, but around the league. It was a well-written, concerned letter and led to several conversations that made me more acutely aware of the feelings of girls in sports and I hope led to some of the better coverage of girls' sports in the area.

The girl was Medley Ann Eberhart, who was active in track and swimming, and perhaps even more active in living and caring about her interests and the interests of others.

Now as a result of an automobile accident on her 20th birthday, Medley is dead. The area, and in a wider sense, the world, has lost a young, pretty, caring human. She, like so many young people that die before their full abilities are realized, leaves a void in the lives that came into contact with her, a void that will not easily be filled."

My sister's death triggered one of the most devastating periods in my life. She showed so much promise and then like a shooting star, every space she had brightened was filled with interminable darkness. I was torn apart on the inside and couldn't really talk about it for more than ten years. Much of my distress derived from deep, deep sympathy for my parents and the realization that I, at that time, was also a parent. That old adage about no parent having to bury their children is more than heartbreaking and excruciating when it becomes truth. Watching my father deal with his daughter's death was agonizing. Thanksgiving was eight days after the accident. As trivial as it might sound, I was distraught watching Dad who never did the dishes, shoo everybody out of the kitchen so he could be alone with his grief. His eventual therapy was to research and write a wonderful book, <u>Music for Medley Ann</u>. At the time, the rest of us in the family discouraged him from publishing it, too personal we thought. Every November 15th, I sit down and read a couple chapters from the book. Not only does it allow me to keep Med's memory bright and alive but

Dad's true essence is woven into every heartfelt word. Though both of them left us way too early, by reading the book every year I'm allowed to spend time with them.

⚬━━◅●▻━━⚬

Music for Medley Ann

Chapter headings

What's in a Name
The House on the Hill
The Animals
Lazy Eye
The Fleeting Years
The Mother Hen
Touring the Estate
Culture and Stuff
Happy Holidays
The Loving and the Kissing
Uncluttering
The Tramp
That Night
Whatever Gods There Be
The Clothes Horse
The Changing Fields
Super Skier
Communications
High School Days
The Best T-P Job Ever
World Traveler
Super Jock
Troubles along the Way
Singing is the Way I Talk

No Strangers in Her Life
The Night the Moose Burned Up
Farrand Hall or Toilet Talk
Poodles the Clown
Castle Gardens
The Language Barrier
First Step toward Stardom
Halcyon Days
The Accident
Todd Smith
The Toy Department
Sisters
Not the end

Not unlike her big brothers, Med liked to party and push the bounds of experimentation with hallucinatory substances. Would she have fallen prey to demon rum like her father? More likely, her perceptive nature indicated a healthy awareness, foresight and determination that hopefully would have stared down temptation. Not only had she seen Dad in the sorrowful depths of his alcoholism, but she was his harshest, yet most compassionate critic. My parents suffered through and survived the tragedy, and later dreadful repercussions (the people with whose car Med had collided sued my parents for further damages beyond what the insurance company paid), but I don't know how. Not wanting to ever face what they did, I have forbidden my three kids from dying before me.

CHAPTER 19

After the longest six months of my life living with Diane's mother in Boston, I found a teaching position in Bath, Maine and we moved into a ground-floor apartment a couple blocks away from the school. The following February in 1980, we welcomed our second daughter, Courtney Ann. I was thrilled because the doctor let me deliver her. From the start, she was out to prove who was boss. We had our challenges with infant Mariah, but she was our first child and after those first few months, we thought we had this parenting thing down. "Not so fast," Courtney squalled. Where we had learned that after 20 minutes or so of crying, Mariah would drift off to sleep, Courtney would howl for what seemed like hours. She also became very adept at projectile vomiting and other assorted tactics meant to cause her parents to pull out their hair.

I came to the realization that I really wasn't cut out to be a teacher. Though I had my successes and got through to a couple kids, I discovered that a good educator is organized and disciplined, not my strengths. After a year and half of teaching at Fischer Elementary, I took a temporary job down the road in Freeport at L.L. Bean, the infamous outdoor retailer and catalog company. My first position with them was in the shoe department which had a side benefit. My parents came to visit soon after I started. Dad's foot issues were flaring and the shoes he was wearing would cave in and put pressure on the wounds. Because I was so knowledgeable, not really, in the subject of footwear, I recommended he try a pair of soft leather shoes that he reported "worked wonders." Their visit coincided with my 30th birthday. When we headed out for a celebratory dinner, Dad was nearly incommunicado from pre-celebration cocktails and ruined my mood for the evening.

Despite myself and my counter-culture orientation, I got a permanent position and began to work my way into the management ranks at L.L. Bean. Diane and I rented a three-bedroom house in the quaint town of Topsham in early 1981. In December of that year, we welcomed our one and only son, Daniel Travis. He was a big boy, eight pounds, ten ounces. Diane and I decided to try the Le Boyer method with him wherein as soon as the baby is delivered, he is eased into a tub of warm water, mimicking the womb. I was amazed at how Travis' terrified little body so completely relaxed when I held him in the water. He's been that mellow all his life. I treasure the fact that all three of my kids entered the world with their own distinct circumstances. Mariah was the first born via the La Maze method in Melbourne, Australia. I delivered Courtney and bathed Travis in the soothing bath. Compare my experiences with my father's, where in his day expecting dads walked in circles and smoked cigarettes in a nondescript waiting room until a doctor came out to announce the birth of his child. Diane waffled a bit about trying for a fourth child so we could have another son. When I convinced her it didn't happen that way, I had a vasectomy and our little family was set.

The house we were renting happened to be owned by a local builder. Just before Travis' first and Mariah's fifth birthday, we moved into a cozy split-level house that he built for us in the Bay Park neighborhood of Topsham. With only one road in and four blocks surrounded by forest, it was a great place for our gang and their friends to spend the first several years of their lives.

* * *

Dad's decision to work only for himself may have been shielding him from the aggravations of other people's rules and regulations, but it wasn't adding much to the family bank account. Once-a-year royalties were helpful, but they were slowly decreasing and not much help beyond the one-time mega-shopping trip. Moreover, he felt his standing among his peers was diminishing, in part due to working at home and being isolated. In his journal, he recounted a reunion lunch with college buddies that though very enjoyable, left him discouraged and demoralized: "I felt like the invisible man most of the time...I would begin to tell a story but then, Les or Keith would start on another subject as if the floor was open — and I wasn't even there. I feel I was more animated than usual, and more witty, but if God gave a pop quiz after the luncheon, my name wouldn't even come up as an alternative answer."

My father's lifelong tussle between dreams and reality only seemed to deepen. In Paris, he sought and discovered a Bohemian lifestyle that was imbued with artistic expression and a freedom of the soul that wasn't overly conducive to life in the middle class. He craved the romantic life and gratification of a writer but had trouble reconciling that with the ordinariness of child-rearing, financial stability and spirit-crushing jobs. To use a tired cliché, for him the grass on the other side of the cultural divide was always greener and more exhilarating. Unequivocally my father had his successes, particularly as an author and historian, but I think he never really achieved the satisfaction of acclaim that he sought, not like Bill Styron or George Plimpton. Dad was known and generally respected, but not necessarily celebrated as he may have hoped, nor showered with financial reward and professional standing. His desire to be acknowledged on his own merit and integrity was noble but incomplete. He wasn't great at marketing himself and he didn't play the political game well which may well have undercut the valiant ambition that fired his soul. In the end, he may have approached the point where Hemingway said, "When you cannot make friends any more in your head is the worst." Dad added to this by musing,

---

Uncluttering 10

Do I look too far and see things dimly?

It was sometime in the early 80s; the family and I were visiting my folks when I headed down the long hallway to Dad's office. He was in the bathroom so I sat in the rickety chair opposite the large, blonde wood desk he had inherited from Grandpa. Feeling thirsty, I reached across the desk to grab a sip from the glass of what looked like iced tea. It was, but nearly spit it out when I discovered it was heavily cut with vodka. Setting the glass back down with a clunk, I fell against the chair back. Dad returned, settled his large bulk on the other side of the big desk and smiled with muted delight that his son was back in town.

I suppose the sour taste still coating my mouth loosened my restraint as I brazenly asked, "Why do you drink?"

Dad looked at the glass, shrugged his shoulders, and said, "I like the taste."

Musing 10

The easiest thing in the world
To raise are eyebrows

'Well, that's a stupid, goddamn reason,' I thought to myself, quite naively I realized in retrospect. Recalling the times I'd seen him fall on his face in a drunken stupor, put his hand through a plate glass window and hallucinate during bouts of delirium tremens, and all because he liked the taste! I did not then understand the disease of alcoholism as I do today, but the scene in his office crystallized for me the nearly insurmountable battle he was fighting, whether or not he chose to accept it. My great grandfather was a fire and brimstone preacher who railed against the evils of demon rum and ardently supported prohibition, yet Dad and two of his siblings fell hard under the spell of alcohol. Uncle Bill told me how the family's fascination, then obsession with liquor seemed to begin at the first family gathering after the war, when everyone was there, including sister Jeanne's boyfriend George. Were they celebrating the end of the war, drowning bad memories or diving headfirst into a new infatuation with all things booze? Bill couldn't say. At the time, he was only 14 and didn't think much about it. These many years later, though, he looks back and is certain that's when the seeds of alcoholism were planted. Even his mother fell into a habit of large glasses of wine every evening.

There were plenty of warning signs for Dad, though how he read them is unknowable. One particularly poignant tale concerned friend Tom Hutton, whom Dad had met at INS. He and Mom became close friends with Tom and his wife, Mary. They lived on a large plot of farmland next door to Westlake the old four-room schoolhouse that I attended in fifth and sixth grade. My brother, sisters and I became friends with the Hutton kids. I loved riding their old horse Betty, and roaming the open fields. Dad reported that Tom Hutton was the nicest guy in the world, until he started drinking, "then it was like Jekyll and Hyde," he said. When Tom got drunk and belligerent in some bar, Mary would call my father to pick up her husband. When Dad showed up, Tom would pick fights just to enlist the help of his "good-sized buddy." The year was 1985 when Mary called to say that Tom had died in a bar fight. Dad bemoaned the fact that there was no obituary in the paper. He called Tom a good man but bemoaned that, "it was a sad story."

I've mentioned earlier that Dad wrote little in his journals or letters about his insobriety. He mentioned offhandedly that he periodically passed out in the back of Mom's car when they were in college. There were the fanciful recollections of drinking champagne, beer, and aperitifs at all times of the day in Paris. In later years, there are a couple of revealing entries such as one written about a presentation to the Historic Boulder committee, where he, "had a little too much to drink before dinner and gave a terrible speech." Or, when in Jackson Hole for a CBC workshop, he stayed in his cabin, didn't eat much, lost weight and was shaking much of the time; "I think from drinking," he wrote. Mom revealed to me many years later that he sometimes fell asleep during meetings and had tried Alcoholics Anonymous but never stuck with it.

His journal noted the sad stories of friends like Tom and Stan Weston. I could not find allusions to his brother Jack's battle with the bottle and ultimate passing because of it, or sister Pat who spent the last years of her life sick and broken because of her alcoholism. It's as if Dad didn't want to see the big red flags. If he did, he shared few insights with me beyond the, "I like the taste." I saw no real acceptance of his condition beyond the offhand comments or weak wisecracks trying to justify his inebriated behaviors. In later years, even Mom wouldn't expose his secrets, though my siblings and I know she was the one who suffered the worst consequences. At some point, he was prescient enough to pen this note-to-self:

Before Next Drink

1. Remember feeling in throat from time to time.
2. Also taste in throat and difficulty in swallowing.
3. The feeling next morning
4. Great fall off of work
5. Weight and blood sugar
6. Worry of kids
7. Promise to Medley
8. Means weakness elsewhere
9. Sleep at night
10. Feeling of throw up in AM
11. Minimum cost up to $10 a day*

* That would be over $100 in today's dollars!

Alcoholism wreaks enough havoc on the alcoholic, but the ones closest to them bear the brunt of their sickness. My mother liked a good cocktail or two or three and I'd seen her drunk a couple times, but the spirits never took control of her life. She, without doubt, enabled Dad's affliction and was under his influence as it were, which is not an uncommon role for the partner of an alcoholic. I'm certain he often coerced her to drink but she didn't deserve to be the target of his inebriated irrationality and rages. He would accuse her of having affairs, perhaps because he felt impotent or incapable of passion. He would push or grab at Mom, telling her she was useless and blaming her for all the ways the world mistreated him. When he chased her through the house, she would jam a dresser against the bedroom door or leave home for days. Eve reported that she always kept keys to the car with her. Mom had a couple of confidantes who stood by her during those times and Dad was supremely jealous of them. After many of these horrendous outbursts, as I previously mentioned, he would sit my sisters down and apologize to them but he never to Mom. Eve affirmed that he was never abusive toward her and Med, but never treated our mother with respect.

Eve asked Mom, "Why do you stay with him when he does all that stuff to you?"

Her reply was simple and heartrending, "Your father is sick, but I love him."

With that eloquent line, she became a saint in my sister's eyes.

One could suggest that he was a product of his times, where old movies and television shows conveyed the myth that cigarettes and cocktails were the norm for the Greatest Generation. Vodka and whiskey became the bogus prescriptions for medicating a distraught mind. Medley's death quite easily and almost justifiably could have been an excuse for Dad to drown an unimaginable pain. The destruction he saw at Hiroshima, I would imagine, could drive even the hardiest of men to drink. All the professional disappointments and missed opportunities were likely assuaged in a shot glass, or several. A nice buzz or three-day bender might transport him back to a sidewalk café on the Left Bank. In drunken reverie, he might imagine discussing Impressionism with Rambeau or the magic of Paris with Hemingway. Real life is unfair and gives us all different tools to deal with its vagaries. Other men travelled parallel journeys to Dad's without the need to seek solace in a bottle. Those men likely lived beyond the age of 64.

Once again, I can only speculate on the motivations and meanings in Dad's poetry, but in this poem, I see an allegory for his journey from a first jaunty beer with his mates on shore leave to that sad confession that he, 'liked the taste.' The mirror may be framed by stacked liquor bottles, flickering neon, men down on their luck, the ambiance of a dive bar. While Part II intimates a love story, is the object of affection and rejection a flesh and blood woman or demon rum in drag? In the end awakening from his nightmare, the face in the mirror tries to fade into the sunset, putting an unrequited love affair to rest. Or, am I reaching too far?

The Mirror Behind the Bar

Great deeds are done, great wars are won
A face may lose its scar.
A man may find or lose himself,
In the mirror behind the bar.

Tomorrow may find a new promise;
Soft memories from afar
Are found in the boundless glimmer
Of the mirror behind the bar.

The altar of an honest man's temple
The gold of a last bazaar
Shine from the glass infinitely
The mirror behind the bar

Your hair was soft and friendly
Your eyes were deep and dear
Your lips curved warm and exciting,
I felt your body near.
And tenderly we talked and laughed
Our hearts glowed again as one.
The reflection had forgotten the bitterness
And the deathly thing you had done
In the glass, all else had left us
My wrong was made a right.
Your look was that of forgiveness.
Our love was again of might.
I lost myself to your vision then
My heart was leaden with tears.
I sobbed for my bitter emptiness
I shuddered from my fears.
I moved to crush and kiss you –
To feel your face and hair.
I wanted to scream and call to you,
But only a sob was there.

III

But you had left your vision to haunt me
A picture that time cannot mar
And I cursed the demon that put you there
In the mirror behind the bar.

A last shaking sob awoke me then –
I knew I had gone too far.
Soberly I tipped my hat and left you there
In the mirror behind the bar.

Dad finished one more book, <u>Ghosts of the Plains</u>, copyrighted in 1986 and published by Swallow Press, now under the auspices of Ohio University. It was to be the first of a four-part collection that would focus on distinct milieus around Colorado. <u>Ghosts</u> was inspired in part by connection to the now, non-existent town of Serene which is not far from the city of Lafayette in north central Colorado. Serene had been a company town for many of the coal mines in the area. Like its sister encampment to the south Ludlow, workers organized under the auspices of the International Workers of the World, also known as the Wobblies, for better work conditions and pay. In 1927 their protests and strikes pushed beyond the tolerance of Governor "Billy" Adams, he declared their activities illegal and sent in the Colorado National Guard. Two guardsmen involved in putting down the insurrection would for a time become fast friends, Fred Eberhart and Carl Haberl. The involvement of his father and future stepfather fueled Dad's curiosity and focus. He went on to challenge the caricature that the fascinating booms and busts of towns of Colorado's flatlands and prairies were not as sexy as the stories from the exalted Rockies. <u>Ghosts of the Plains</u> sold well and continues to generate royalties to this day.

CHAPTER 20

In addition to the blasé admission that he liked the taste of booze, there was just one other moment of candor I remember Dad sharing with me about his drinking, and maybe his lifestyle, I'm not sure. The year was 1988, not long after I had completed my coast-to-coast bicycle ride, the family and I were again visiting from Maine. Little did I know it would be my last visit with him.

Just before we came to town, Dad had been in the hospital a few times for several ailments, the specifics of which I can't particularly recall. There was the time Mom called to tell me that he had died on the operating table only to be revived after several attempts. He was in the hospital when we planned our trip to Colorado but he had checked himself out so he could spend time with his grandkids in a more pleasant setting. The two of us were sitting in the living room of the small condo he and Mom had bought. His body was emaciated and showed the ravages of internal functions that were all but destroyed. After some catching up, he paused for a long moment and stared out the window into the golden Colorado sunshine.

His voice barely audible, he murmured, "Dan, don't do to your body what I did to mine."

I was overwhelmed at that moment with a flood of empathy and loved him absolutely for that truthful confession. After I'd returned to my home 2,000 miles away, I pondered his words and got angry. I wanted to ask, "Why the hell didn't you admit that profound sentiment to me many, many years earlier?" Would his candor have opened doors to communication that kept us from really knowing each other and growing the bond between us? I don't know. When did he honestly confront himself about his addiction? Between his own health issues, AA, the deaths of close friends and family, he knew all the signs and consequences. All those grueling stays in the hospital could have been avoided if he'd stopped drinking because he knew it was bad for his diabetes. Did it actually take 63 years for him to admit the truth to himself, if not to his son?

My father died on January 13, 1989. He was 64 years and 161 days of age.

The stated cause of death was cardiac arrest, but the doctor confided that cirrhosis of the liver had ravaged his body, his organs gave up after years of mistreatment.

Mom did receive many condolence cards and calls from lifelong friends and associates of Dad's. I was disappointed though, that his prominence in the state didn't prompt any formal, public memorials or even enhanced coverage in the local newspapers. His groundbreaking books and accumulation of community involvements, I feel, warranted more acknowledgement. Dad's personality must have kept him below the radar—who's to say? The family did have a small ceremony in the backyard of the Niver house, where his ashes were spread over his treasured rock garden. I've often wondered and chuckled over what future owners of the house might have thought had they known my father was still in residence in their backyard.

* * *

Dad's death imposed a particularly devastating burden on my mother. Her role in life and source of stability had been dependent on the only two men she ever really cared for, her father who passed away in 1963, and Dad. When he died suddenly, sadly though not unexpectedly, her role as caretaker and defender was taken away. Within six months of his death, she had a mental breakdown. I was with her when the deterioration began. In a clamor to cleanse her life of the depressive triggers that reminded her of Dad, she scrambled to clear the house of his "stuff." I came back from Maine to lend help and comfort. At one point, Mom ran down the hall, upset and in a tither. With tears in her eyes, she cried, "He's not the man I married!"

The moment resounds with me because I distinctly remember enfolding her into my arms and letting her sob into my shoulder. The moment was more poignant because I could not remember ever holding her so close to me. She recovered and began instructing me on items to give away and those that I might like to take home to Maine with me. That's when we contacted the Denver Public Library and they gladly accepted what became 39 boxes of his unfinished manuscripts, research, notes and documents from his community activities. In my ignorance, we also gave them the collections of his creative writings, that I would not delve into for another 20 years. Mom and I then devised a plan to rent a pick-up truck to drive my mementos back to Maine. That included the eight boxes of photographic slides that still today sit in my basement, waiting for me to sort through them. She would drive with me, we would make an adventure out of it. It was still wintertime but nature was on our side as we encountered little weather-related difficulties. I couldn't say the same for Mom, she was very high-strung and scatter-brained. One of the symptoms showed itself soon on the long, interminable drive across the featureless Midwest interstates. She had always been a great power napper, able to close her eyes for 15-20 minutes and awake rested. Sitting across from me in the truck, kind of scrunched down in the corner, she'd say, "I'm going to take a little nap." She'd snap awake a mere few seconds later and ask, "Where are we?"

"Only a few miles down the road," I'd tell her. She did that several times a day during the drive.

An unrelated, yet sad event compounded her state of mind when we hit New York State. She'd heard that her Aunt Sadie was in the hospital in Westchester County. We detoured there so Mom could visit the relative she hadn't seen in decades. We found the hospital and went in looking for Aunt Sadie. Outside her room, one of her sons informed my frazzled mother that his mother didn't want to see her. Showing no signs of sadness or discouragement that would have made me furious, Mom turned to me and said, "Let's go, then." My heart hurt so bad for her even though I knew she was never very close to her extended family.

There was a back story to this encounter that I found out much later after Mom's passing. Apparently Granny had purposely kept her only child and husband estranged from the Tecklin side of the family. My brother, sisters and I didn't learn much about that side of the family until many years later, although I did visit with some of them when I took a trip to New York City and Long Island when I was 15. After Granny and Grandpa died, there was some reconnection as a few first and second cousins ventured out to Colorado.

A few years ago, my brother Pete, through his genealogical excavations, found some Tecklin relations, George and David in New York. As became our modus operandi, Pete would find them and I would visit them. I met George in 2015 at his home in New Rochelle on Long Island. From him, I learned how my grandmother whom they called Carrie, had kept my grandfather Max from interacting with his family and he said, 'even tried to poison my mother's relationships with her aunts and uncles.' Pete's detective work found another distant cousin. Bonnie Tecklin on Facebook. I visited her and her wonderful husband Manny soon after they'd moved to Las Vegas, Nevada from Los Angeles. She'd heard some of the chatter about Carrie and, more or less, corroborated George's reflections.

Mom's travails weren't over when she left our home in Maine. I was leery of her flying home by herself but she insisted she was fine. Though being a seasoned traveler using her flight privileges on United Airlines, we heard later that she had wandered aimlessly around the airport in Pennsylvania, where she was supposed to change planes for Denver.

When Mom returned home, she was diagnosed with mental health issues that required pharmaceutical intervention. She soon valiantly overcame and managed her challenges, emerging with the caring and sunny disposition that won over most everyone who came into her orbit. Well, except the asshole that key-scratched her car in the Safeway parking lot!

On the beach in Water Mill on New York's Long Island where she spent summers as a young girl, Mom's lifelong love of the water blossomed. As her life got sorted out after Dad's death, she moved to a townhouse in Castle Rock, down the street from my sister and her family and became a regular at the recreation center swimming pool. With Eve coaching the local team, Mom competed in the Senior Olympics; she placed third in the 1,500m freestyle, second in the 50m freestyle, and second in the relay.

Bound and determined to retire from United so she could travel wherever her fancy took her, fate as fate will, messed with those plans. Even though Mom and Dad had taken great advantage of the flying perks, sadly he passed away before she retired thus she lost her travel buddy. Then, her body rebelled soon after her last day of work. At first, arthritis was diagnosed in her spine which resulted in several surgeries to relieve pain and retain mobility. A hip had to be replaced, but the worst setback was aggressive neuropathy that left her with pervasive numbness in her legs. She became confined to a wheelchair which put a major crimp in her travel dreams. No cause was found; she was never diagnosed with diabetes, which is the most common cause. Despite the impairments and broken dreams, she never lost the smile and compassion that inspired genuine love in friends and especially family, and it didn't stop her from swimming. She campaigned and raised funds for a contraption at the rec center that would lift her from her wheelchair and into the swimming pool. Once, when I was visiting and went down to watch her, I was overwhelmed with emotion to see the pure delight in her eyes as she floated in the water and, for a few minutes regained glorious freedom from corporeal bondage.

Soon after my mother retired, she and a friend embarked on a long-anticipated trip to China. Mom could barely walk by then and regrettably could only sit in a wheelchair at the base of the Great Wall. Despite the disappointment, her love of life persisted and she assertively instilled the love of travel in me. Mom encouraged me to go to those anywheres and everywheres that she never made it to. I don't think any mother could have been happier, indeed many might have been terrified, when her little boy became a truck driver who would drive over one million miles, through every state and on every interstate as well into Canada and Mexico. She even installed an '800' phone line so I could call free from wherever I was and give her a full run down on all the details. My travels also benefitted from the maternal severe storm warning center.

"Be careful, Dan, there's a tornado watch in Oklahoma."

"Thanks, Ma, but I don't think that'll be a problem up here in Seattle."

"There's a major snowstorm in New York, they've closed the turnpike."

"Mom, I'm in California."

She got it right a few times.

I love to call Eve a Christian's Christian. She is the first one to show up when a friend, neighbor, or even stranger is in need; she makes dinners for those that are grieving, grocery shops for elderly shut-ins and is there to listen when her brother needs a shoulder to lean on. After their brothers flew the coop, Eve and Med were left to weather our parents' tumultuous years but were each other's lifelines. When Dad died, Eve kept Mom nearby and was there to provide invaluable love and support when Mom's legs crapped out. Eve would opine that as the youngest in the family, she was a spoiled, whining brat but as far as I'm concerned, she evolved into the family's rock.

My mother passed away in June of 2003. As if knowing the end was coming sooner than later, she prepared for the end of life in a very pragmatic manner. All the t's to be crossed and i's to be dotted were spelled out for us, even who to call to collect the body she wanted donated to the University of Colorado Medical Center. When she passed away, she left behind of legacy of warmth and love that to this day leaves friends, family and even acquaintances teary-eyed. I portrayed my father's love for his mother as verging on worship. He strived all his life to make her proud of him with hopes that he could make up for all the hardships she faced when he was younger. Indeed, she was his guiding star. Would I say that about the reverence I held for my mother? I suppose I can be faulted for looking back through rose-colored glasses, but I remember Mom more as an ally, a sounding board and even an instigator. While Dad was the disciplinarian, Mom was more like a companion, almost a partner in crime. She was an artist and loved finding innovative ways to do things. Her vision was more worldly as she saw an endless collection of places to be visited and an infinite number of people whose acquaintances to make. She instilled much of that in me, for which I am eternally grateful. Especially in later years, when she vicariously lived her life of travel and adventure through my journeys Down Under and over the road. Did I worship her the way Dad did his mother? I think not, but I bathed in the sunshine of Mom's smile, the mischievous twinkle in her eye and her subtle way of making me accept responsibility when I needed it. She encouraged me to go beyond my hesitancies and push the boundaries, but she shared my fulfillment rather than setting it as a goal to which I should aspire. I don't think I worshipped her but more regretfully cannot recall many times when I told her that I loved her. Being in her orbit was what I sought, and I still miss her presence in my life every day.

Dad wrote the following lines, but I'd like to borrow them to express the adoration I held for my mother.

Uncluttering 18

Why I love you:
 You are a haven my roaming mind can settle to
 You are training and taming the tempest of my soul

A bizarre yet poignant addendum to my mother's story emerged twelve years later. As I mentioned, Mom had her body donated to the University of Colorado School of Medicine in hopes that it might help them with their research to find causes for the neuropathy that bedeviled her later years. My sister, brother and I never heard what came of the donation until 2015 when Eve got a curious letter from the Colorado Anatomical Society asking what should be done with our mother's ashes. Apparently after her body's usefulness had been usurped, it was cremated, put in a nondescript urn and placed on a shelf somewhere. When they were returned, the three of us decided to divide them up amongst us and our children, her grandchildren. I made a rather elaborate effort out of purchasing ornate little tin containers and pasting a portrait of Mom on the side to present to my daughters and son. Travis offered a unique suggestion. Since I was a truck driver at the time and Mom had loved to travel, he said I ought to take her remains and spirit with me on the road, spreading the ashes in various, exotic locales. Couldn't quite bring myself to do that, but I did take the opportunity to spread them in some of her favorite places around the country. She now lies in ashy repose on the shores of the lake in Watermill and next to her old friend Zdena's house in the Sea Ranch, California, though she didn't know it. A few blocks from our house in Denver, she lies at the base of a bench that looks out across Washington Park to Mount Blue Sky. The last bit I took to the place where I hope to join her, the 12,000-foot summit of Loveland Pass.

CHAPTER 21

My father died way too young and missed a lot. I could not have been aware back in 1989 the many and varied ways he would continue to affect my life. His presence in my life remains strong, his spirit stays bright and his words continue to speak to me.

The trajectory of my work life was not as rocky as Dad's had been, but like him, I was never a model employee. When I landed in 1980 at the catalog legend L.L. Bean, the company was riding the crest of popularity and innovation. Customers trumpeted their undying loyalty, many for almost as long as the company had been in business; during my time there, we celebrated 75 years. We had a soft-spoken, benevolent president, Leon Gorman (grandson of L.L.) who was genuine in his care for employees. Business growth was phenomenal; when I started with the company as a shoe clerk in 1980, total sales were $100 million. In 1991, when I was the Returns Department manager, the company had $100 million in returns, and almost $1.5 billion in retail sales. I benefited through a series of promotions, the first of which was as eclectic as it was amazing. The Director of Personnel took me under his wing and, until he had designed a specific role for me, sent me on a six-month training regimen that allowed me to spend time in each department of the company, learning the tasks performed therein, but most importantly getting to know almost every employee. Other Bean benefits included a significant employee discount on merchandise, an employee use room where we could check out canoes and tents, and great retirement benefits. The company also paid for me to get a Masters of Business (MBA) degree.

Yet, I was not far from my father's maverick ways. Though I had Leon's support, I rubbed more than a few people the wrong way with my unconventional approach to problem-solving and obsessive defense of the "little guy," the workers. According to my supervising manager in the Distribution Center, my benefactor to whom I've been eternally grateful, I came close to being fired more than a couple times. In the end, I know that being at L.L. Bean during what we Has Beans (ex-L.L. Beaners) call the halcyon years benefitted me immensely as I was to discover in succeeding years.

Despite the good times, Dad's need to be true to himself and Mom's wanderlust made me restless. In 1991, L.L. Bean had its first management level layoff to save expenses. They offered a good separation package, six months continued salary, and out-placement resources to volunteers. In my mind, I had arrived at the point where I saw no upward growth in the company so I decided to take them up on their offer. In hindsight, one of my biggest failings in that decision was not being open to my wife Diane's reluctance. The desire to move on became fervent in me. As much as I loved Maine for its beautiful autumns and rugged seashore, I needed more sunshine and was excited to move back to Colorado or somewhere new and exciting. During the process, I discovered that I like looking for work more than actually working. I earned lots of frequent flier miles jetting around the country for interviews. Dad would've loved that!

Ultimately, I accepted a position with the Tog Shop, a women's wear catalog, based in Americus, Georgia. I was offered the position of Vice President of Customer Service and Human Resources. Being honest with myself now, I guess I was enticed by the title and moderate bump in salary. However, the company was one-tenth the size of L.L. Bean and the implications took very little time to establish themselves. The executive team included one other vice president, a corporate financial officer (CFO), two marketing execs and VP of a satellite catalog. The president was an arrogant transplant from the Midwest, a penny pincher and decidedly not a people person. While I had good relations with my subordinates that included promoting the first black woman to a supervisory position and making many budgetary improvements to my operations, it became obvious that my real draw to the president was having L.L. Bean on my resume. He and the other executives were not interested in the positive business and employee management practices I'd brought with me. The executive team met weekly in a small conference room where cigarette smoke hung like a cloud over the proceedings. The contentious discussions over operational changes were tolerable, but what really irked me was the penny-pinching when it came to determining pay increases for the employees. Even though we had supervisors and managers to determine and recommend raises, the president had the executive team fighting over miniscule and, in my mind, demeaning incremental increases. I remember arguing to get a top employee a half cent per hour raise. Dad would have been proud of me for standing up for the workers and I'm sure he wouldn't have been surprised that after two years, I fired myself. When the president rejected my entreaties and ignored the positive changes I'd made, saying I'd be affecting my management bonus, I walked. Subconsciously, I know I was channeling my father's dignity and resentment.

My next foray went about the same. In 1994, I found a position as Director of Customer and Member Services at a trade association in North Carolina. Once again, I uprooted the family and headed north to Chapel Hill. Though the change was difficult at first, Diane and the kids came to love their new residence, particularly Courtney and Travis who felt most at home in the state and became ardent North Carolina Tar Heel fans. Mariah, not so much, as she was used to being a big fish in a small pond and Chapel Hill was unequivocally a larger pond. We let her move back to Americus for her senior year so that she could graduate from high school there. Once again, I'm sure L.L. Bean got me in the door but, in practice only led me to ruffle more feathers. In retrospect, I think I made some constructive changes, but as at the Tog Shop, when you report to only one person, it's best not be a rabble rouser. In September of 1996, they showed me the door. I could just imagine Dad ranting and extending a middle finger to my boss.

Diane and I had separated a year earlier, much as a result of my restlessness. We worked hard to ease the disruption for the kids. By then, Mariah was off at her first year of college, Courtney and Travis were in their last years of high school. When my latest corporate job fizzled, I did a disappearing act by throwing my bicycle in the mini-van and heading west. I rode my bike to the top of Independence Pass in Colorado and said to myself, not unlike Dad many years earlier, "Fuck it! I'm not working for anyone again!" The days of being a square peg officially ended. The contours of my rebellion took the form of truck driving. I told the trade association if they paid the $300 for me to get a Commercial Driver's License (CDL), I'd relieve them of the thousands of dollars they were going to spend on yet more out-placement services for me. That was an easy sell!

I might have been tasting Dad's frustration of being rudderless in a metaphysical gale and not knowing how to trim the sail; though by then, he wasn't around to commiserate with. Although he had left us almost a decade before, my brother and I seemed to be shadowing his footsteps. While I was going through my changes and escaping the bureaucracy of corporate employment, Pete was bailing out from the suffocation of being a techie in Silicon Valley in California. He shared his father and brother's penchant for champing at the bit and reviling nonsensical bullshit in suffocating workplaces. With a significant buyout of stock shares, Pete started buying vacation properties and old trucks. Over the course of years, he's tried many ventures, but today he is sitting on top of the world playing jazz piano in San Francisco. I'd like to think Dad found some gratification in the professional world, but Pete and I may have been able to move on from where he left off.

Dad penned the following lyrics with lofty goals, yet embedded with personal motivations. I interpret his words as holding oneself to higher goals, whether in the bigger sphere of industry or in the intimate sanctum of morality. Not only were Pete and I infused with Dad's altruism and brutal inner honesty, but I see many of the same traits making their ways to my brother and sister's heirs.

❖

My Job

Freedom is a living thing
It battles alone against the treachery of man to man,
It consoles the suffering and hurt.
It stands against tyranny, against evil.
Its seed grew from the heart of strong men,
It was fertilized with the blood and suffering of
 countless ages.

Freedom is the good in man.
It is not a selfish thing.
All the treasures of the ancient kings cannot buy it.
All the treachery of all the schemers in the
 World cannot win it.

Through knowledge,
Through suffering,
Freedom was born
 Of strong men
 Of ideals
 Of knowledge

God bestowed upon me the gift of Freedom
In a world where freedom is a luxury.

My job is to repay the privilege.
My job is to earn the privilege.
My job is to keep my freedom
To wear it proudly.

My job is to repay all the dead patriots for the hard-
earned prize
My job is to continue their work,
To keep my country strong, and growing,
To keep freedom from dying,
My job is to seek, to know, to understand.
Knowledge is strength.
My job is to cleanse myself of petty prejudices.
Pettiness, selfishness and ignorance gnaw away at
    Freedom and make it weak.
My job is to spend my birthright,
To make it a living, growing thing.
My job is to participate honestly
So that I can carry the banner before the world,
In the knowledge that I have earned the privilege of
Freedom
That I am truly a free man,
That I have done my job.

The depth of one particular impression my father made on me was a long time in coming and, unfortunately, crystalized a few years after he died. I never came face to face with the brutal possibility of dying in a faraway land like Dad did, or regretfully understood the inner turmoil he suffered as a result of his military experiences. In that long-ago kitchen, he started me on my journey from skeptical warmonger to anti-warrior whose goal was to not face the brutal horrors of combat nor have anyone else face them. He managed that by asking me difficult questions and causing me to reflect on my naïve beliefs. What he didn't do was share his wartime experiences to the extent that I might truly understand what he saw and did.

Too many years later, in retrospect, did I find that I had a comparable situation to that kitchen discussion with my son. It was 1996 and Travis was about the same age I was back then, almost sixteen. I had dropped him off with his cousins in New Jersey on my way to visit a friend in New York City. On our way back to North Carolina, I decided to take a quick detour into Washington, D.C. The Vietnam Memorial (the Wall) was opened in 1982, but this was my first opportunity to see it firsthand and what a learning experience I thought it would be for Travis. On a Sunday afternoon, it wasn't hard to find a parking space on Constitution Avenue but we had to wait to cross the street. Bill Clinton and his motorcade were passing by. Waving to the President of the United States certainly added weight to the moment. As we walked across the lawn and through the cherry trees, the ground seemed to drop away from us. The memorial is built into the side of a hill that faced away from us. We came around to face one pointed end of polished black granite that rose to a 10-foot pinnacle in the middle and stretched almost 500 feet to its other pointed end. I felt like I was in the shadow of a gargantuan black bird spreading its wings and preparing to soar into the heavens. As we walked along the wall, our strikingly clear reflections moved among the more than 58,000 names chiseled into the smooth stone. A lump grew in my throat and my eyes teared up as I tried to explain the magnitude of the Wall to Travis. I was suddenly hit by the realization that a majority of those 58,000 names had been kids like me, kids whose lives had been sacrificed for a cause that was dubious at best. There are small pedestals covered by glass to protect hefty directories that locate individual names on the Wall. With Travis at my side, I found three of my high school classmates. My heart was heavy and voice pretty silent as he and I walked slowly back to the car in the dimming light.

Sadly, I don't recall my father ever visiting the Wall. If he did, we never discussed it. The opportunity was lost forever that he might have told me what inspired the following poem. In particular, there's a reference to his father, wounded in World War I, who returned to be, "...your agent [God]...A minister, but not a minister of love." Oh, how I wish I could go back and learn all the back story. Looking at the polished black granite of the Wall, I can almost hear the voices behind the chiseled names express solidarity with Dad.

I was Afraid of You God

I was afraid of you God when I went to war
- Afraid to question — so I believed.
But in the face of nearer dangers, I lost my fear.
But I was vulnerable and afraid in the jungle
And I prayed to you for a shield
As I knelt, suddenly, I could not feel you near
I became transparent — I felt a chill
And the jungle was dead and musty with loneliness
I cried, I cried for you, God,
Somewhere in the soft azure above
Somewhere above the dark world gone mad
Somewhere there must be a God.
I was driven on

Then I trudged the muddy profanity of the southern sun
Looking and searching for you.
I peered the vileness, the dinginess, the blackness
Where wretched humanity lies contorted and bleeding
Where hating humanity awaits the dawn — to kill again.
I saw a bloody arm on the beach at Manus
Was it once lifted to you in prayer?
I don't see You — but irony
In the bloody body lying cold on the beach
In his body, I saw youth, and gaiety, and love
But in his eyes, opened skyward, I saw death
And a question.
Did my brother come to you before –
Before a shell at Ardeimes took his leg
A friend opened his heart to you often
Now he lies, a silent vigil, at Bizerte –
Love, and life and humanity were shelled
And bled from my father at Verdun.
He returned to be your agent
A minister, but not a minister of love.
Is this your world God?
Are you in the handsome youth
That turn into howling savages,
Do you condone the hate, blood, butchery
That has smothered the world for all time
Not improving but only become more universal and
effective
At Iwo Jima, Murmanck, Tunisia.

All the large-scale business wars
To the small personal wars
Moses murder of the heathen at Phoroa
A lynching of a negro at Atlanta

Every man since time began has had faith
Just as strong and just a believable as mine.

———◦◦———

Every time I'm in the Washington D.C. area now, I make a
pilgrimage to the Wall. While it reminds me of the opportuni-
ties I squandered to have in-depth discussions with Dad about
war and pacifism, I can also look fondly back on that day in
1996 when Travis and I saw the monument for the first time.
That somber yet illuminating occasion has inspired me to talk
more openly with my son. I'm striving to be the open book
that my father wasn't, a failure for which I must share blame.
Not only war, but I hope we can talk about the myriad other
issues that sons need to hear about from their fathers such as
parenthood, careers, finances, and even relationships, though
I still haven't mastered the finer points of that one. As well, I
want that book to be open to my daughters and four wonderful
grandchildren. I may not be a sagacious font of wisdom, but
I'm now relishing opportunities to converse with them about
the world, its wonders and troubles while hopefully instilling
in them desires to make their own differences in it.

* * *

As I mentioned earlier, my transience and lack of direction
placed a lot of stress on Diane and our marriage. We divorced
in 1997 and I found my version of freedom as an over-the-road
truck driver, soon to be followed by the acquaintance of my
muse as a wannabe novelist. The dramatic change was very

tough on Diane but she, the kids and I have, over the suc-
ceeding years, navigated ourselves to bonds much richer and
more compassionate. One upshot of the moves, despite my
best Mile High efforts, is that Mariah, Courtney, and Travis
have become Southerners at heart.

My truly nomadic life began as I shared an address with
Mariah in North Carolina but rarely stayed long enough to
call it home. The truck was my dwelling; the tractor I drove
had a sleeper cab called a condo unit because it had bunk
beds. It was also equipped with a television and refrigera-
tor. I added what was called a trucker's stove, a small black
construction-type lunch box like a small hot-plate oven. My
bicycle was my constant companion, strapped to the back of
the cab so I could explore where my truck couldn't go and
I added cross-country skis for the winter. I drove 47 of the
lower 48 states in thirteen months, with another couple years
before I added North Dakota to complete my list. Over ten
years of driving, I logged 1.3 million miles. I used my travels
as opportunities to visit family and look up old friends and
college roommates, many of whom thought they'd seen the
last of me years before.

I distinctly remember when inspiration hit, when I discov-
ered the daughter of the muse my father had found in Paris
almost 50 years before. Late night, I was rumbling westward on
Interstate 70 about to cross the Big Muddy. Ideas started swirl-
ing in my head and coalescing into the basics of a story that I
needed to write. As words, ideas and themes came together, I
got so excited, I was literally jumping up and down behind the
steering wheel of my big rig. Just as my fervor was reaching its
peak, the Gateway Arch rose over the bright lights of St. Louis.

From that point on, I utilized rest stop picnic tables and coffee houses to craft what would become my first novel, <u>Quadrangle</u>. My initial manuscript was a grand mix of handwritten, type-written and finally computer-generated pages. To finally be following in my father's, his mother's and the family's creative footsteps has given me immense pleasure.

Truck driving proved to be halcyon in more ways than the independence of the open road, it brought me regularly back through Colorado and the home I'd never really left. I swapped Mariah's address for that of my Mom's condominium in Castle Rock which was down the street from my sister and her family. Forever lovingly burnished in my memory, Mom is standing on her balcony, waving and smiling the world's biggest smile as I pulled up my rig across the street. At the time, she was playing Bridge with a Mensa group (they're really smart people!) and had befriended, as she called her, "a for-tyish young lawyer." Her name was Karen and she had grad-uated law school from Mom's alma mater, Duke University. Karen introduced Mom to her mother, Ann, and they became fast friends. By the time I came on the scene, our families were already connected. Sadly, Mom passed away before that young lawyer and I got married in 2006, but would be delighted to know that the fire she kindled remains blissfully bright these many years later.

Little did Karen know how the game of Bridge would change her life. Soon after our mothers had brought us together and shortly following my 49th birthday, I ended up in the hospital. Midway through a cross-country jaunt, I was close enough to Denver that I parked my 18-wheeler down the street from Karen's house, grabbed her bicycle and rode downtown to join her and a couple friends for dinner and beers. Pedaling my way back to Karen's house, about the time I hit Washington Park, a burning circle of pain settled in the middle of my chest and started sending spasms down my left arm. When I got to her living room, I could not get comfortable, lying down or sitting up. In a rare moment of common sense, I told Karen that maybe I should go to the hospital. Soon after we arrived at Porter Hospital, about a mile from the house, they took me in the ER and declared that I was in the midst of a moderate heart attack. The excellent staff stabilized my condition and admitted me. A stent was placed in my heart two days later to facilitate the flow of blood. Though I came through the procedure with flying colors, I was not allowed to drive for four weeks. Did I mention I was a nomad and didn't have a permanent address? Karen graciously allowed me to move in with her. That was in September 1999 and as the saying goes, the rest is history.

One of the few regrets I have in life is that Karen never got to meet my father; I never got to meet her father Luis either, as he died of cancer in 1984. Aside for their shared love of Bridge, I would have loved to watch Karen and Dad debate the issues of the day. They shared much in common with the depth of their involvement in Denver's growth and stature as one of the nation's premier cities. Many of the folks Dad had worked with during his days with SPARC and his other activities were still around to engage Karen in her responsibilities as an Assistant City Attorney. She has also become my cherished companion as we use Dad's books and infatuation with Colorado to track down ghost towns and mines that he wrote about.

Though Dad didn't get the chance to meet Karen, I think he possessed clairvoyant inspiration to write this poem that would capture my feelings for her.

Ode 2

Please take my worldly kingdom
As minor as I might be,
But of all the worlds of every time,
It is the greatest one to me.
Please take each little second
That made the life I live,
Of all the time of a million years,
It is all I have to give.
You have given my life the mettle
To consecrate my soul.
You have given my life a reason
You symbolize my goal.
Please take all my life forever,
And lacquer each jointed part;
To guide and gild my steps above
With the gold within your heart.
Please — please take the love I offer,
And pull me to the shore.
I have no throne or battlefield to honor it
But I could not love your more.

EPILOGUE

---◆---

Who Am I?

Who am I?
This, the poet asked as he fingered the sky.
The _____ asked as he dissected the firmament.
The tyrant, the lover, the sneak.
They asked.
All life is a question, history is a series of tiny answers.
So, who am I to ask who am I?

I am the answer to date — half-born, ignorant.
Bear with me.

For I was born naked in the year of our lord 1924.
Clothed in dreams and fed on glorious fables.
I trudged through the sparkling corridor of youth
following the
       arrow –
Turning the right corners, mumbling the prepared text,
smiling, laughing,
       fighting, playing, praying in proper order.
A fine figure they said.

A good boy they said –
And they patted my head.

Then, slowly as I approached that faraway island of man –
    the fog lifted.
Through the mist I met manhood –
A fiery initiation of man's war, his games — his
god's world.
One by one the fables and the dreams departed, seared
away by
    the world that is.
I linger on the threshold, wary of entering, but weak to
stop the
    flow.
As I pause, I stand once again — naked,
And ask who am I?

Before me lies a jungle of symbols and masks, paper
thin and phony.
In a beauteous cove, I see man lives in an abscess of
bricks and steel —
    chipped and faded.
A pushbutton world of kaleidoscopic slides, and actors
paint
    sparkling on and off, slicing the night.
Here man is rooted, but the roots are shallow and sick.
Everything is up for sale — at bargain prices.
The priest and the politician hide in their temples,
reading the script
    and counting the change.
Love and truth are celluloid images, negotiated by the
turn of the dial.
Life is a well-rehearsed farce, crackling silently.
Reality is a rare disease for which man is striving to find
a cure.

The soul is buried
Deeper and deeper.

Nothing is real.
The words, the pictures are as old as sin, newly tailored
to sell.
Bluff is in power, the lieutenants are the liars, the man-
lovers, the
    looters.
And the herd is spoon-fed on lies, to enjoy the scraps.
God is success, and success is gold.
Every man is alone, the mold is the same.
He views the beauty a moment, self-consciously, then
returns to bury
    the surface roots.

I wish I could know when this brutally honest, sad and cynical poem was written. Was Dad looking back on his life when the end was near, evaluating the lessons he'd learned? Might he have been unburdening himself from the ravages of experience? At mid-life, was he tallying up wins against losses and determining that he'd lost more than he'd won? I'm left only to speculate on his message and state of mind when he penned this harsh portrait of life.

Were I to write a companion poem it would be titled, 'Who Was He?,' and would paint a different portrait of my father, as seen from the artist's perspective. I would first talk about a man who was borderline genius, quick-witted and insightful. He was inquisitive and very well-read, from books and literature earlier in life to the later years of newspapers and periodicals. As for the rest of society, television seeped into our lives hoarding time away from the more intellectual pursuits. Dad was probably one of the few people that, for a while, could simultaneously manage both. Three televisions would be stacked in a pyramid, each tuned to a different football game. His recliner would be surrounded by newspapers and magazines from around the state. I would ask him what was happening in each game or what he was reading about and amazingly, he would answer specifically without hesitation. As headlines became more sensational and the world shrunken by cable news and mass media, his perception of humanity became more and more inflamed. That was before the internet. My brother, sister, and I ruminate on how Dad would've handled the onslaught of social media and the digital age.

I'd allude to Dad and Mom's love of music, starting with their collaboration on Colorado Songs from Timber Tavern days. It celebrated the power of folk music on college campuses. Their infatuation infected us kids, there was nary a moment when music wasn't filling our house or car as we all sang along with folk songs, soundtracks from Broadway musicals and Tennessee Ernie Ford spirituals on Sunday morning.

Dad's intellect and intuition were captured in his love for the game of Bridge, the card game he learned in the Navy and became most proficient at. He came to take the game very seriously and I marveled at how he could read a person's hand from their first bid. I also vividly remember how my ex-wife, Diane, bested him during a game while he and Mom were visiting us in Australia; Diane dances around the room while Dad pouted and acted like he'd lost the Super Bowl!

I couldn't write my verse without extolling my father's love of sports and especially football. He discovered that he had some talent in high school that was reignited when he returned to CU after the war. My Uncle Bill recalls that Dad was touted for his potential, but for some reason only played one play in one game and he was penalized for being offside! After that, he traded playing for partying, but his infatuation with the game was epic. Even when he lived in Paris, he imposed on his mother to keep him informed of scores. He loved the challenge of picking winners, to the point of making a science of filling out the weekly football pools in the Rocky Mountain News. Aside from the gridiron, we kids were proud. Although, we should have told him more than we did that he was our number one fan, sometimes the only spectator in the stands for our games, matches and swim meets, but always the most boisterous and fervent.

'Who Was He?' would highlight the insight and strong opinions that fueled Dad's Liberal politics, which one could almost say were bred into him. From his grandfather who published the only Democrat paper in Yankton, to his outspoken single mother, Communist stepfather and all the progressives with whom he surrounded himself, Dad was the consummate Left winger. I remember him blaming Ronald Reagan for every ill that disaffected the 1980s. I can only imagine the fury and indignation he would gin up in today's divided and antagonistic world. Even if the names and events are not familiar, it's hard not to miss the sarcasm in this poem that would be relevant in today's world.

The Politician

You won with a smile, your homily style
The battle-winning path you've trod
Your speeches had charm and did you no harm
Sprinkled heavily with home, mother and God.

And you promised us loads of homes and roads
And schools to put the kids in.
You mentioned hospital beds and as for the Reds
You wouldn't give them another smidgen.

To Labor you vowed smartly, "another look at
Taft-Hartley,"
Implying the utmost of charity.
You bestowed the same charm on the family farm
With promises of full parity.

So, if the figures aren't false, you won in a waltz -
Showing what promises can do.
But after we voted, you, (on) whom we doted –
Why, man, you?

You unleashed the McCarthys, McCarrens, the money
barons, "Bird-dog" Wilson, and then, son,
You brought on high interest rates, Nixon, Dixon and
Yates
And Ezra Taft and Benson.

You gave us the power lobby, Oveta Culp Hobby,
The gal who couldn't "foresee."
You even dug up "Uncle" Herb, we had to curb
Way back in thirty-three.

There were the Georgia trips and Dulles quips,
And guys like Talbott, Wenzell and Bowes.
You gave it away through Mitchell and McKay
And opened up shop to the Matusows.

You condone the Nixon "smearings," the army hearings,
And fired guys like Corsi and Ladejinsky,
And some 6,000 others whom even their mothers
Couldn't prove were the least Bolshevinsky.

***

My poem would celebrate Dad's status and celebrity as an expert of Colorado history. Tom Noel, aka Dr. Colorado, said Dad was the go-to guy for knowing how to get around our beautiful state and telling its story. Dad took great satisfaction in being conferred with the title of Authority. Doors opened, people came a'callin' and cared about what he was doing. Having been battered for years and having his credibility called into question far too often, at last, Dad was in control of his destiny. He was inspired to dig deeper and cast his net farther to glean the secrets and stories of the state and region he loved. How fulfilling to turn one's passion into an avocation! For quite a while, some financial reward followed, allowing the affirmation that money can provide. He honed his craft to the point where he was considered a writer of renown, especially to his eldest son, who would one day attempt to follow in his footsteps.

The Oxford dictionary defines a (human) maverick as an unorthodox or independent-minded person. My poem would confirm Dad's bona fides as a maverick. It was based on the lofty ideal he penned numerous times, "be true to yourself." To him, that meant in life you will face many challenges, fight many battles and have your heart torn out, yet you take principled stands, follow difficult paths and hopefully reap some reward. Even if in the end, you are a shadow of yourself. Being true to yourself keeps you from being a hypocrite and Dad strived mightily to do that. He got beaten down a lot, but all those of us who knew and loved him understood that he believed he was doing right. The maverick spirit means that its bearer does not always follow the crowd, it bends and even breaks a rule now and then, but doesn't suffer fools or foolish situations.

Regardless of what they had done in life, Dad believed each and every person deserved to be treated with respect. There's good in everyone, though you may have to look deeper to find it in some more than others. Even the most heinous characters are human, have mothers and can feel pain, though the evidence may be buried at the bottom of their souls. That is not to say their bad deeds should go unpunished. In my poem, I would celebrate his attempt to find the redeemable in each person and thank him for passing it onto me.

Dad had to look deep within himself to tolerate those who played games or were unscrupulous and arrogant. My verse would exalt his capacity for avoiding that trap and those people when he could. I would accentuate his tenacity for putting up with their deceit and lack of ethics for as long as he could, though he lost many of the battles. Dad wasn't a game player, a wheeler-dealer that connived, manipulated and made bargains with devils in disguise. Those inabilities cost him dearly and further tarnished his dreams. Being a maverick meant believing in and living by firm principles. I'd like to think that he cultivated in me the maverick spirit and that it flows into our next generations as well. The disenchantment of being a maverick is that we're smart enough to have some or even considerable success while periodically getting ourselves into trouble. Dad and I experienced heartbreak from shattered dreams but wouldn't have been happy or contented if we'd forsaken what was important to us just to get ahead. Satisfaction comes with making positive differences without losing one's soul. I've lived long enough to accept and relish my successes, even if they weren't earth shattering. Sadly, dying way too soon deprived my father of looking back to treasure the good things he'd done and let the stings of failure fade into shadows. I would have loved sharing that contentment with him.

The ode to my father would not dance around the fact that he had his flaws. The ones that stand out most to me are steeped in alcohol. Dad knew others who more or less drank themselves to death: Brother Jack, Sister Pat, Stan Weston, Tom Hutton and a few others who might come to mind. He wrote about them in his chronicles but the implications never seemed to resonate enough to foresee the same happening to him. Maybe he did at some point or another; Mom let on that he did try AA a few times but obviously escaped its healing embrace. When he was diagnosed with diabetes, he celebrated by purchasing a keg to share with the neighbors. "What the hell? What does it matter now?" he wrote. In the throes of alcoholic madness, he harassed my mother, then sobered and apologized to my sisters. What makes a man throw away his life for the taste of liquor? I could brainstorm reasons why he might have been caught in that death spiral: it was in his genes; medication to forget what he saw during the war; the pressures of being a newspaper man; the weights of self-doubt, -worth, -image, -confidence; possessing a high intelligence that saw wrong with the world, but disappointment that he hadn't made a difference; and unbearable guilt from his treatment of his wife. There's no absolution in that mountain of excuses, but the reality of his weakness certainly robbed him of self-forgiveness and longer life.

My poem, 'Who Was He?,' would end bemoaning the fact that our connection could have been so much richer if we'd each tried a little harder. I would lament the unshared confidences, anxieties and heartfelt sentiments. I would chastise myself for being more of a passive observer than a soulmate. My poem would end mourning the depth and breadth of what I'd lost when he died.

In 'He Dropped a Minute of Time,' perhaps Dad was adding an addendum to 'Who Am I?'

He Dropped a Minute of Time

He dropped a minute of time
He missed the soft sun — green of a farther
    field
He heard the soft cry that wasn't
    heard
and his heart broke open.

Dad didn't tell me a whole lot about his father Fred, nor did he write much about him in his journals. My blood grandfather was never around much so most of Dad's memories are gleaned from odd, short visits and mixed ruminations from his mother. His mother never outright disparaged her husband, though in her writings she recounts fighting to keep the family together despite his philandering and petty thievery. Consequently, Dad didn't really have a good role model for a father but I think he tried to be a better one for me. Why has it been that, long after he's gone, that I'm only now coming to fully appreciate the lessons and guidance he did provide me? In tribute to him, I aim to take up the mantel and foster stronger bonds with my son and daughters before it's too late.

On the journey to discovering my father, I arrived at another way station of insight. I realized and accepted that a parent never stops seeing their child as, well, their child. Even after a son or daughter has long entered adulthood and is thriving on his or her own, many of us parents are never quite able to slough that last shred of nurturing. My offspring often remind me of this fact.

"Stop treating me like a child, I'm an adult now, Dad!"

"Don't worry Dad, I got this."

"Please Dad, we'll be okay."

All such admonishments are lovingly and gently delivered in response to my sage advice garnered from years of experience, hard work and mistakes learned from. It's all part of the universal cycle of children looking up to fathers, then miraculously becoming very capable of figuring out the world themselves. Harry Chapin captured that migration in his classic song, 'Cats in the Cradle.' The journey from the first verse...

> "My child arrived just the other day
> He came to the world in the usual way
> But there were planes to catch, and bills to pay
> He learned to walk while I was away
> And he was talking 'fore I knew it..."

...to the last...

> " 'When you coming home, son?'
> 'I don't know when,
> But we'll get together then, dad
> We're gonna have a good time then.' "

...represents, I think, every father's fear that opportunities to bond with his offspring will pass like ships in the night. Deep beneath the urge to share insights gained on the excursion through life is a perilous desire to keep our kids close to our hearts even if they may physically be a thousand miles away. I learned too late that my father craved that closeness during the separation scene in the family living room when I told him that I was leaving the family nest. He must have perceived that confrontation as a major threat to our attachment.

That's not to say Dad and I didn't have some grand experiences together, we did. There were the car trips around Colorado and New Mexico, the tick perched atop his big belly, the drive-in movies in Durango that scared the hell out of me, the football games in Boulder. And then there was the time he took me fishing in Estes Park and I caught a duck. As I got older, there was a Bronco game here and there. He and mom visited us in far-flung parts of the country and world.

Unfortunately, as age and obligations bore down on us, opportunities diminished to cultivate the robust connection of shared hobbies, adventures and sadly, casual chats. There was unfinished business that neither of us was ready to admit, much less address. I would have loved for him to be a mentor when I started writing. Sitting with him, just the two of us, sorting through all the big issues: our kids, surrounding ourselves with the wonder of grandkids, love, our fondness for Colorado...Oh, the things we could have pondered! Regret is one thing I've tried to avoid, but my biggest one is that I barely knew my father's innermost thoughts. I touched upon the top third of the iceberg but was woefully ignorant of the bottom two thirds where he buried the failures, disappointments, dashed dreams, destruction caused by alcohol, the meat of our relationship, essentially all the stuff we should have discussed but never did.

What stands in the way of sons and fathers not exploring the depths of their relationship, much less the challenges of life? Male pride, I suppose, is a big part of the conundrum. What is pride? The Oxford dictionary defines it as, "the consciousness of one's own dignity." That's a meaningful description, but begs the question, what is dignity? "The state or quality of being worthy of honor or respect," says the same dictionary. By way of consolidation, male pride, then, is a man's sense of his own capability for honor and respect. Between a father and a son, each has a need to preserve their self-worth which is defined by their sense of dignity. To me, the sword is double-edged in that the son wants the father to lead him in his search for that dignity, while at the same time being proud of him for finding it on his own. The pressure on the father is even greater because he needs to be perceived as respectable and worthy of the son's reverence.

I'm not sure I can't say that my perception of my father's role as revered sage didn't take some of the same turns. He died too soon for that narrative to unfold and I was too self-absorbed to ponder it while he was alive. What kept me and Dad from knowing each other better? Did years of pummeling by forces outside himself cause him to suffer from insecurity and a damaged self-image that might have made him feel he wasn't living up to what he perceived as my expectations of him? If I'm being honest, and that's why I'm here, maybe he did fall short but that's also my problem. I didn't take the opportunity to pry from him his disillusions and how they contributed to his self-reflection. I never spent much time evaluating his feelings about me and the way I was living my life. For the most part, I know he was proud of me but the unsent letter of disappointment where he called me a sissy proves that wasn't always so. Very much to the point, why didn't he send the letter or discuss his concerns and criticisms with me? I must also ask myself, why was I so oblivious to the indications that he was unhappy with me?

As this lyric expresses, there is a holy center in the core of the bond between father and son but sometimes we have to swim dark seas to find it.

Uncluttering 6

The temple of man:
> Through the tyranny of his own invention.
> He is rising like a mountain emerging from the
> dark sea.

⸺⸺◆⸺⸺

Thinking about me and Dad gave me cause to wonder about other fathers and sons. Were Dad and I typical or outside the norm? So I set out to uncover what other guys thought about their fathers and their relationships. In a very unscientific and random survey, I interviewed male friends and family members, in particular, those whose fathers had passed away. What follows is a summary and synthesis of the comments so freely and unreservedly provided.

The first of my discoveries was finding that rapport covered a full spectrum from closeness and connectedness to estrangement, seemingly independent of the years since the father had died. One friend felt most of his accomplishments weren't much appreciated by his father and that he was "totally pissed" when the son didn't follow the career path that the father had envisioned for his boy. Another buddy reported that he was essentially raised by his father; they went out to dinner once a week, talked about anything and everything. Later, when this friend was well into his professional career, his father invited his workmates to weekends and activities at the family lake house. Reflecting on those friends' assessments,

I'd put my relationship to my father as somewhere in the middle trending toward involved, yet distant.

Dads were described in many ways. One was frugal, a religious reader of the evening newspaper, loving to play games and entertain. Another had a good logic about him, offered good advice and was a mountain of support. Many were a balance of "good and bad." Some never wanted to show vulnerability, kept their cards close to their chests and tended toward suspicious. One childhood friend said his father was a perfectionist, making the son feel like he could never get anything right. His father also passed down his depression and anxiety. Another buddy went from hating his dad for letting the family down to re-establishing a connection later in life. Commonalities across most of the relationships were that the fathers were unemotional men, never outwardly proud and rarely shared a lot; sons had to ask the questions and some felt they were never talked to as equals. Particularly for those fathers who served in the military, we sons knew very little of their wartime experiences, which isn't surprising given the depths to which veterans bury their memories. To the positive side of the scale, our fathers were our biggest cheerleaders when it came to our athletic endeavors.

Another commonality seemed to be that our dads consciously or subconsciously modeled for us sons the men they wanted us to be, but never really told us what that was. As I mentioned, my father hadn't a good role model which seemed to be a common thread. Our dads raised during the Great Depression, tried to do better than their predecessors with mixed results. A couple of my friends did speak highly of the examples set by their fathers to the extent that they went into the same occupation.

One friend shared this about his father: "My sister recently showed me a photo of [our father], who was a vice president at his company, working a ceramic press. Here he was in a white shirt and tie engrossed in and operating this large press. I realized that I am very much like him in that regard. As I kept advancing up the technical ladder, I have always been very involved in all the details from design through implementation."

I'd have to say the strength of Dad's example for me was more in the philosophical, contemplative vein. He inspired my creative instincts, strong political bent and love of learning. When I think of the parenting and relational skills he modeled, they were more like billboards along the way not necessarily tangible lessons that we explored together.

The norm for our fathers' generation was that the husband should be the provider and moral leader for the family. Some of my friends lived that life, though their dads just worked and didn't contribute around the house, but that isn't to say that the kids were deprived of a happy home life. For others, the man wasn't always the breadwinner which reflected mixed results. To make men out of their sons, some fathers provided tough love, leaving the boys to earn such things as private school tuition and basic expenses outside the home. One friend actively defied his father's expectations by taking a totally opposite tack in life. My dad worked and strived to provide for the family yet Mom was the more reliable wage-earner.

Most all of us discovered stuff about our fathers after they died that affected us in different ways. The most poignant comes from my brother, and I did not know this. My mother sadly recalled that the night before he died, my father casually said to her, "You know Sandy, I love you." That is an earth-shattering revelation to me because, over the years I lost sight of the affection they shared; I'm still dealing with that.

Another friend learned like me about his father's wartime exploits, not directly from the man himself but from his World War II diaries. He discovered that his father had flown 34 missions in B17s as a navigator/bombardier, then 35 missions in B-26s in Korea and was shot down over Belgium but was able to walk away; for his actions, his father received several medals and an oak leaf cluster. Another buddy knew his dad was a lifelong hypochondriac but discovered that that was his way of prying attention away from his two sisters. Also his mother had threatened serious bodily harm, which started an enduring affliction of anxiety attacks that father passed down to son. Another friend discovered that his father was born six years before his grandmother married his grandfather.

My one friend who was estranged from his father harbored no regrets and wasn't particularly saddened by the lack of a relationship. Others felt that while not perfect, they were happy with the bond they had shared with their dads. Most of the group shared regrets from not having their fathers around anymore. Their reticent comments included:

> "I think he would have enjoyed seeing my poetry chapbook, but alas, it was written somewhat as a result of his dying."

> "Would have liked to play catch with Dad one more time; that was his way of connecting."

"We never had the chance to sit down and share a beer."

"He didn't get to meet his grandson."

"He never knew my [second] wife; they could've been kindred spirits...maybe I was attracted to their similar energies."

"I regret not being able to really listen to his stories about his family and writing them down."

"Oddly, while he wrote one novel and a memoir, we never really talked much about writing books."

"Our kids never, it seemed, got to see Dad's gregarious side."

"I never got the chance to see if we might find more common ground."

"My father missed seeing how my life and loves turned out, leaving me to wonder if he would have been proud of me."

There's sad optimism in the hope that many fathers and sons arrive at a point in life where old habits drop away and they begin searching together, sharing and commiserating. My father's premature death deprived me of that sweet spot. Seems like I'm not alone in suffering that ache. Dad would now be in his mid-90s and at best, I could be taking care of him, helping us both navigate the vagaries of the twilight years. We'd spend many quiet, late afternoons gazing at Rocky Mountain sunsets, hopefully chatting about everything and nothing. Had we another couple decades to interact, I think we'd have learned so much from each other and become prouder of each other. In this scenario, I hope that I would've found he yearned for and found a life lived with purpose, that his life would have found the meaning in 'Ode 5.'

Ode 5

Every day and every death helped make our birth
As every rain and every wind made our earth......
....some life my death shall make.

Several years ago in the springtime, I was riding my bicycle along the South Platte River. Late afternoon sun highlighted budding new leaves and ripples on the fast rushing water. Around a bend, just before the downhill that went under a railroad bridge, a small but prominent sign sat in a lonely patch of grass between me and the highway. It signified this small area was named for a man whose name I vaguely recalled. Dad must have known him, I said to myself. I wondered how and why this guy got a park named after him, even though it was just a little clearing in an obscure location. That got me to thinking, my father had done a lot for Denver and the state of Colorado, wouldn't it be nice if he was accorded some sort of public recognition? As I continued to ride Denver's streets and paths over the next few weeks, I kept an eye out for an edifice or piece of land that would be suitable for a sign or plaque dedicated to W. Perry Eberhart. A pedestrian bridge erected near Confluence Park where the South Platte River and Cherry Creek converge caught my eye. It was just down from the newly built Joe Shoemaker Park which sort of lorded over the Confluence. That bridge could be a perfect tribute to Dad as he and SPARC were instrumental in laying the foundation for much of the redevelopment that Shoemaker would later make happen. The bridge exhibited the uninspired moniker, 15th Street Bridge. Armed with the conviction that this name certainly could be improved upon, I struck out to get it renamed for my father. I began by picking the brain of my Assistant City Attorney wife who practiced real estate law for the city of Denver. She pointed me in the direction of the Parks and Recreation department where I researched the guidelines for getting things named. Armed with what I had unearthed and a dossier on my father's accomplishments, I met with an associate at the city planning board, who directed me to the city councilwoman who represented that area of Denver. To my despair, she was less than encouraging as re-naming roads, parks, and other community entities was fraught with politics and bureaucracy. I found with building frustration that the bridge was not in fact, under the purview of Parks and Rec, but Public Works. From them, I learned that while they had a few named landmarks in their stable, they didn't have guidelines for labelling things. That would entail having the city council develop criteria and mechanics to formalize the process. I had this impending sense that I will most likely have passed on and my offspring might be trying to get something named after me before that happened. Dad's poetic reflection on another minute of time aptly portrayed my vexation.

Musing 18

I plucked a minute from a tree
polished
sucked it
ate it
and threw away the pit — ugly

Joe Shoemaker, for whom the plaza on the Confluence was named, also initiated the Greenway Foundation which not only spearheaded early revitalization efforts but assumed stewardship for the river valley by building recreational facilities as well as developing a host of programs to promote and protect the waterway. I had met Joe's son Jeff, at a few civic and social gatherings. Jeff had inherited the Greenway Foundation's executive director position from his father and was still active in that role some thirty years later. His door was open when I approached him with my scheme to get some tribute to Dad along the river. Jeff was very complimentary of Dad and his accomplishments even trumpeting the fact that Dad had been honored as a "Friend of the River" in 1988. While supportive of my quest, he significantly tempered my expectations. My growing sense of exasperation deduced that serious financial contribution to city coffers was most helpful in getting the type of public recognition I was seeking. Fund-raising hadn't been a strong suit of Dad's, nor was it of mine. Graciously however, Jeff offered the Greenway Foundation's support and would contribute to a commemorative plaque placed wherever I saw fit. In the end, though exasperated with bureaucracy as Dad had been, I accepted and thanked Jeff for the offer. Through the auspices of the foundation, I got a 4" x 6" plaque affixed to a park bench overlooking the Confluence across from Shoemaker Plaza. Not interested with a simple "in Memoriam," I insisted that the plaque read:

"A tribute to
Perry Eberhart
A true Colorado visionary
He knew what Denver was
and what it could be
He saw into Denver's
past *and* future"

With that small but nice accomplishment, I set my sights higher. In addition to his good deeds in Denver, my father did much for the state of Colorado. His four books, sold world-wide, heralded the state's treasures and contributed to its already lofty reputation. He had been integrally involved in major events and activities that celebrated the state. My bias tended to think that men who had done less for the state and the city were memorialized in parks, on roadways and even intersections. In the end, Dad was just not the type of guy to beat his chest and posture for attention. A few people will say they remember my father and that he did some good things, but no one has taken up a banner to get him officially venerated, except me. The plaque at the Confluence notwithstanding, after considering my fruitless struggles at the local level threading the vagaries of statewide bureaucracy could only be worse. With my tail between my legs, I withdrew into my recollections and allowed my ultimately futile efforts to die a smoldering death. As I have excavated his immense collection of papers, awards, photos and memorabilia, my motivation has been resurrected. Though the name Perry Eberhart may not adorn a park or highway sign, it will now receive loving tribute in this book written about him.

Dad did not write the following passage, but he clipped and saved it among his treasures. It was written anonymously and reprinted in an Ann Landers column, dated March 28, 1986. The poem reminds me that, despite my efforts, his memory and spirit are larger than any sign in a park or on a bridge.

———◦———◦———

My Grave

Do not stand by my grave and weep.
I am not there, I do not sleep.
I am a thousand winds that blow.
I am a diamond glint on snow.
I am the sunlight on ripened grain.
I am the gentle autumn rain.
When you awake in the morning hush.
I am a swift uplifting rush
Of quiet birds in circling flight.

I am the soft starshine at night.
Do not stand by my grave and cry.
I am not there....I did not die.

———————◆———————

What is a legacy? Among the many definitions and characterizations I found, most of them involve the conferral of financial well-being and material gifts; moolah, trusts, land, treasured keepsakes, etc. On a website called Love to Know, I found a connotation that more aptly describes what my parents left to their next generations. To quote, it states, "The richness of the individual's life, including what that person accomplished and the impact he or she had on people and places. Ultimately, the story of a person's life reflects the individual's legacy." That, to me, is much more meaningful than the inheritance of a few bucks, piece of real estate or fancy relic.

Neither of my parents left much in the way of a will that bestowed money or property. When Dad died, there was the house on Niver Avenue but its sale barely paid off the second or third mortgage he and Mom had on it. When she died, we were left with the condo in which she had lived the last twelve years of her life but it too was sold at little profit. Amusingly, the only contested item Mom left behind was a collection of VHS tapes on which she had meticulously recorded many 'Northern Exposure' episodes, our favorite television program. When my brother Pete found out that I had asked her if I could have them and appropriated them after her death, he got very upset. In the end, I bought him a DVD of the first season, that sort of appeased him.

Despite the meager material inheritances, the richness of my parents' lives indubitably flowed to the next generations that comprised four offspring, eight grandchildren and sixteen great-grandchildren thus far. Their love of music flowed into our hearts and permeated all our lives, as well as their loyalty and pride in all of us. My father weathered many ups and downs yet his intellect and benevolence touched many people, as well the eminence of his beloved state and community. His heirs need only to look around beautiful Colorado, along the banks of the Platte River and on any library bookshelf to see the fruits of his labors. My kids and their cousins remember a boisterous yet caring and intelligent man who loved to sit them on his lap and tell them stories. Tales about him, tall and otherwise, are continuously passed down to the great-grandchildren by us reverential offspring and our progenies. Though the latest generation never knew him, they are easily awed by the breadth of his accomplishments. For example, my grandson Jacob loves to tell and show off the books that his grandfather and great-grandfather wrote.

Our mother, Sandy, had a million-dollar smile and kind word for everyone who came into her orbit. She was genuinely attentive, authentic and an eternal optimist even in the toughest of times. In an eclectic yet intimate way, to an individual all her grandkids remember fondly sitting on the couch with Grandma and watching tennis, her all-time favorite spectator sport in which she was pretty good in her day. I was amused by the fact that she wasn't particularly adept at dealing with the grandkids when they were babies and toddlers, but as they matured they found in her an life-force filled with love and warmth.

So, I can sincerely say that my parents' legacy blessed us with a heritage of idealism, love and persistence that helps us soldier on through lives filled with achievements, disappointments and assurance of a better future in spite of monumental challenges. In this poem, Dad gave us our marching orders.

One Child

As long as one child is not allowed to reach
as far as he can reach...
There is work to do
As long as there is a reason for war in the world....
There is work to do....
As long as one man is held back because of
the color of his skin, the church he goes to
There is work to do....
As long as there is hurt, bitterness or unhappiness
instead
of the music of mankind in man's heart....
There is work to do

My brother recalls that he overheard our neighbor on Niver Avenue, Marge Beaver, say that "Perry was the happiest man [she] knew." The statement caught me off-guard because I was steeped in this later-in-life image of Dad as an unsatisfied, discontented man much of the time. I also was poisoned by the crass rejections he faced in the workplace, social settings and among people he considered friends. Those concerns tended to make me forget that he was a laughing, insightful, and gregarious man. He reveled in his children's successes, Mom's artistry, a challenging game of Bridge, a good party and especially a winning season from the Denver Broncos; alas, he didn't live long enough to see them win the Super Bowl. Too often, liquor took him away from his happy places. I was intrigued by Marge Beaver's recollection and while she has passed on, I'm still good friends with her son, Randy. I called him to verify or dispute his mother's reflection on my father. I got so much more than I bargained for. In scratching out the fodder for his own memoir, he wrote at length about living across the street from the Eberharts. I have taken the liberty, with his approval, of synthesizing his ruminations about Dad, our family and the Niver house:

> "My parents had virtually nothing in common with The Eberharts other than proximity, parties and love for a good game of bridge. They were beatnik artists who had lived in Paris. My people were tightly wound, Oakley, Kansas born Republicans. Perry was a big man, tall, square-shouldered and around 230 pounds. He was a totally unconventional author in the Hemingway mode, wily in discourse, making outrageous statements and debatable pronouncements, just to get us going. Sandy, my second mother, had an IQ of 170 plus, quirky, liberal and street wise. She was a Mensa scholar, Bronx oil painter. Both of them were well ahead of their times. They both killed at Scrabble. I liked that Perry did not like Kansas either; his advice; 'The best thing to do with Kansas is to use it to explode a few atomic weapons and flood the crater so that Colorado could have an inland sea.'

The Eberhart house: Fishnet draped over the planter in the hall, piles of logs, wood scraps and newspaper next to the flagstone fireplace. Dusty stacks of Look, New Yorker and National Geographic magazines, records and books piled everywhere and Sandy's paintings on the walls. A desk so buried in detritus that it was hardly discernible in the front room. Pantograph rolls of paper, wooden blocks, Mr. Machine parts, a gray sectional couch perpetually covered with clothes. Odd driftwood lamps. Pet rabbit 'Too Ti' nesting behind the upright piano, a complete catalog of Peanuts and Dr. Seuss. Ancient turntable with NY show tunes. Downstairs, more bedrooms, a playroom. Art books full of naughty photos, bullfighter and travel posters on the walls. They did not bother to take down the old ones, it just didn't matter. In 'The days of Wine and Roses' EVERYONE had a bar in the basement. It was 'cool' at that time to have a basket bottomed Italian wine bottle in the middle of a wooden cable spool table with copious streams of colored crayon wax melted down the sides. A suburban shrine to insidious creeping Bohemia, as close to 'paraphernalia' as we got. Pool and ping pong tables.

Kids RULED the Eberhart house. If you made a big mistake with an exploding can of spray paint, or say, a plate of spaghetti on the wall; No Biggy! Sandy collected partially filled paint cans free, somewhere. The walls in the basement playroom were all different colors, and it didn't matter. IT DIDN'T MATTER!"

Thanks so much for that, Randy!

*   *   *

The world lost a man. Why this man and why then?

I struggle to understand why the life of W. Perry Eberhart transpired and expired the way that it did. He left behind a voluminous treasure trove of pieces with which I've tried to put together the puzzle. My efforts will fall far short of being complete and accurate. Were he alive to edit my work, I'm sure he would make enough revisions and deletions that the whole piece would probably end up in the trash can. While I can't be sure about his reaction to my efforts, there are many noteworthy indications that he felt his life worthy enough to document and collate for posterity. A significant portion of *everything* he collected included letters, journals and what would become a late-in-life chronicle. The wealth of his reflections and insight prompted me to wonder why people keep journals and diaries. They can be vehicles for self-enjoyment through nostalgia and contemplation, but are such records undertaken with the intuitive optimism that someday, someone will read their deepest meditations, ideas and creations, seeking to delve into the soul and spirit of the person? Many a journal or diary has been used as the basis for the next great best-selling memoir, but for us common folk, I have to believe there's a simple satisfaction in laying out for the individual and maybe a few descendants their version of their lives. I feel there's an essence in Dad's writings that conveys a wish that his legacy would be more than stories told around the dinner table or campfire or other gatherings of family and friends. There are his successful books, but I think the preservation of his life's works, loves, and reflections was a labor of self-love meant to cushion him from the roller coaster of life experiences. Did he crave a more rewarding level of recognition and accolade beyond repute as a local historian and community activist, something in the romantic mold of a cowboy Bohemian? For a good part of his life, he rubbed shoulders with luminaries, intellectuals and achievers who garnered praise, people to be emulated and revered. Perhaps too lofty a goal, but I'm sure he would have desired such a dignity to validate a life lived well and with purpose.

I do think Dad was looking to the future, and though at times feeling like I plagiarized a bit too much, I think he would be pleased that his story is being told. After the disappointment of discovering what I didn't know about the man and being inspired by what more I came to understand, this book is my effort to elevate his soul and forge for myself a clearer, more meaningful picture of a complicated man. The life story I've put together here is without doubt imperfect, but to quote Joan Wickersham in The Suicide Index, "I'm not a professional biographer...I'm his child." What's it all about? I'm just a boy that wants to follow in a father's metaphorical footsteps, emulating his successes and avoiding the calamities.

A life story such as this one needs to end on a high note, happy and heartwarming. I'm an Atheist so there's no afterlife for me but I love the idea that our lost, loved ones are up there somewhere, appearing just the way we remember them at their best, looking down on us. I envision Dad, with Mom and Medley, watching over all of us, clapping hands and laughing at our fun times, sniffling and commiserating when the times are rough.

Dad loved a good song, and if he really loved it, his loud, boisterous voice would be heard throughout the house as he sang along. The theme song from the movie 'Alfie' was one of his favorites. As a single, its theme song, 'What's It All About, Alfie?' earned a Grammy Award in 1967for Dionne Warwick, one of his favorite artists. I think he would like me to send him out on the essence of its beguiling lyrics and the certitude that he'll be singing along at the top of his lungs.

"What's it all about, Alfie?
Is it just for the moment we live?
What's it all about when you sort it out, Alfie?
Are we meant to take more than we give?
Or are we meant to be kind?
And if only fools are kind, Alfie
Then I guess it is wise to be cruel
And if life belongs only to the strong, Alfie
What will you lend on an old golden rule?
As sure as I believe there's a heaven above, Alfie
I know there's something much more
Something even non-believers can believe in
I believe in love, Alfie
Without true love we just exist, Alfie
Until you find the love you've missed, you're nothing, Alfie
When you walk, let your heart lead the way
And you'll find love any day, Alfie
Alfie

{Burt Bacharach and Hal David, 1966}

ACKNOWLEDGEMENTS

First and foremost, I want to thank my brother Pete and sister Eve for their loving support and thoughtful input. I hope they feel this story is written for them as well as me. The spirit of our sister Medley provided inspiration and depth to our story as well.

I couldn't have written this book without hearing Uncle Bill's stories and recollections. As the last of his generation in our family, he is the wise patriarch to whom we nephews, nieces and grandchildren look for family history from someone who was there.

Speaking of family, I want to thank my cousin Cheri for her insightful project, <u>Apron Strings</u>, a thorough compilation of family history as seen through the eyes of its strong women. Also, my Grandmother Lucile's memoir, <u>A Bridge Named Harriet</u>, which was written under her pen name Eve Bennet, was an invaluable resource. My ship sister Lisa Bittle, provided the spark to my project by sharing invaluable background for our fathers' time at sea during World War II. I'd also like to thank the staff at the Denver Public Library for their organizing and stewardship of my father's papers.

In the Epilogue, I alluded to an unscientific survey I undertook to learn about how others navigated the bond between fathers and sons. I appreciated the willingness and learned a lot from the thoughts of my brothers-in-law, Monty and Brian Aviles, my brother Pete and friends Brian Brown, Mike McDermott, David Demarest, Randy Beaver, Doug Heath and Mike McCabe.

No author can complete a comprehensive work without feedback from fellow writers. For me, those wonderful people include Alison Preston, Mike McDermott, Jeff Therrien, Rick Ginsburg, Sharyn MacArthur Cerda and my cousin Steven Hart.

I benefited greatly from the insight and knowledge of professional editors Alyse Knorr and the folks at Silly Goat Media.

Lastly, this and all my endeavors would not be possible without the love and support of my partner in life, Karen.

ADDENDUM

WHAT SHALL I TELL
MY CHILDREN BY EVE BENNETT

My six and I, we live on relief. I have heard it said that any-one worthwhile wouldn't take charity. I used to think so, too. I am proud and sensitive. I have dreamed dreams. I fought for months, trying to stave off this relief business. I looked every-where for work. I wanted to take care of my family myself. But there isn't any work that would provide a living for one mother and six children and pay for competent care for the children while I am gone, so that they would run the streets and get killed, or worse. So, we are on relief.

II

I live alone with my six children in what the social workers speak of disparagingly as a "broken home." I married, when I was young and very foolish, a man who was talented, and incorrigibly weak and irresponsible. I stuck to him for four-teen years, following his wandering footsteps uncomplain-ingly, because I believed in loyalty and love and "the faith that will move mountains." Now, some of my women friends who have an enviable amount of self-sufficiency, say to me: "You were a fool not to leave him long ago. You would be far better off today."

I counter, "But then I would not have my children."

They answer, groping to be gently tactful, which hides from me not at all the depth and positiveness of their inner convictions: "But your six children — if you can't support them...."

I go on: "But I would not have a clear conscience if I had not given my children every possible chance."

Their answers, kaleidoscopically, go round and round, but always come out here: "But you would have been able to acquire material comfort for yourself by now."

I love my children. Almost all mothers love their children. I bore everyone of mine in poverty, under humiliating conditions, without any alleviating small luxuries — and I wanted every one of these six; I loved them from the moment of their conception. From my youth up I have studied to be a good mother. I am fairly intelligent, fairly well educated. I pride myself somewhat that I have been more farsighted than many of the superficial women of today who say, so glibly: "We can't afford children. We don't think it fair, you know, to bring a child into the world if you can't support him properly." I think they mean they won't give up their cars, their permanents, their overstuffed suites, their bridge parties, their quota of wine and cigarettes, their smart seasonal outfits, for a baby's soft, warm arms, a baby's smile, a little boy's trust, a little girl's love. Somehow, I think I am wiser. Yet I must find means with which to equip my children to face an unjust world — or the world must be changed for children!

III

My nine-year-old comes in on dancing feet. Her eyes are dancing, too. She has had a treat, a penny to spend.

"Mother, I bought some two-for-a-penny suckers and when I was coming past Elaine's, she wanted me to play, so I gave her one, too."

I look at her and thrill to the sparkle in her rich brown eyes, the sunshine of her smile. She's a precious, lovely thing....I say smug, motherwise, "That was nice of you to share with Elaine." Then, as an after-thought, "Where's Elaine now?"

"Oh, she had to go in. She said her mother wanted her."

A little later she is in again, my young daughter. Hurt quenches the glow of her. "Mother, Elaine went by with a whole sack of candy, and she wouldn't even answer when I said 'Hello.' "

I look at her again. I am troubled with her trouble, angry at that little snip of an Elaine who has done this before. I am silent. I was raised a Methodist, in an old-fashioned, virtue-esteeming home.

Shall I say to my daughter: "Turn the other cheek....for with what measure you mete, it shall be measured to you again....if any man take away thy coat, let him have thy cloak, also...."? Shall I say, with increasing asperity, but still within the bounds of conventional platitudinism: "Be not deceived, God is not mocked, whatsoever a man soweth, that shall he also reap"; "....Elaine is selfish and shallow and treacherous — someday she'll be sorry. You did right. The meek shall inherit the earth....."? (Question: what's to stop Elaine from taking that, too, if she wants it?) Or shall I say, as would Elaine's mother:

"Well, I'll wring the neck of the little brat, next time I see her. Let this learn you something — don't never give away your candy; keep it for yourself!"

IV

I was talking the other day to the boys' adviser in one of the largest junior high schools in the city. He is new at his job, and very young. He has the pale, ascetic look of the idealist. He said to me: "You know, some of these problems here just get me. One of the teachers said, 'Oh, you're too sympathetic; you'll get over that.' But you know, some of these children come to school hungry! Why, look here –" and he showed me an information blank filled out by a pupil. "Look! Eight in the family, income forty dollars a month....and some families have even less! I feel I must do something. But what?"

I hope he'll not get over that feeling, this kind young man. I hope he'll keep on worrying at the problem of economic insecurity until he helps do something about it. And I hope he learns with age and experience, so that he broadens his understanding, for he went on to say: "I'm here to help all the boys I can. I want, especially, to help those boys who have a nice attitude. If a fellow won't co-operate, is surly and ungrateful, then I don't feel he deserves so much sympathy."

Well, I wanted to start an argument, but I didn't. You see, two of my boys are in that school, and he likes their "attitude." And "it is the truth, if I do tell it myself as shouldn't," as an old Dutch friend used to say, those two middle school boys of mine are fine, manly little tykes. One is by the way of being a homespun philosopher with a twinkle in his eye. The other is serious and sweet, an idealist. The neighbors tell me these two lads of mine are outstanding in their willingness to do any kind of work that will earn a little money. They are growing up firm in the conviction that, by working and saving, they can get through college, and then, equipped with an education, with ideals, with training for hard work, they can conquer the world. I am their mother. I was brought up to believe children should be steeped in such ideas. But sometimes to myself I whisper, "Oh, yeah?"

V

I am worried about my oldest boy. He is a super-sensitive boy and has always had an abundance of what is commonly termed false pride. The depression has hurt him in spite of me. He goes to the high school where are some of the richest and some of the toughest youngsters in the city. My son is envious, resentful. I haven't been able to convince him that "clothes do not make the man"; that he should "seek first the kingdom of God and his righteousness and all these other things will be added unto him." His experiences at East (high school), being a humble pedestrian among boys who drive big cars, who carry away the girls, who ruin everything and have all the fun, have convinced him that money is a vital necessity. He doesn't care that "it is harder for a rich man to get into heaven than it is for a camel to get through a needle's eye." He'd like to be rich and get into some of East's biggest social functions…. He wants money very badly — too much. He has suffered humiliation too long without it. Sometimes my younger daughter, five, shows like tendencies….

To go back, then, to the boys adviser. Instinctively, you know, I rise to the occasion and assume the proper role every time. I teach my boys to have a "nice attitude" as much as possible. I haven't exactly told them that God is responsible for all our blessings and that if you believe that and practice good works, you'll be fairly deluged with all the good things of life; I've seen too much of the tendency to depend on God for things while those not so religious (but more practical) snatch them. No. I go diddling along down the middle of the road, preaching a sort of feeble doctrine: be nice, keep your ideals — and watch out like everything!

Anyhow, I couldn't have that boys' adviser thinking my youngsters have a dangerous radical for a mother. So I didn't argue with him. I didn't say what I thought: How can a child who is starving have a nice attitude? Why should an underprivileged child be grateful? Wasn't it Oscar Wilde who inquired why a child should be grateful for crumbs at the rich man's table when he should be seated at that table?

He admitted, this tender-hearted young teacher in his natty tailored suit, that he had always lived in security himself. I wanted to say: "But suppose you had been born down under the viaducts some place? Suppose you had never known anything else but ignorance and poverty and disease? Suppose you had never really been warm or full in your life? Suppose, in the miserable scrabbling for existence in your environment, that no one had ever had the time or heart to teach you a 'nice attitude?' Suppose, all that being so, that you go to junior high school: you start for school in the morning out of your background, squalor, hungry, weak, perhaps cold; along the way to school you pass a cop and he leers at you — you've long ago discovered that you automatically become an object of suspicion just by being born on the 'wrong side of the tracks'; when you get to school you spend the day in competition with more privileged children; you meet with the hard-boiled light in the eyes of the teacher who got over being 'too sympathetic' and you observe that the class bully is sleek and smug, well fed and well dressed, fairly reeking of security. Would you be grateful for a few kind words, for a bowl of soup in the school lunchroom? Would you leap to be co-operative and friendly? How could you? Why should you? You've been robbed of your fundamental rights ever since you were born! If a bandit with a large, business-like machine gun, who has robbed a bank of thousands of dollars, should, in a whimsical moment, walk into the office of the bank's president and return just one of those cute little packages of dimes which banks have, is that bank president apt to be grateful to that bandit? Very likely the bank's president won't display a nice attitude after all — he'll summon all the police in town as fast as ever he can. He'll want all of his money back — and he'll want revenge, besides!

"Have you ever been a little child who goes to school suffering from malnutrition (and likely, bad teeth and tonsils) — and tried to keep up in your schoolwork? Have you ever smelled food close at hand but not for you, hungry though you may be, because you have no money? Have you ever been taunted by other children because your clothes are cheap and ragged? Have you ever known what it is to return daily to a home where fear and want and insecurity are constant guests, so that your mother looks old and sad and cross, and your father never does anything but growl, or maybe retreat to drink?

"Have you ever, as that child, grown older, and tried without any sympathetic help from any side to go straight? To keep on starving, and not steal? To keep on hurting, and not grow twisted and bitter? To keep on being beaten, and not stay beaten?"

VI

My baby is exceptionally bright. At two years, he could use, with full knowledge and ease, six hundred and twenty-five words. Will I be able to develop his potentialities to the utmost? How? Will I be able to pay for a good education for him? And, if I do, after college will there be a fit place for him in the world?

VII

My landlady is a fat, sloppy woman, a dyed blonde. She drives an expensive car and tells me importantly of her stylish friends. She intersperses broad a's and prominent spots in her speech — and then lapses forgetfully into bad grammar when she get excited. She shrills personal insults at me through her adenoids if I don't have the rent ready when she comes for it. Her husband is a slimy, fat toad of a man with watery eyes. The neighbors tell me that, periodically, he buys his way out of trouble with the law. He, poor dear, is miscast. He would star, I'm sure, as the villainous landlord in stage melodrama; he seems sadly wasted in his dusty offices designated somewhat vaguely as "Mining Stocks, Inc."

My landlady says, in a rarely mellow conversational moment: "My god, you can have all the kids you want — just so I don't have to have any! Anyhow, should I ruin my figure for a man twenty years older'n me?"

In three years' time I am thirty dollars behind in the rent on my twenty-a-month "dump" — home to us. My landlady has never put out a cent on repairs for us. Screams she: "I ain't putting any repairs on a house where there's six kids!" I have never lied to her; I have paid her as regularly as has been humanly possible. I have taken her abuse silently (though I admit that, if it is true that "as a man thinketh in his heart so is he," I have been Mrs. O'Meara's murderer many times!).

Why has Mrs. O'Meara the right to hound me, to scream at me? Is she more honest, more fair, more intelligent, more industrious, more kind? She is vulgar and common and stupid and hard. But — she has money and I haven't. She has a fine home, an empty, selfish, childless home — but it's all hers. I have a shabby, overcrowded little home, full of children's love and laughter — and it's hers too!

You know, sometimes I think I have just as much right to security as a childless, selfish woman. Sometimes I get quite aroused in my conviction that every child has a right to a happy childhood!

VIII

My father was, at one time, the editor of the only Democratic daily in a certain Midwestern state. My father almost worships Franklin Roosevelt, as he did also William Jennings Bryan and Woodrow Wilson. And all the partisan politics aside, I believe in the principles of President Roosevelt, too. My father thinks that stern ideals, hard work and the Democratic

Party can pull the United States through anything. Now, at sixty, my father, after a lifetime of hard work, straight living, loyalty to ideals and party, has lost his business and his property. He and my invalid mother face hardship — now, when they should be at peace and secure in the "sunset of their lives."

When I was a little girl, I did not speak to any of my friends around election time, because they (though they didn't really care) were all Republicans and mostly "wets"; I, who did care, passionately, and ridiculously, was a Democrat and a "dry (Prohibitionist)." (The terms are not always synonymous, I realize!) Those were the good old days! We were all so firm in our various faiths....

I'm not firm, now. I'm not sure, not sure of anything. How can I, what shall I teach my children? I'm too steeped, yet, in superstition, idealism and conservatism — and cowardice — to tell my children: "Only selfishness and greed will bring you any security. The way things are now, too much character is a handicap..."

Not so long ago a mother in New Jersey had her children taken away from her because she taught them communism. I, too, am a reprehensible mother. I don't teach my children communism. I drift along with them under a system which has done these things to us and to many, many others — and I say nothing....

What shall I teach my children?

Hiroshima

The buildings along the dock were untouched and busy.
I was so happy that the world was untouched.
Then we walked a block and it hit us –
Across the street was another world,
A world extending to the hills miles away
The rubble of a city lay at our feet –
A different rubble, for we had seen much rubble.
The city had been inoculated a month before,
And it was still unconscious and unmoving.
It lay like molten dust hugging the ground
With only lonely charred and twisted trees,
Like the black naked props in a Frankenstein movie,
Standing above as eerie monuments.
    As we walked and saw deeper into the wreckage,
We saw the ruin as it really was — a molten mass –
Not crumbling and dusty like the others, but smoothed over
Like brightly-colored mush, frozen and lumpy;
Between the lumps a substance had run.
It had hardened as it ran — like peppermint candy.
But the recipe called for different ingredients –
The heated fusion of the elements-
A man's house, a man's furniture, a man's child.
A shipmate joyfully found an unbroken vase –
With a big glob of peppermint hardened on it.
He would take it home and place it on the mantle,
And wind proud tales around it for all
interested listeners.
    This was Hiroshima to a few victorious sailors.
Walking through it — getting close to it.
Further off — when we could lift our heads –

At the foot of the hills and along the water
On the other side, too far to walk,
Were the naked and twisted girders of steel.
Once living buildings, their bodies had been undressed,
Their skeletons had been twisted by giant angry hands
That you and I cannot comprehend.
    I could go on building my humble description,
But I cannot build it for there is nothing to build.
You have all seen living pictures since,
And heard higher words than mine — and
have forgotten.
I have merely walked through it and cannot forget it.
To me it was no more than a molten wreckage –
A crushed and dead city. What more can I say?
Materials may be destroyed by man and built up again,
Spending only time and money — but there is plenty.
People could be killed and fused into the elements,
And nobody but their families would miss them;
But families would soon die and forget them.
I saw more destruction in the living.
Yes, people still walked over the paths of the city –
Thoughtful, convenient paths, through the dead debris.
The living, people picking and searching,
Not looking for anything — and finding it.
Ragged and dirty women walked in Hiroshima –
A species different from my mother at home.
    Their eyes were empty, cold and old,
Plodding along, feet tattered and smudged
Coming from nowhere and going nowhere –
No cause to live — no use to die
A species different from my mother at home,
Followed by their numerous, straggling urchins,
Their dirty young heads seared and scarred.
The light had dulled in their hardened eyes.

They picked with as much gusto for their father's
remains
As they did for the cigarette butt of a sociable yankee;
They were ugly and old and cynical at six.
    Once a man shot us a smirk of hate;
Another winced and walked away.
But there were more mothers and their children
And understanding and caring shown dead in their eyes.
    I was trapped in this land within the low hills.
I tried to see another world beyond them,
But this was all time and everywhere.
There was no world of gay, tripping girls
Sparkling over a soda in a well-lit fountain;
There was no plump, red-cheeked men
In flashing suits — doing their daily business.
There was not a color nor a bar of soap in the world,
There was no ugliness and beauty — nothing;
Just this meaningless, boxed-in world — all was dead.
    Then I don't know why — but I laughed.
I bit my tongue until it bled to keep my laughter
to myself.
Others were looking deep into the ruins,
Making with the profound remarks expected of them,
Gathering as much as they could to take back
with them.
But as spontaneously I laughed to myself — hysterically,
I laughed at men — plump men in flashing armor,
Who studied and labored endlessly — at a
thankless task –
To put scars and burns on little heads,
And to take a mother's light out of a mother's eyes —
To fill other eyes with fear and hate;
How complete lives can be absorbed in the amiable
pursuit —

To find the most effective way of destroying cities;
And how, by destroying another man's home,
Everybody loses and nobody wins in the long run.
So the cities will be built again and again,
And other men will come and study and labor
And bicker and debate and give orations
On the most effective way to destroy cities –
To mutilate babies and empty mothers' eyes,
While the fear and hate created in another man's eyes,
Will work to destroy others before his own can be
destroyed again.
- And at home they punished a single murder
And put a suicide in the headlines.

    As we left — for the first time in my life,
I suddenly felt empty and wasted also.
I felt as if the body I was given
Was no more than a plaything to dabble with
A few years and then discard.
I felt like a helpless suffocating little mass
At the bottom of a heap of humanity.
Humanity — groping back and forth — back and forth –
Diddling while they wait to discard their bodies;
Awaiting the dawn so they can awaken
And then go back to sleep again.
    As we left the docks of Hiroshima,
I noticed the sun was shining on the dark waters –
Shining from a deep-blue, cloudless sky.
It had been shining all the while, it felt hot and heavy
on my back,
But it was a callous harsh heat and
    I had stopped laughing.

3.   **God Wore No Uniform**

I left the green valleys of youth,
I left the hills of happiness and love,
I left God –
When I sailed to a world at war
- in the beautiful South Pacific;
To trudge through dust, and heat, and fear,
Dark fear — dark jungle fear,
Fear of a leaf, a godly ripple,
Fear of a star-filled night,
Fear of myself.
My only protection was the right to kill,
My only possession was a weapon.
My luck was not with God
For the dead died with their faith –
The bloody stump on the beach
Had once been lifted in prayer.
The helpless and twisted dead
Lay in godless mounds.
Knowing only blood, and dust, and sweat
God's golden parables crawl in and through
Their bodies — like maggots.
The strange dead enemy
The stranger I hate — I shook him
To ask if his faith was as strong,
His god as perfect,
He didn't answer — he didn't even smile.
I looked up to see the gods warring in heaven,
But I thought I saw them sitting in the bleachers,
"Have a hotdog, God."
"Are you enjoying the game?"
This one is better than the last

- or do we die in vain?
We've had the benefit of a brilliant coach,
To meet with a so able foe
- and made also in Your Form;
To make our minds such monsters –
So able to hate, and kill, and not wince;
To condone the second wrong –
The right to kill the unfortunate –
You made — barely different from us.
    And then the world tires,
And we are dispersed to rest.
Dispersed to mingle our profanity,
Our brutality — with the wisdom which is God's,
In the sparkling world of romance and music,
And the distant ripple of laughter.
My green valleys are blotched with blood,
And the hills are piled high with superficialities;
Those dead are left alone and cold,
We were fortunate to escape
To practice petty hates and hopes;
And the world sweeps the battleground clear
And searches for a new enemy,
A new god, a new war ground, a new reason –
And another 'big game'
That no god can explain away.

4.   Unnamed 4

Our love it seemed was perfect
I loved her completely and unselfishly,
And I felt that she loved me the same
Each blissful moment together
Blinded me to all the world
Apart from her I felt like half a man
And thirsted for the moment, so far away
That we would be one world together again
More than all the gold in the world
I wanted her to be happy.
I lived for her smile and her laugh
I would mortgage all my vain pride
And petty ambition to establish this aim
I wanted her to forget all the ugly things
And to see only the beauty of love
To find her strength in me
I struggled to be perfect in her eyes
Not by my wanderlust (*or*) by my deeds
I was happy in my love and strength
I felt her happiness the same
   Then one day an unknown mood
Caught a foolish word from another world
A mood is feeling sorry for oneself
And this word jabbed in-between the filaments
Of my love and permeated my foolish thought
Our love was so perfect I wanted to defend it
I couldn't believe a foolish thought
I tried to force the alien element from me
But it would not leave me.
The more I forced it, the stronger it became
An effective martyr for my mood

And it soon discolored my whole life
The elements produced fear which cleared
Space for all of its foolish cohorts
And not only my thoughts warped
But my actions became guided
By the dragon from Eden's garden
    I began to look around corners
And see things in the shadows
Where there was nothing to see
New fuel fired my fear
And the ugly feeling grew inside of me
Unsaid words and unmeaning looks
Fortified the growing venom
And tore my love apart
To salvage with but the skeleton
I went on the defensive side and tried
To cover my tracks by being aggressive
My actions hurt my love and changed her too
She became as little as I.
We both wanted to win the defeat
We commenced cutting competition
To gain the upper hand.
    Slowly I began to fear our meeting
My thoughts and actions were guided by the desire
As my fear given the fire spread
I felt she was thinking in her mind
Behind the mask she wore
That I was ugly and that she hated me.
I felt like I was groping for land
In a dark, tortured sea.
Groping with the only weapons I knew
As would a child, I began to hate her
I lied and tormented my way
Into being more separated from her

I began to loath the girl
I had once loved in perfection
And all these petty children of fear
Clouded the beauteous world
And made it a raging, endless stream
I became a madman, I became desperate
And finally in self-defense
I killed the love that had been perfect
To win the defeat I had won
But now I am dead

5.   A Handful of Dust

From <u>Guide to Colorado Ghost Towns and Mining Camps</u>
(Swallow Press, 1959)

>   The mountains were there when man came west.
> Shoulder to shoulder, they marched tall out of
> the plains,
> Their silent profile born of unheard fury and sound,
> Their wrinkled brow washed by the snow of ages,
> And whipped by the unheard winds of the millenniums.
> Here volcanoes roared,
> Storms were born,
> First life crawled onto shore,
> Mighty beasts lumbered over the land,
> First man felt the sun's warmth briefly, and died.
> Here in the mountains
> All things lived and died.
>   The mountains were still,
> The trees were green and full,
> There was the same blue sky
> When the red men came.
> Their bronzed bodies walked through the centuries
> And through the trees.
> Here was their happy hunting ground,
> A pagan playground for the sober ritual of living
> and dying.
>   Long ago the Spanish came,
> In shining armour and with fine, black horses.
> Somewhere in that snow-capped jungle
> Is Eldorado, the city of shining gold.
> The Spanish had their moment,
> And were gone.
>   Eldorado remained.

Then came the explorers.
One by one they fought their battle with the mountains.
They lost, or won little victories.
Cautious Stephen A. Long walked over what he called
"the great
    American desert" to the foot of the mountains.
He looked up.
Invulnerable, he said.
Of course, the mountain men didn't believe him.
Kit Carson, Broken Hand Fitzpatrick, Charles Baker, Jim
Beckworth
    And others didn't believe him.
    A young fellow named Fremont,
John C. Fremont, didn't believe him.
He walked to the top of the mountains
And looked down....
A matter of perspective.
He and Kit began cutting the mountains down to size,
Moving them apart.
    But when the gold was discovered in California,
When the wagons started rolling,
They cursed the mountains and went around them,
Leaving them to the savages, the mountain men, and
John C. Fremont.
    They knew there was gold in Colorado.
The Spanish said so.
Pike said Purcell, or Pursley (What was his name? Who
was he?)....
He found some.....in 1806 or 1807.
The mountain men told of gold,
Fremont said "Parson" Bill Williams found it in the
South Park in 1846.
"Buck" Rogers found a mountain of it on the way
to California.

Col. William Gilpin, in 1849, searched the mountains
for Indians,
And found gold, or evidence of gold, in five areas:
South Park,
    Pikes Peak, Cherry Creek, Clear Creek, and the
    Cache La Poudre.
Georgia hunters told of gold they found on the Cache
La Poudre.
The Ralston brothers found gold on the South Platte
in 1850.
Another California-bound prospector named Norton
found gold in 1853.
Mexican miners from Sonora panned gold above Cherry
Creek in 1857.
Fall Leaf, the Delaware Indian guide, displayed the gold
he found.
    But the mountains were still too formidable.
Besides, there was enough gold in California and
Nevada for everyone.
    William Green Russell was more a symbol than
    a beginning.
He was a symbol of the end of the California and
Nevada romance,
Of hope of prosperity after the depression of 1857.
Of escape from the burning slavery question.
H represented a need....
A need for a new gold rush.
    He didn't find much....
Just a handful of dust on Cherry Creek,
But his find, traveling through the troubled air,
A handful of gold dust in a depression
Became a new Eldorado back east.
    There was gold in Colorado....gold in Colorado!!!!
    There was gold in Colorado!!

And they started coming.
In wagons, wheelbarrows, or walking,
From the far pockets of humanity,
They started coming.
Maps and guidebooks to the new wonderland sold at
a premium.
The guidebooks were all wrong....
But they sold well.
Except for bits and snatches,
What did they know of the mountains?
To an easterner all Colorado lay in the shade of
Pikes Peak.
Pikes Peak was three mountains....
All the mountains rolled into one.
But the guidebooks were more than that,
They were tickets to the new Eldorado,
A fresh start, new hope, a chance on a fortune, a ticket
to heaven.
And by thousands they came.
Starving, ragged, stumbling and dusty they came.
Their eyes on the horizon;
The Mountains were their goal.
Many didn't make it.
Many died on the way to Eldorado.
Many tarried along the road....
The dream was too much for them.
The Parade couldn't wait.
Here came the farmers, lawyers, doctors,
ne'er-do-wells.
Here came the best and the worst,
Southerners, northerners, the English, French, Chinese.
There were cannibals, the slaves, the barons,
But mostly just average men after an honest fortune,

There was George A. Jackson, Gregory and
A. D. Gambell.
They found more gold in one week that Russell found
all last year...
Just in time, too.
They put an end to talk of a "Pikes's Peak Fiasco."
Here came Rose Haydee, the first "pinup" girl in
the mountains,
Jack Langriche and "Drinking" Ed Daugherty,
They saw the mountains as a stage
Silver heels and her flashing feet,
She lost her beauty but gained immortality.
Here came H. A. W. Tabor whose dreams were as big as
the mountains,
Too big to see beyond.
Others found gold,
Pat Casey, John Morrissey, Tom Bowen, methodical
Winfield Scott
    Stratton, Thomas Walsh,
Some illiterate, some carpenters,
All dreamers.
For some the dream was never finished.
For "Chicken" Bill, Dick Irwin, "Cowboy" Bob Womack,
    and "Commodore" Stephen Decatur.
Some dreamed too much.
Take Mark M. "Brick" Pomeroy, for example.
To some not even the mountains were too big,
Like Otto Mears,
The little man who could see over 14,000-foot peaks.
And there were Hagerman, Rollins, David Moffat,
and others,
Who weren't afraid.
    The Mountains had room for everybody.
A widescreen stage for the Reynolds farce,

A hiding place for the "Bloody" Espinozas.
A burial plot for Bob Ford, "that dirty little coward."
There was even room for "Mr. Howard" in
California gulch.
There was elbow room for Soapy Smith, and plenty
of suckers.
There was a stage, a boudoir, a rose-covered castle for
the ladies,
For Augusta Tabor, afraid to dream'
For Baby Doe, who dreamed enough for both.
There was "Silk Stockings,"
Who found respectability in a parlor house;
There were the dealers in human flesh:
Mollie Purple, Mattie Silks, Six-foot-two Rose Vastine,
    Better known as Timberline.
There was "Calamity" Jane, smoking a stogie;
The "Unsinkable" Mrs. Brown,
Who found Denver society too small to handle her.
    There were the men behind the badge,
Good men and gunslingers
There was Sheriff Billy Cozens, Matt Duggan, Jim Clark
and Matt Dillon.
There were the men of God,
Father Dyer, Bishop Machboeuf, two-fisted Reverend
Uzzel and
    Sheldon Jackson,
Their eyes on Heaven.
Their feet in the mud.
There were the chroniclers, the poets,
Cy Warman, David Frakes Day, Eugene Field,
Damon Runyon.
    There were others, many others,
Big and little people,
As mountains are big and little,

As hopes and dreams are big and little.
They cut impossible trails through impassable
mountains and forests.
They gave life to such temporary towns as Buckskin Joe,
Tin Cup,
    Caribou, Slabtown, Camp Bird, Rosita, Irwin, Gothic,
    Royal
    Flush, Silver Heels, Whiskey Park, Crazy Camp
    and Poughkeepsie.
Each sought God on the mountain tops.
Their search was furious,
But short.
They are dust now,
Their names, their dreams, are but dust....
Scattered in the mountains.
    Some found their gods,
Some didn't.
Maybe the Indians were right.
Maybe the mountains are the real gods, after all.
More than a happy hunting ground,
More than Eldorado,
More than gold and silver....and uranium.
More than a handful of dust,
But hope and dreams and fear,
Loving and laughing,
Living and dying...
And more....
Because when the hoping and dreaming,
When the loving and laughing,
The living and dying are done,
When the echo of the gold is gone,
The mountains remain.

Milton Keynes UK
Ingram Content Group UK Ltd.
UKHW022339011124
450602UK00005B/91